Alone in a World of Wounds

Alone in a World of Wounds

A Dharmic Response to the Ills of Sentient Beings

Shodhin K. Geiman

CASCADE *Books* • Eugene, Oregon

ALONE IN A WORLD OF WOUNDS
A Dharmic Response to the Ills of Sentient Beings

Cascade Books
An Imprint of Wipf and Stock Publishers
199 W. 8th Ave., Suite 3
Eugene, OR 97401

www.wipfandstock.com

PAPERBACK ISBN: 978-1-6667-1496-8
HARDCOVER ISBN: 978-1-6667-1497-5
EBOOK ISBN: 978-1-6667-1498-2

Cataloguing-in-Publication data:

Names: Geiman, Shodhin K., author.

Title: Alone in a world of wounds : a dharmic response to the ills of sentient beings / Shodhin K. Geiman.

Description: Eugene, OR: Cascade Books, 2022. | Includes bibliographical references and index.

Identifiers: ISBN 978-1-6667-1496-8 (paperback). | ISBN 978-1-6667-1497-5 (hardcover). | ISBN 978-1-6667-1498-2 (ebook).

Subjects: LSCH: Buddhism. | Dharma (Buddhism). | Buddhist precepts. | Zen Buddhism.

Classification: BQ9286 G22 2022 (print). | BQ9286 (ebook).

To Michael, who was there every step of the way.

But when the notion of suffering and beings leads him to think
"Suffering I shall remove, the weal of the world I shall work!"
Beings are then imagined, a self is imagined,
The practice of wisdom, the highest perfection, is lacking.

—*The Perfection of Wisdom in Eight Thousand Lines*

Contents

Introduction | 1

PART I. Going Alone

1. This Holy Life | 19
2. Taking Saṃsāra Seriously | 51
3. The *Nos* Delusion | 72

PART II. Alone in the World

4. A Distinctive Compassion | 99
5. The Bodhisattva of Compassion neither Plots nor Schemes | 122
6. The Ultimate Austerity: Patient Forbearance | 142
7. The Social World Endured | 162

PART III. Upāya Born of Emptiness

8. *Justice* Is a Word not Uttered by the Wise | 183
9. All the Time in the World | 206
10. Nowhere Abiding | 228

Conclusion: Not Quite So Alone | 251
Postscript | 259

Bibliography | 261
Subject Index | 267

Introduction

An observation by the great American ecologist, Aldo Leopold, provides the title for this book:

> One of the penalties of an ecological education is that one lives alone in a world of wounds. Much of the damage inflicted on land is quite invisible to laymen. An ecologist must either harden his shell and make believe that the consequences of his science are none of his business, or he must become the doctor who sees the marks of death in a community that believes itself well and does not want to be told otherwise.[1]

I find this a compelling observation because it captures so many things that hang together but are hard to express all at once. There are things to be known that are not apparent to most people. Because most people do not know them, they act in ways that are quite often harmful to themselves and others. The person who does know these things can't get much of a hearing from those who don't, simply because they cannot see what he sees. He is then faced with the choice of either retreating into his own space set apart to watch the ensuing damage unfold, or of exposing himself further to the thankless task of being the misunderstood and unwelcome bearer of a truth only a very few are able to hear. In either case, the ignorance-driven harm continues. In either case, he stands alone. Put in the simplest terms possible, the world is mired in hardship, and there is not much one can do to put an end to it.

Expressed in such simple terms, this might seem to be the end of a very short story, and Leopold himself doesn't offer much beyond his sober observation. As it is, however, this simple fact of life is only the very beginning of a rather longer tale, because while we don't need much

1. Leopold, *Round River*, 165.

convincing to see how accurate it is, what we do need convincing of is what is skillful and appropriate in light of it. That, in a nutshell, is the subject of this book.

Yet another mass shooting takes place in the United States. Before the last of the responders has left the scene, the media chatter begins: "What could have been done to prevent this?" "How can we keep this from happening again?" Advocates for just about every possible cause imaginable weigh in: "We need better psychological screening and services in the community." "This speaks to the need for tougher sentencing in the courts." "This shows we need to restrict gun access and regulate possession."

Another report on the dramatic global effects of a rapidly changing climate is released, and individuals and communities exclaim, "We should do what we can to put a stop to this!" That the "this" in question is the sum product of the activity and choices of countless numbers of human beings, that those activities and choices grew out of activities and choices stretching back as far as historical memory goes and longer yet, that the use of the word *stop* in conjunction with this process smacks of a misunderstanding of what that verb could possibly mean—none of that stands in the way of the heartfelt sentiment expressed. Plans for consciousness-raising events, resolves to lessen one's carbon footprint, and decisions to get one's electricity from ever-greener sources ensue. Although the impact of these actions on global phenomena is admittedly small, the hope is held that "if everyone would just do as much" effective change might be forthcoming.

Other examples come to mind, but we need not lay them out here, because in the end the particular situations and talking points are not as important as the assumption that the responses to these scenarios and others like them all share, namely that this troubled world is somehow fixable, if we but figure out the right way to fix it or to empower those who presumably can.

The assumption of the world's fixabilty is of relatively recent provenance; it is hard to find much of the language of social transformation prior to the late eighteenth and early nineteenth centuries in Europe. What had long been an observation of how the world works, namely *that* things change, turned rather quickly into something of a moral injunction that people like you and I *should* change them. Marx's eleventh thesis on Feuerbach ("The philosophers have only interpreted the world in different ways; the point is to *change* it"[2]) found echoes in practically every moral and social philosophy and movement of the last two hundred years or so—from utilitarianism, socialism, anarchism, social-democracy, and the various civil rights movements, to fascism, jihadism, and state-centralized socialism—right up to the present day, regardless of ideological leaning. To be sure, each of these positions could dig deeply into the history of philosophy and religious thought in the West for some support (Christian language of the coming of the kingdom on earth as in heaven and the Jewish invocation of *tikkun olam* come to mind), but the urgently transformational rhetoric and thought forms prevalent in all of them are distinctively modern.

This newfound tone was not limited to philosophical or political circles, and religious institutions were soon pressed to make their stand relative to this call for social transformation as well. Leo XIII's 1891 encyclical, *Rerum novarum*, addressed head-on the spirit of revolutionary change in the face of capitalism's excesses, followed forty years later by Pius XI's *Quadragesimo anno* addressing the reconstruction of the social order. The intervening years saw individuals and groups, such as G. K. Chesterton and the Catholic Worker Movement, blend Christian teaching with anarchist theory as developed by Peter Kropotkin and others. Some sixty years later, the opening lines of *Gaudium et spes*, the "Pastoral Constitution on the Church and the Modern World" of the Second Vatican Council, set the stage for what would come to be developed as a "Preferential Option for the Poor": "The joys and the hopes, the griefs and the anxieties of the men of this age, especially those who are poor or in any way afflicted, these are the joys and hopes, the griefs and anxieties of the followers of Christ."[3] Liberation theologians took up this programmatic point in earnest, weaving scriptural exegesis with the language of revolutionary socialism to create a system of thought and action that saw the liberation of people from oppressive economic and political and social structures as a necessary prelude to—or expression of—the salvation of all in Christ.

Even when not explicitly tied to a particular political doctrine, the active participation of clergy and religious in the protest movements of the 1960s and beyond made it seem, if not obvious, at least not

2. O'Malley, *Marx: Early Political Writings*, 118.

3. Second Vatican Council, *The Documents of Vatican II*, 125.

unthinkable that persons of faith would involve themselves directly in activism aimed at altering the social landscape. Frs. Daniel and Philip Berrigan, Ven. Thích Quảng Đức, Rev. Dr. Martin Luther King Jr., and Archbishops Oscar Romero and Desmond Tutu, to name but a few, stand out as examples of those who took the step, in some cases with their lives in addition to their actions, of drawing attention to or trying to change prevailing conditions. Around that same time, any number of primarily lay religious groups and organizations were founded that, taking their cues from the religious pacifist groups of the early part of the twentieth century like the Fellowship of Reconciliation, took on the job of addressing matters of peace, economic justice, racial and sexual equality, environmental degradation, and the like.

Buddhism entered the popular consciousness in the West around this time, and many who were among the first to take up practice were also keenly attuned to—and taking part in—the developments of the day. The prominent names will be familiar to many in Buddhist circles in North America and Europe. Robert Aitken, cofounder of the Diamond Sangha in Hawai'i, was also one of the original founders of the Buddhist Peace Fellowship, now one of the most extensive networks of socially engaged Buddhists. Gary Snyder combined Buddhist teachings with his poetry, anarchist politics, and deep ecology, leaving a body of prose and verse that calls for a thoroughgoing renewal of personal lives and social structures. Bernie Glassman, Taizan Maezumi's Dharma heir, was also an entrepreneur who created businesses providing training and housing opportunities for the socially marginalized. His own school, the Zen Peacemakers Order, continues that legacy. And of course one cannot here fail to mention Thich Nhat Hanh's incomparable influence in fashioning a socially conscious Buddhism from the sixties onward that has served as the inspiration for thousands here and around the world.

A good amount of effort has been spent in the intervening years developing the parameters of what is called "Engaged Buddhism." The various contributors to this field constitute something of a single chorus in that they echo at almost every turn the words Gary Snyder first penned in 1961: "The mercy of the West has been social revolution; the mercy of the East has been individual insight into the basic self/void. We need both."[4] Approaching that dyad from the Buddhist side, the criticism is

4. Snyder, *Earth House Hold*, 92. It is nothing short of remarkable the way that quote has stood—and continues to stand—at the head of so many books and articles in Engaged Buddhism. For some sixty years now since the essay was first published

generally made that Buddhism has hitherto remained something of an archaic, private, self-oriented form of practice that, as such, needs a hand, and that hand is to be found in the progressive social tradition of the past few centuries in the West. From the social revolution side, Buddhist teaching is proffered as something of a kinder, gentler, more spiritually committed approach to social transformation than militant secular activism has often proven to be.

Serving two masters is never easy, and there is a price to pay in trying to remain in the employ of both: one will tend to cling to the one and tend to reject the other. For the most part, it seems fair to say that of the two, the Dharma and activism aimed at social change, it is activism that has won out over the Dharma in most expressions of Engaged Buddhism. I say that social activism has taken primacy over the Dharma here, because there is very little, if anything, in the collective expression of the teaching over twenty-five hundred years that can underwrite at all the assumptions that lead to the calls for social change of the kind—and certainly on the order of magnitude and with the particular kind of focus—envisioned by most of these writers. Of course, many engaged Buddhists are all too ready to concede this, and they have no hesitation in calling for the Dharma to be "updated" as a result.[5]

But it is not just that the tradition has simply been silent on these matters. Even the casual reader of the sutras and the Dharma Ancestors will be struck at the difference in tone and outlook one finds in Engaged Buddhist literature relative to these earlier sources, and there is a certain amount of cognitive and spiritual dissonance in passing from the one to the other. Should one take the time to return to the sources, one soon finds that it is not just that the teaching of the Buddha and the Dharma Ancestors simply *neglects* to address many of the root assumptions and theoretical commitments that lie at the heart of the Engaged Buddhist program, it directly *challenges* them. Yet even now as differences between the tradition and Engaged Buddhism are becoming distinct enough that forms of engaged Buddhism are being trumpeted as a new development of Buddhism for the modern world, one rarely finds many attempts critically to assess the basic assumptions of the rhetoric and practice of social transformation from the perspective of the legacy that has been handed down. I attempt to do some of that work here.

in 1961, those lines have been simply restated by countless others as an obvious commonplace on the present-day status of the practice come down from the Buddha.

5. See Loy, "Buddhism and the Modern World," 411–12.

The Dharma of the Buddha is unique in human history. Whatever similarities it shares with other religious or philosophical schools (and it does, indeed, share many), in the end what separates it from the rest of them is the singular point that the source of our troubles is not hardship or difficulty (which all conditioned beings necessarily share) but the *dukkha*, or suffering, that emerges out of our own self-generating streams of ego-fashioning, or *tṛṣṇā*, in response to them. Expressed as the Noble Truths of *dukkha*, *tṛṣṇā*, *nirvāṇa*, and *mārga*—frequently rendered as suffering, craving, the cessation of craving, and the path to its cessation[6]—the Dharma offers a clear diagnosis of the ill, its etiology, its overcoming, and the way to overcome it.

What makes the Dharma worth aspiring to is that the path to the cessation of dukkha indicated by the Buddha is *efficacious*. In every age since its first promulgation, men and women have found in it a sure path for overcoming their hindrances, abandoning obstructive mind states, confronting their attachments, and attaining to (some measure of) liberation and release. Others, seeing their efforts come to fruition, have in turn taken up the practice and pursued the same end. If today's practitioner can begin to see with the same eye as the Buddha and the Dharma Ancestors, it is because coming to realization is not an idiosyncratic phenomenon or historically constituted reality but the recognition of the plain truth of all things. Simply—and unblushingly—put, *there is awakening*.

This path, however, is also *difficult*. The liberative teaching of the Buddha was developed within the parameters of a renunciant-contemplative form of practice, and the broad contours of that practice continue to inform it to this day. Even as it is most often cast as the work of bhikkhus and bhikkhunīs, the paths of the layfolk and ordained have ever been considered to be one and the same—seeing into and severing the roots of ego attachment that bind them to their churning worlds of saṃsāra. All, whether lay or ordained, are invited to tame their unreflective drives, overcome their hindrances, develop the mental factors that conduce to awakening, and attain to a samādhi free of all mental projections on the basis of which alone the realization of wisdom (*prajña*) might break through. This invitation to cross the threshold of awakening (*sotāpanna*,

6. For the sake of clarity, the Sanskrit terms *dukkha*, *tṛṣṇā*, and *nirvāṇa* will be kept throughout.

kenshō) through the abandonment of delusion has consistently been coupled with the understanding that it requires an enormity of effort and the expectation of continual adversity. Monks and nuns face this in the very structure of renunciant life, and while householders may be exempted from the training rules (*Pātimokkha*) of the homeleavers, they have their own constraints to work with as they carry out this practice while at the same time navigating family and work in an ever-uncertain social and economic and political environment. As the *Sutra on the Upāsaka Precepts* consistently concludes almost every one of its sections, "Good son, there are two kinds of bodhisattvas: (1) lay and (2) ordained. It is not difficult for the ordained bodhisattva . . . but it is for the lay bodhisattva. And why is this? Lay people are bound by more unfavorable conditions."[7] The conditions may be different, but the task is one and the same.

Now it has to be said that even as more and more people find themselves drawn to the teaching of the Buddha in popular culture, the company of those who have crossed (or who are seeking to cross) the threshold of awakening is quite small indeed, and it has to be admitted that at many temples and practice centers even the very prospect of coming to awakening is downplayed, redefined, or altogether ignored. For most of those who have begun to cross, it has required the kind of investment of time and energy—and the kind of divestment of ego-attachment—that the general run of the population is either incapable of mustering, or unwilling or uninterested in making. The Buddha understood that most people would neither understand the teaching nor set themselves to practice, so such a dearth of aspiration should come as no surprise or be of much concern generally. It is, however, vitally significant for any proposed *Buddhist* social theory, because so much of what is said in the tradition concerning the nature of compassion and wisdom and right action and the like that gets marshaled in support of Engaged Buddhism presupposes that the threshold has, indeed, been crossed—or, at the very least, that one is actively set on crossing it.

The Buddha and the Noble Ones give us a view *from the other shore*, as it is put, and to take what is the prerogative of the awakened and awakening ones and to assume that it is equally applicable to everyday persons or to society at large is to invite, at best, a category mistake and, at worst, a point of confusion by making as if coming to awakening were not at all germane to the claims that are made concerning living out the

7. Shih, *Upāsaka Precepts*.

Dharma. Far from being "a fetish," as one Engaged Buddhist declared it,[8] enlightenment—or, as I will be phrasing it here more accurately and in a less charged way, the cessation of tṛṣṇā in nirvāṇa or the unshakeable deliverance of mind—is the very *raison d'être* of the Dharma, and it simply runs counter to both the tradition and to sound common sense to suggest that the spiritual benchwarmers are on par with the spiritual athletes. If the sports metaphor seems a bit of a stretch, one can easily refer to the pastoral one in the *Dhammapada*:

> One who recites many teachings
> But, like the negligent, doesn't act accordingly,
> Like a cowherd counting others' cows,
> Does not attain the benefits of the contemplative life.
> One who recites but a few teachings
> Yet lives according to the Dharma,
> Abandoning passion, ill will, and delusion,
> Aware with mind well freed,
> Not clinging in this life or the next,
> Attains the benefits of the contemplative life.[9]

In either case, the point is the same: simply appropriating the language and maybe even some of the outward forms and techniques historically associated with Buddhism is not the same thing as setting oneself to the realization of the Dharma.

So perhaps we need to distinguish between *Buddhism*, engaged or otherwise, and *the Dharma*. One can well be *a Buddhist* and not commit to the practice of awakening or even entertain it as part of one's life. Countless men and women the world over attend services, engage in devotional exercises, support temples and monasteries, attend Dharma-related talks, pursue scholarship on Buddhist sources, and perhaps even practice some form of meditation—all without having given rise to the "mind proceeding toward awakening" (*bodhicitta*) that marks the threshold of realization.[10] Their self-understanding and their heartfelt activity are not to be made light of or scorned; we all practice what we can to the best of our abilities. But if one has set oneself to realizing the promise of

8. Jones, *Social Face of Buddhism*, 101.

9. Fronsdal, *Dhammapada*, 5.

10. Śāntideva describes the threshold between simply "desiring awakening" (*bodhi-praṇidhi-citta*) and actually "proceeding toward awakening" (*bodhi-prasthāna-citta*) as the distinction "between a person who desires to go and one who is going, in that order." Śāntideva, *Bodhicaryāvatāra*, 6.

the Dharma—if one would be a *noble disciple* rather than an *ordinary disciple*, as these are cast in the tradition[11]—then one needs carefully to consider how many of the prevailing conceptions and practices of this (or any) age one simply loads onto the Buddhist bandwagon, no matter how appealing and noble-minded they might at first appear.[12]

As I read the relevant literature, there are several areas where the impetus for social change as expressed in the various manifestations of Engaged Buddhism runs up against key elements of the Dharma. The first would be what I would call *modern exceptionalism*, the idea that there is something so distinctive about contemporary life that a significant reworking of the core teaching is in order. There is no denying that the conduct of life throughout much of the world today is technologically and scientifically much more sophisticated than any other age has known, and that this has brought with it a concomitant increase in speed and complexity and reach. A consumer good may now be made of parts from three different continents and assembled in a fourth. News travels in instants rather than at the speed of a horse or a ship. We can splice genes and split atoms. Bombs can now take out tens of thousands where a spear or arrow or musket could at best take out one. Trade policies enacted in some national capital by politicians and bureaucrats impact

11. Bluck, "Path of the Householder," 18, draws attention to this long-standing distinction:

> The difference between monastics and lay Buddhists in the Pāli Canon is more quantitative than qualitative. The monastic life provides ample opportunity for spiritual progress, but of course the individual monk or nun has to make the effort for themselves. The household life has many distractions, but for the determined lay disciple these need not be barriers to spiritual progress. In the Pāli Canon—and by implication in historical and contemporary Buddhism—the progressive path of morality, meditation and wisdom is open to monastics and lay-followers alike. The essential distinction, both then and now, is not between the monastic and the lay-follower, but between the "ordinary disciple" (who may still be a devout Buddhist rather than a merely nominal one), and the "noble disciple" who has glimpsed Nibbana and who is genuinely committed to the understanding and practice of the Dhamma.

12. Sulak Sivaraksa's "Buddhism with a small b," for instance, might enjoy some widespread renown and some superficial relationship to this or that aspect of the Dharma, but it is not a guide on the path to awakening, nor does it claim to be. B. R. Ambedkar was quite upfront in indicating just how far he was distancing himself from the Dharma with his "Navayāna Buddhism," and rightly so. It is, of course, no coincidence that both Sivaraksa and Ambedkar were Western-educated, and their use of the Dharma was rather consciously tailored to the demands of transformative social theory in the Marxian framework prevalent in the academic and social environment at the time.

the ability of families in distant lands to secure food. Collectively, human activity has altered the climate of the planet. While this means there are different phenomena, or *dharmas*, in play, it would need to be shown not simply that these dharmas are different in *degree* (which, of course, they most assuredly are) but also that they are different in *kind* such that the dukkha that arises in conjunction with them would need to be overcome in a way that differs from the path indicated by the Buddha. I have seen little that makes that argument *while at the same time* holding to the soteriological aim of the cessation of tṛṣṇā in nirvāṇa.

Second, built into much socially oriented Buddhism is a rather breathless elevation of *activism* as a key element of practice. Ken Jones makes this point quite unequivocally: "For the mature social practitioner neither [a just social order nor awakening] is primary. There is only a single, seamless practice experience, and activism."[13] Activism, it should be remembered, is a distinctive form of social engagement that emerged under certain historical conditions. It takes on many forms, but all of them share this much: they seek to change policy and social structures in light of the view held by comparatively few people who consider their particular position on an issue to be superior to and more beneficial than the prevailing ones of the day. They all share the assumption that the proper and right solution to social troubles is to leverage minds and institutions and to change laws and policies in the ways that they deem fit. Even as one will rightly acknowledge moral non-equivalence among them, environmental activists and anti-abortion activists, gun rights activists and transgender rights activists, the alt-right and antifa, the Buddhist Peace Fellowship and Focus on the Family are in this respect all cut from the same cloth. It is hard to make the case that the Dharma was ever conceived of as a practice that would function in this way at *any* point on the political spectrum—or even that it is coequal with such practices *at all.*

Finally, one cannot fail to detect in much Engaged Buddhist literature a deep-seated doubt about *the reality of awakening*. Where it is not dismissed outright as either archaic or out of touch or a pipe dream, it is so reworked that awakening now gets reduced to the commitments of progressive social thought ("awakened people combat racism," for example). This is not an argument against progressive social thought and engagement but against its being cast as a fitting manifestation of the

13. Jones, *Social Face of Buddhism*, 214.

Noble Path. Where one would expect a discussion of abandoning the hindrances and overcoming delusion, one finds instead a litany of social ills and broad gestures toward a society free of them.[14] The silence surrounding realization and the nature of the path to its attainment in this context is nothing short of deafening.

These are the issues that will be addressed here, in various ways, across the whole of the book, even as some chapters take them up in greater detail and other chapters provide background or support. My aim across the whole is to sketch out what can be considered a skillful response to social ills that hews much more closely to what is most unique and, above all, most profoundly liberating in the Buddhadharma—seeing clearly into dukkha and its cause by following the path and coming to its end. Although I will not hesitate to indicate those points where that skillful response departs from the assumptions of Engaged Buddhism, my aim here is not so much to critique that school directly as much as to indicate how close attention to the core of the tradition leads to a very different assessment of, and response to, social ills from many of those currently being advanced.

Part I is devoted to clearing some ground. Chapter 1 sets the core teaching of the Buddha, dukkha and its end, within its root framework as a form of life marked through and through with the spirit of solitude and renunciation. After briefly touching on the Noble Truths of dukkha, tṛṣṇā, and nirvāṇa, I follow the gradual training sequence outlined in the *Nikāyas* as an illustration of the Noble Truth of the path manifested in what the sutras call *the holy life*. The pursuit of the Dharma is often criticized as a self-serving enterprise, wholly focused on the individual and his or her attainment. In seeing just how demanding each step along the path is in terms of what distinguishes everyday life from the holy life, we can see why the oft-repeated charge that the pursuit of the Dharma is self-servingly individualistic—the very charge that underlies so many attempts to render the Dharma more socially oriented—misses the mark. Because so much of what is to follow in subsequent chapters will rely on the technical vocabulary and distinctive elements of training in the Dharma outlined here, this chapter is necessarily on the long side, and I would beg the reader's patience while these foundations are being laid.

14. Loy, *Great Awakening*, 18–40. David Loy puts a good amount of store in the idea of *social dukkha*, but by his own admission this is not the dukkha the Noble Truths address.

Chapters 2 and 3 unpack the oft-echoed exhortation, "We must change the world," first with reference to *the world*, and second with reference to the presumptive *we*. The teaching on saṃsāra shows that, because my world arises out of my own additions of tṛṣṇā to the perceptible, it is more accurate to speak of myriad "worlds" when considering many beings. Calls to change *the* world tend to over overlook both the thoroughly idiosyncratic nature of samsaric worlds and the overwhelming effort it takes for any one of us to see through our own. Taking saṃsāra seriously means, first, attending to the depths of my own delusions and, second, appreciating how beings, absent awakening, only ever act with reference to their own. As there is no collective saṃsāra, there is no collective coming to its end.

One of the purported advantages of appending a social theory to the Dharma is that it avoids the trap of getting overly caught up in considerations of self. But the issues surrounding selfhood at the individual level (the "I" or *ego*) are not mitigated by replacing it with a social self (the "we" or *nos*), since that, too, bears the marks of nonself (*anattā*), conditionality (*anicca*), and dukkha. The saṅgha would seem to stand as a counter example to this, but already in the sutras the Buddha indicated that the sociologically describable saṅgha was subject to corruption, and he counseled a bhikkhu to be steadfast and ready to practice alone—*as an island*—if need be. Indeed, the saṅgha in which refuge is taken is not the everyday assembly but the *āryasaṅgha*, the saṅgha of the awakened/awakening ones, but even here there is no communal structure and identity to be found. Finally, I briefly touch upon the idea, often appealed to in socially oriented Buddhist literature, that the interconnectedness of all things itself constitutes the parameters of a collective identity such as would be sufficient to orient action. While the interconnectedness of all things rightly indicates the inseparability of dharmas, it does not go so far as to provide a collective identity to go along with it.

The chapters in Part II make up the core substantive contribution of this study: a presentation of compassionate action in the world that hews quite closely to the soteriological aim and practice of the Dharma. Chapter 4 takes up the *brahmavihāra* of boundless compassion (*karuṇā*). As the sutras make clear, the exercise of compassion is only possible after following a concerted and difficult course of renunciation and meditative training leading, first, to samādhi which makes the practice of the brahmavihāras at all possible, and then to prajña, which allows one to see their emptiness (*suññatā/śūnyatā*). Without that concentration and insight, the most one is left with is a "near enemy" of compassion, as Buddhaghosa put it, one that is still tied up with attachment and aversion, gain and loss. Action aimed at ameliorating the samsaric conditions of individuals shows itself to be an instance of this near enemy, and, as such, misses both the boundlessness and the emptiness that characterizes karuṇā proper, throws one off the path to greater awakening, and curtails in the process the fullest possible expanse of compassion. This stands counter to the common idea that bodhisattvas somehow "defer" their awakening in the name of compassionate action aimed at bettering the world.

The analysis of compassion in chapter 4 is illustrated in chapter 5 with a close reading of chapter 25 of the *Lotus Sutra*, which describes the activity of Avalokiteśvara, the Bodhisattva of Compassion. It is clear in the *Lotus* that the Bodhisattva's skillful action does not to consist in altering samsaric conditions but in becoming an occasion (*nirmāṇa*) for another's awakening as an outgrowth of her further striving in the direction of Buddhahood. The *Śūraṅgama* and *Kāraṇḍavyūha Sutras* echo the *Lotus* on this distinctive understanding of skillful means (*upāya*). Far from underwriting a transformative social agenda, the picture of the bodhisattva presented here speaks to the skillfulness of a selfless and agenda-less moral exemplarism that, contrary to popular understandings, cannot be translated into determinate actions aimed at making the world a better place.

Chapters 6 and 7 offer an extended engagement with Nāgārjuna's exposition of the perfection (*pāramitā*) of patient forbearance (*kṣānti*), first with respect to the harm caused by another person and second with respect to the harm prevalent in the social environment. Because the bodhisattva does not seek to change conditions, she is still subject (like everyone else) to the ill effects of sentient beings' actions. Her response, following Nāgārjuna, is to endure them with forbearance. Chapter 6 follows Nāgārjuna's treatment of the kṣānti pāramitā in the *Mahāprajñāpāramitā Upadeśa* in addressing patience with respect to beings. Lack of patience with respect to beings, Nāgārjuna indicates, is a form of the defilement (*kleśa*) of anger that reveals, as he puts it, a kind of "stupidity" concerning the nature of those beings' conditioned nature. Chapter 7 continues his treatment of the kṣānti pāramitā, now with reference to dharmas, *social* dharmas included. As Nāgārjuna shows, lack of patience with respect to social formations is of a piece with lack of patience with respect to any other conditioned phenomenon, and hence another occasion for the "stupidity" of anger and aversion to take hold.

In Part III I sketch out some of the implications of the foregoing chapters. It is widely acknowledged that *justice* is not a word in the lexicon of the Dharma. Returning to the *Nikāyas* in chapter 8 we can see why. The Buddha, like John Stuart Mill many centuries later, located the source of the drive for justice in the feeling of resentment. Mill thought it only natural that we should resent those who do us harm and seek justice in response. The Buddha did not disagree that it was natural to resent those who harm us, but he did not see fit to put forth the pursuit of justice as a skillful response to that harm. Concerning situations that give rise to resentment, he countered simply, "What can be done about it?" indicating a path by which one can put an end to resentment itself. This is not a mark of apathetic resignation but an invitation to look again at the reality of saṃsāra, to appreciate its "stickiness," and to see that there is no skillfulness in trying to discharge one's resentment by trying to rectify the situation with appeals to justice. To do so is to fail to see what right view in such situations entails. This view is described in the account of action in the *Mahākammavibhanga Sutra*, which further highlights the unskillfulness of linking retribution or reward to transgression or compliance by pointing out the limits of what can be possibly be known about actions and their attendant fallout (*karma*).

In chapter 9 I take up the issue of time. Action aimed at social change looks for measurable results within a graspable time frame in which past, present, and future are clearly marked out. The Buddha challenged such attachment to past and future states, pointing out that "invincibility" is found only in the present. Following Dōgen's reflections on time in *Uji*, I show how fecund that present is and how it can school us in the exercise of patient forbearance. The chapter concludes with a reflection on the skillfulness of invoking *kalpas*, those immeasurable expanses of time (and not unrelated to the immeasurable expanse of karuṇā) as a tool for freeing the mind from attachment to localized, temporally frameable, outcomes. It is this understanding of time that makes the bodhisattva's great vow to liberate all beings more than empty words.

Finally, chapter 10 addresses the curious and troubled relationship between religion and politics in contemporary life. When asked for a brief summary of the Dharma, the Buddha replied, "A bhikkhu has heard that nothing is worth adhering to."[15] One way that insight manifests is in the surrender of the impulse to weigh in on current events and to influence others. Beginning with the Buddha's injunction against what he identified as "pointless talk"—which included talk about society and politics—we can see that the drive to function as a social watchdog that would "speak truth to power" reveals a kind of hubris that is wholly incompatible with the surrender of self so integral to the path that leads to dukkha's end. If there is a role for the practice of the Dharma in the public sphere, it would consist in simply being a living manifestation of the holy life in its exercise of solitude and non-attachment, a selfless and agendaless demonstration of the key point that "nothing is worth adhering to."

The Dharma is often viewed as something exotic come from the East, even though it has always presented itself simply as a clear-eyed account of the nature of things. By way of conclusion, I offer examples from the Christian tradition that exemplify some of the themes taken up here. Although for the sake of analysis I have had to differentiate key elements of the Dharma from certain ideas found in the Christian tradition throughout the book, my point was never to take issue with Christianity was a whole. In fact, the Christian tradition is replete with accounts of those who, like the Buddha and the noble disciples, understood that "nothing is worth adhering to," set aside all conceit of the self, and gave themselves over to the wholehearted pursuit of the holy life of solitude and surrender.

I should add that I have felt free to move among the *Nikāyas*, Theravādin commentators, Nāgārjuna and other Madhyamakans, the Zen tradition, and contemporary teachers in all schools, not because I do not recognize or appreciate the subtle differences among them, but because I have been profoundly struck by the one voice they all share when it comes to the core of the Dharma. No Lion of the Dharma ever lived at a time when everyone was fed, the laws equally administered, the weapons of war stilled, or nature in its pristine beauty and wonder kept free from human threat, yet all of their fingers seem to point toward the One Moon all the same.

15. Ñāṇamoli and Bodhi, *Middle Length Discourses*, 347.

To sum up: "Social revolution" is not "the mercy of the West." It is a construct that grew out of some very specific turns in late-eighteenth and early-nineteenth-century European philosophy and political practice. It has never entirely freed itself from the self/other metaphysics of the West, as any number of critics by now have pointed out. It is also not a key element of the Dharma, nor can it be without losing what is most distinctive about the Dharma, the unshakable deliverance of mind from all that has hitherto constrained it. Returning one last time to Snyder's language—and this, in a nutshell, is the driving thesis of this book—if one has realized (as he phrased it) "individual insight into the self/void," one will *not even begin* to entertain talk of "social revolution."

I

Going Alone

1

This Holy Life

THROUGHOUT ALL THE YEARS of his teaching, the Buddha insisted that he taught one thing and one thing only: dukkha and its end.[1] Other religious or philosophical systems may offer perspectives on how best to manage one's day-to-day life, how to deal with interpersonal relations, how to understand one's place in the universe or society, or how to conceive of the whole of the cosmos form start to finish, but none other sets out to address—as directly or as exclusively—the issue the Buddha addressed: dukkha and its end. This is the Buddha's unique contribution to the world, profound in its straightforwardness and efficacy. Whatever else may have attached itself to the practice of Buddhism over the course of the centuries, whatever ideas or concepts or practices may have eventually come to be associated with it in its movement out of India and beyond, and whatever interesting philosophical or religious ideas it might raise in the speculatively minded, if there is any standard by which to measure just how near or far any of these are from the heart of the Dharma, it is to be found in the degree to which they hew to the teaching of dukkha and its end.

The Buddha was under no illusion that this teaching was going to be to everyone's liking or comprehension. According to the canonical account, the newly awakened Buddha was in fact quite loath to teach what he had come to know given the strong likelihood of a poor reception:

1. Bodhi, *Connected Discourses*, 938.

> "If I were to teach the Dhamma and if others would not understand me, that would be wearisome for me, that would be troublesome."
> Thereupon these astounding verses, not heard before in the past, occurred to the Blessed One:
>
> "Enough now with trying to teach
> What I found with so much hardship;
> This Dhamma is not easily understood
> By those oppressed by lust and hate"
>
> "Those fired by lust, obscured by darkness,
> Will never see this abstruse Dhamma,
> Deep, hard to see, subtle,
> Going against the stream."
>
> As the Blessed One reflected thus, his mind inclined to living at ease, not to teaching the Dhamma.[2]

Then Brahmā Sahampati, seeing the impending loss, intervened and persuaded the Buddha to teach by pointing out that there were at least *some* human beings "with little dust in their eyes" who would otherwise perish without the Dharma. This was just enough:

> Having seen this, he answered Brahmā Sahampati in verse:
>
> "Open to them are the doors of the Deathless:
> Let those who have ears release faith.
> Foreseeing trouble, O Brahmā, I did not speak
> The refined, sublime Dhamma among human beings."[3]

And so the Wheel of the Dharma began to turn—but only for those few with ears to hear and eyes as yet just a little clouded over.

As we begin this exploration of a Dharmic response to the ills of the world we do well to keep the Buddha's initial reluctance in mind. Many aspects of the practice come down from the time of the first promulgation of the Dharma now enjoy a certain broad familiarity and even popular appeal, and it can be hard to see what the Buddha's reluctance could possibly have been about. Frequently enough the association is made between the Dharma and meditation, for instance, particularly in the West, and, to be sure, the practice of the Dharma does make use of meditative techniques and, as a rule, gives much higher importance to

2. Bodhi, *Connected Discourses*, 231–32.

3. Bodhi, *Connected Discourses*, 233.

them than, say, ritual observances. The ones the Buddha taught were, however—from the beginning stages to the most advanced—the ones he himself had learned from his own teachers,[4] and there are clear parallels between these mediative practices and certain forms of contemplative prayer in other traditions as well. They are included in the practice because they are skillful ways of cultivating the tranquility (*samatha*) and insight (*vipassanā*) that help clear the mind and so conduce toward realization.[5] Tranquility, insight, and the meditative practices that develop them are important, but they are still not the heart of the Dharma.

Or again, many have been swift to praise the ethical dimensions of the Dharma, but one would be hard-pressed to see in the precepts much of anything that is not part and parcel of most other religious and philosophical ethical teachings as well. The five core precepts (*pañca śīla*)—not to kill, not to take what is not given, not to engage in sexual misconduct, not to lie, and not to indulge in intoxicants—are foundational for any spiritual practice, no matter what tradition it is found in. But they are foundational for any decent human life, too, and the Buddha reminded his disciples that anyone who would praise him for keeping these would only be focusing on "inferior matters,"[6] and that even the more focused ethical practices of the renunciant life—refraining from adornment, idle entertainment, luxurious accommodations, not harming the environment, and the like—are still not particularly extraordinary, are found in other renunciant-contemplative traditions, and can be easily appreciated as praiseworthy even by many everyday people. All the same, they do not, of themselves, necessarily reflect anything about the heart of the Dharma.

The aim of the Dharma is not simply to make us better meditators or even more ethical people, as worthwhile as these might be. Its heart lies elsewhere:

> This holy life, bhikkhus, does not have gain, honour, and renown for its benefit, or the attainment of virtue for its benefit, or the attainment of concentration for its benefit, or knowledge and vision for its benefit. But it is this unshakeable deliverance of mind that is the goal of this holy life, its heartwood, and its end.[7]

4. Ñāṇamoli and Bodhi, *Middle Length Discourses*, 256–59.
5. Bodhi, *Numerical Discourses*, 152.
6. Walshe, *Long Discourses*, 68–73.
7. Ñāṇamoli and Bodhi, *Middle Length Discourses*, 290.

And it is that unshakable deliverance of mind that is so uncanny, so counterintuitive, and so against the stream that the Buddha had a hard time imagining it could possibly draw the least interest—let alone understanding—from anyone at all. This is because it consists of nothing less than the complete abandonment of every form of attachment, and it is so thoroughgoing that when the Buddha was asked by one of his senior disciples, Moggallāna, if he recalled ever having given a short summary of the Dharma, he responded:

> I do recall doing so, Moggallāna. Here Sakka, ruler of gods, came to me, and after paying homage to me, he stood at one side and asked: "Venerable sir, how in brief is a bhikkhu liberated in the destruction of craving, one who has reached the ultimate end, the ultimate security from bondage, the ultimate holy life, the ultimate goal, one who is foremost among gods and humans?" When this was said, I told him: "Here, ruler of gods, a bhikkhu has [seen] that nothing is worth adhering to."[8]

The slightly more expanded formulation of the Buddha's succinct "nothing is worth adhering to" is, of course, nothing other than the Noble Truths of dukkha, its origin, its cessation, and the path to its cessation.

We do well to take the time at the outset of this study to familiarize ourselves with this heart of the Dharma itself, both in terms of what it teaches *and* in terms of what conduces to its realization. Both are essential. The Buddha called what he had to say the *Dhamma-vinaya*, the teaching-*and*-discipline, and not without reason. The teaching informs the discipline, and each step of the discipline helps one to see for oneself—unshakeably, not just intellectually or affectively—the core truth the teaching expresses: nothing is worth adhering to. Together their exercise constitutes the holy life (*brahmacariya*), as it is called in the early sources, a life that, down to its least aspect, is one devoted to that honest and utterly straightforward practice of identifying without filter and without fear every last instance of one's attachments in order to surrender them all. In this respect, such a life is best characterized as a renunciant-contemplative practice, and it is the kind of spiritual work that one can only do for oneself—both because no one can do it for me, and because I cannot do it for others.

8. Ñāṇamoli and Bodhi, *Middle Length Discourses*, 347. I have substituted *seen* for *heard* here. In everyday English, someone who realizes something is said to have seen it. As the sutra continues, it is clear that what is being referred to is not the auditory reception of someone else's verbal message but the clear realization of the truth of things.

Starting with what can only be the barest of summaries of the first of the Noble Truths of dukkha, its cause, and its end, I offer here a somewhat fuller account of the fourth Noble Truth. Although it is well captured under the rubric of the Eightfold Path, it is perhaps best understood when viewed in light of the *gradual training*, as it is referred to in the *Nikāyas*, the developmental stages in the cultivation of the holy life from start to finish. My aim here is to provide a framework and an orientation for the discussions in the remaining chapters by setting out some of the broad lines of thinking and more specialized vocabulary that will be used along the way. More specifically, I am looking to ground any discussion of social action that would accord with the Dharma squarely within the renunciant-contemplative practice out of which it emerges and to which it necessarily returns.

What is noteworthy about the Buddha's teaching on dukkha is not that dukkha exists; everyone will agree as much. No one will deny that life has its share of heartache and pain or that even small joys are fleeting and large dreams are never quite fulfilled. Its distinctiveness lies in the realization that, as far as the everyday experience of conditioned phenomena, or dharmas, goes, there is *nothing but* dukkha. When the Buddha declared that "birth is suffering, aging is suffering, illness is suffering, death is suffering; union with that is displeasing is suffering, separating from what is pleasing is suffering; not to get what one wants is suffering,"[9] he was not listing seven particular things that constitute dukkha but rather indicating dukkha's sheer *comprehensiveness*. There is no discernible state of affairs that is immune from it, and there is no alternative state of affairs imaginable in which it would not also be present. The substantive content of every "If only . . ." ever uttered, were it to come to pass, would itself be a further occasion of dukkha as it fails to live up to expectations or, even if it should, simply fail to endure. The simple and straightforward claim of the Noble Truth—*there is dukkha*—cuts to the root of every form of wistful or magical thinking, any hankering for what might have been, or any hope that (at least some) effects do not follow inexorably from their causes and conditions.

9. Bodhi, *Connected Discourses*, 1844.

This disappointing character of all phenomena is part and parcel of what it means to be a phenomenon in the first place. When I look closely at things, events, or psycho-physical conditions, I cannot help but notice that they rise, change, and fall in conjunction with the circumstances around them. Because they are only ever conditioned (*anattā*) in this way, they are also impermanent (*anicca*). If they were self-generating, they could, in principle, maintain themselves forever. But such is not the case—not for anything around me nor even for myself. Here again, most religious and philosophical systems are in agreement with the broad contours of this claim concerning the fleetingness of life. The distinctiveness of the Buddha's teaching is that there is in experience *only* non-self; there is no discernible state of affairs that is without a proximate cause, and there is nothing discernible that is itself uncaused, unchanging, or abiding that underlies or perdures through it.

Distinctive, too, is the identification of where, exactly, the source of dukkha lies. When the Buddha listed the various forms of dukkha, he summed them all up in one simple statement: "In brief, the five aggregates subject to clinging are suffering."[10] The five aggregates (*skandhas*) are the identifiable, mutually conditioning, moments in having any experience at all. Any experiencing is owed to the fact that there is a living body (*rūpa*), a field that opens on to the world in certain kinds of ways and not others. Its particular way of opening on to the world, generally referred to as the senses, allow for sensations (*vedanā*) to arise that come to be associated with each other, giving rise to the apperception (*saṃjñā/saññā*) of a certain object or state of affairs that can be interacted with or not (*saṃskāra/saṅkhāra*) based on whatever else is going on at the time. If someone asks, it is possible to report on all of this because there is a conscious awareness (*vijñāna/viññāṇa*) of what is happening as well. Taken together, the skandhas exhaustively account for "what is going on" as far as my experience of myself, others, and the world goes.

Tṛṣṇā emerges at the point at which the content and conditions of experience are overlaid with the conceit of a self that recoils at the thought of being subject to the marks of dukkha, anattā, and anicca like everything else. Simply put, tṛṣṇā is what transforms "things experienced" or "things that happen" into "things related to me"—a *me* I have a vested interest in seeing turn out one way rather than another, because of—or

10. Bodhi, *Connected Discourses*, 1844.

despite—the fluctuating nature of experience. The *Nikāyas* give a rather clear picture of how this works, here with tṛṣṇā rendered as *craving*:

> Bhikkhus, I will teach you about craving—the ensnarer, streaming, widespread, and sticky—by which this world has been smothered and enveloped, and by which it has become a tangled skein, a knotted ball of thread, a mass of reeds and rushes, so that it does not pass beyond the plane of misery, the bad destination, the lower world, saṃsāra. Listen and attend closely; I will speak . . .
>
> There are, bhikkhus, these eighteen currents of craving related to the internal and eighteen currents of craving related to the external.
>
> And what are the eighteen currents of craving related to the internal? When there is [the notion] "I am," there are [the notions] "I am thus," "I am just so," "I am otherwise," "I am lasting," "I am evanescent," "I may be," "I may be thus," "I may be just so," "I may be otherwise," "May I be," "May I be thus," "May I be just so," "May I be otherwise," "I shall be," "I shall be thus," "I shall be just so," "I shall be otherwise." These are the eighteen currents of craving related to the internal.
>
> And what are the eighteen currents of craving related to the external? When there is [the notion], "I am because of this," there are [the notions]: "I am thus because of this," "I am just so because of this," "I am otherwise because of this," "I am lasting because of this," "I am evanescent because of this," "I may be because of this," "I may be thus because of this," "I may be just so because of this," "I may be otherwise because of this," "May I be because of this," "May I be thus because of this," "May I be just so because of this," "May I be otherwise because of this," "I shall be because of this," "I shall be thus because of this," "I shall be just so because of this," "I shall be otherwise because of this." These are the eighteen currents of craving related to the external.[11]

This passage is worth reading in full, because of all the descriptions of tṛṣṇā in the *Nikāyas* this narratively structured presentation is one of the most useful and certainly one of the clearest. It squarely situates the source of dukkha in the introduction of the idea of a self, an "I," into what is otherwise the mutually conditioning functioning of the skandhas (the "this"). It also highlights just how downright *psychotic* tṛṣṇā is—a persistent drive to break with what is simply going on by trying to commandeer a very dynamic, changing, and ultimately ungraspable interplay of

11. Bodhi, *Numerical Discourses*, 586–87.

phenomena into a storyline that agrees with my projected self-concept. Moreover, it demonstrates just how banal and commonplace tṛṣṇā can be, a willingness to tether the self to anything at all, since the *this* in question covers anything from the most trivial to the most sublime.

Tṛṣṇā is the broadest name given to this compulsive drive, but it can be further broken down according to its modes of operation. I can either try to latch on to dharmas that serve my self concept (greed/attachment, or *rāga*), seek to eliminate or protect myself from those that seem to hinder or harm my self concept (anger/aversion, or *dosa/dveṣa*), or I might just simply be stymied as to what is going and where I fit into it altogether (delusion, or *moha*). In the *Nikāyas* and commentarial sources these three defilements (*kleśas*) are called the "three unwholesome roots"; in the Mahāyāna they are designated the "three poisons." They are, as it were, the power source that keeps the churning of tṛṣṇā in motion. Further refinements of the kleśas are based on the kinds of dharmas they manifest in conjunction with: the taints (*āsavas*) are particular ways in which the kleśas leave the world altered in their wake,[12] and the five hindrances (*nīvaraṇas*) are perduring mental habits and dispositions that obstruct the attainment of tranquility and insight.[13] Whether viewed as kleśas, āsavas, or nīvaraṇas, all of these obstructive states have their origin in a fundamental ignorance (*avidyā/avijjā*) of things as they really are.

The end of dukkha lies in the cessation of the tṛṣṇā that gives rise to it. This cessation of tṛṣṇā is *called* nirvāṇa. Far from being some kind of mystical experience, altered state, or place, the cessation of tṛṣṇā is simply that—a cessation or extinguishing, however brief at the start, of the compulsive drive to pass all experience through the registering and assessing filter of the self. The endless production of "I am" statements that ordinarily arise in conjunction with matters of body, speech, and mind when driven by the kleśas simply goes on hiatus.

If the five aggregates subject to clinging is the definition of dukkha, the end of dukkha can be understood as the five aggregates *not* subject to clinging. There is still sensing, ideation, awareness, and the rest, but they rise and change and fall as conditions warrant without any felt need to evaluate how a presumed self might be faring through all of that, whether it be in my immediate context or in the broader picture of something I might fancy as *my life*. Ajahn Sucitto describes something of how this

12. See Ñāṇamoli and Bodhi, *Middle Length Discourses*, 91–96.

13. See Bodhi, *Connected Discourses*, 1591–92, 1597–98, 1631.

might manifest in his description of *sotāpanna*, or stream entry, the first limited and fleeting cessation of tṛṣṇā:[14]

> Stream-entry is the beginning of being completely composed on the path. With that level of clarity, there is no longer the instinctive need to hold on to any image, physical or psychological, as one's self. Someone who's "entered the stream" relates to their body as a part of nature . . . They regard the bundle of learned habits, emotional patterns, and attitudes as an acquisition, a product of conditioning, and of old kamma. Stream-enterers are not trying to make the world fit their personality, nor are they trying to abolish their personality . . . Finally, doubt, uncertainty about the Dhamma, is quelled because through applying himself or herself, a stream-enterer has sensed "the deathless," nibbana.[15]

Everything one happens to be and think is ever just exactly as it is, but now one has begun to see that none of that is at any point constitutive of an *identity* that needs to be cultivated, protected, and cherished. The subsequent stages of renunciant-contemplative development hone, refine, and further purify that initial clarity and clear away any remaining defilements.[16]

Nirvāṇa is often referred to in the *Nikāyas*, as here, as *the deathless*. Given a cultural horizon in which the phrase, *eternal life*, is frequently used in conjunction with ample speculation about postmortem existence, there is good reason to be cautious about using such language. A less fraught—but certainly more fecund and equally canonical—appellation would be *the fearless*.[17] With the cessation of tṛṣṇā, one comes to see that there is nothing for a self to be afraid of. No longer clinging to a self-concept, both the fear of it becoming otherwise (birth) and the fear of it being annihilated (death) simply do not arise.

The end of dukkha does not just happen willy-nilly. Having been so inured to dukkha, so ignorant of its cause, and so doubtful about the very possibility of its extinction, it might seem easier just to gut it out until the

14. Broadly speaking, *kenshō* or *satori* in Zen correspond to *sotāpanna*.

15. Sucitto, *Turning the Wheel*, 126–27.

16. Whether considered as sotāpanna, kenshō, or satori, it is understood that this initial insight is but the first glimpse, so to speak, of nirvāṇa. In the Theravāda, there still remain the levels of once-returner (*sakadāgāmi*), non-returner (*anāgāmī*), and arhat; in the Mahāyāna this is the first of ten levels or grounds (*bhūmis*) of bodhisattvic attainment on the path to Buddhahood.

17. See Bodhi, *Numerical Discourses*, 550–52.

end, hope that it passes of its own accord, or pray that it be taken care of by someone else. Then again, I might try to do something about it, so I cast about for some way of improving my lot by manipulating circumstances with the intention of putting more painful ones at bay and promoting more pleasant ones. While any of these might make me happier, calmer, wealthier, or better adjusted as these are commonly reckoned, none of them quite does the work of helping to see clearly the reality and the cause of dukkha. In fact, engaging in these various strategies only serves to further the churning of tṛṣṇā as I try my utmost to leverage myself to a better situation.[18] On the other hand, I might go in the opposite direction and, sensing dimly that there is a connection between dukkha and my bodily and mental states, try to cut to the chase and just eliminate my embodied form. Suicide, of course, stands at the farthest limit of this strategy, but all forms of mortification have this same end in view.[19] The mistake here lies in the thought that the self is somehow caused by the skandhas and that in order to become "selfless," I need to be free of those causes. Using one's body or one's abilities as a tool or taking aim at them as the source of troubles is still a way of playing the game of "May I (not) be because of this."

The path outlined by the Buddha offers a way to come to the cessation of tṛṣṇā without at the same time getting caught in the trap of self-improvement or self-destruction.[20] Each component of the Eightfold Path—right view (*sammādiṭṭhi*), right aspiration/intention (*sammāsankappa*), right speech (*sammavācā*), right effort (*sammāvāyāma*), right action (*sammākammanta*), right livelihood (*sammā-ājivo*), right mindfulness (*sammāsāti*), and right concentration (*sammāsamādhi*)—provides a skillful approach by which an aspirant might come to see for him or

18. Therapeutic applications of the Buddha's teaching need to be counted among these as well. No doubt mindfulness training in clinical settings and other such exercises bring some measure of relief and comfort to those who practice them. Still, such uses cannot be counted among the factors on the path to awakening.

19. While the Buddha never flagged in his praise of *renunciation* and a moderate *ascesis*, he had no hesitation at all in pointing out the misguidedness of all forms of *mortification*. Renunciation is understood here as the setting aside of something that is no longer considered worthy of my time. Asceticism is the discipline undertaken to facilitate that task. The term is derived from the Greek *áskesis*, which means exercise or training. It calls for the resolve to do what needs to be done, even if it involves physical, mental, and even emotional hardship. Mortification has the Latin *mors*, or death, as its root. It is nothing but fruitless self-mutilation.

20. Classically these are referred to as the *thirst for existence* and the *thirst for annihilation*.

herself the conditioned nature of all phenomena (one's self included), become dispassionate towards them, and come to be free of the tṛṣṇā that gives rise to dukkha. They do this by schooling the aspirant in the art of setting down the burden of always trying to fiddle with phenomena in order to game their conditioned nature to some advantage or another.

Right view stands at the forefront of the eight because it indicates at the outset the kind of view that is required to take up the other seven aspects of the path at the same time as it indicates their aim: "Right view comes first. And how does right view come first? One understands wrong view as wrong view and right view as right view: this is one's right view."[21] The first moment of right view is the very basic recognition that there is even a difference between right view and wrong view at all. Wrong view fails on this point from the outset:

> And what, bhikkhus, is wrong view? "There is nothing given, nothing offered, nothing sacrificed, no fruit or result of good and bad actions; no this world, no other world; no mother, no father, no beings who are reborn spontaneously; no good and virtuous recluses and brahmins in the world who have realised for themselves by direct knowledge and declare this world and the other world." This is wrong view.[22]

Wrong view obliterates differentiation of every kind. Actions are seen neither as skillful nor unskillful, and persons are not distinguished in the least. There is no separation between attainment and non-attainment, and all of experienced reality is affirmed as a monistic, seamless lump of facticity. We should not be too hasty in overlooking the perduring attractiveness of this position and in so doing miss the need to identify it for what it is. "It's all good" or "It is what it is" might be everyday versions of wrong view; other variations might be "we are all the same" or, in a religious context, "all spiritual paths are valid." The largesse of spirit such statements purport to show hides the fact that such a view is both vacuous and vapid—it says nothing particular, and in overlooking significant ethical distinctions among persons and actions ("We are *all* saints" or "We are *all* sinners," for example) it roundly fails to orient action.

Right view stands counter to wrong view in two ways: "There is right view that is affected by taints, partaking of merit, ripening in the acquisitions; and there is right view that is noble, taintless, supramundane,

21. Ñāṇamoli and Bodhi, *Middle Length Discourses*, 934.

22. Ñāṇamoli and Bodhi, *Middle Length Discourses*, 934.

a factor of the path."[23] The first of these stands directly counter to wrong view:

> And what, bhikkhus, is right view that is affected by the taints, partaking of merit, ripening in the acquisitions? "There is what is given and what is offered and what is sacrificed; there is fruit and result of good and bad actions; there is this world and the other world; there is mother and father; there are beings who are reborn spontaneously; there are in the world good and virtuous recluses and brahmins who have realised for themselves by direct knowledge and declare this world and the other world."[24]

This view is right in that it acknowledges the lay of the land in all its differentiation. There *is* right and wrong. There *are* saints and scoundrels. There *is* a difference between unawakened and awakened. This view is right in that it avoids the stupidity and torpor that comes with denying such distinctions. With this form of right view, it makes sense to strive to be free of the attachments and dark paths that have hitherto proven obstructive because I can discern relative merit and gain and loss. One possessed of this first kind of right view is clear on the point that there is something at stake in spiritual aspiration, that there are skillful and unskillful actions, and that reality in all its myriad diversity and complexity is not to be glossed over in the process.

This form of right view, however, is not without its drawbacks. It is still "affected by taints, partaking of merit, ripening in the acquisitions," and as long as these are operative, one is still caught up in the push and pull of dharmas and will continue to define oneself with reference to them. This may not matter much for everyday persons, and it is fair to say that most religious and philosophical systems remain at the level of this first kind of right view—disagreeing on the details, perhaps, but nevertheless remaining fundamentally committed to the dynamics of such oppositional pairs as right and wrong, holy and profane, just and unjust, better and worse. If wrong view leaves one indifferent to the diversity of phenomena, the first kind of right view leaves one fretful and fidgety in always trying to see to it that the preferred side of any of those pairings has the upper hand.

23. Ñāṇamoli and Bodhi, *Middle Length Discourses*, 934.

24. Ñāṇamoli and Bodhi, *Middle Length Discourses*, 935.

The practice of the Dharma is unique in that it conduces to the second kind of right view, going past both lethargy and restlessness by cutting to the heart of the matter:

> And what, bhikkhus, is right view that is noble, taintless, supramundane, a factor of the path? The wisdom, the faculty of wisdom, the power of wisdom, the investigation-of-states enlightenment factor, the path factor of right view in one whose mind is noble, whose mind is taintless, who possesses the noble path and is developing the noble path: this is right view that is noble, taintless, supramundane, a factor of the path.[25]

The second form of right view is the direct awareness of the Four Noble Truths. To the extent that I begin to see that *all* dharmas—the ones I call right *and* the ones I call wrong, the ones that I label exalted *and* the ones I label profane—are still dharmas, still of a nature to be inconstant, still without abiding substance, and hence all still unsatisfactory, I can slowly come to live and move without pinning my identity to them. My thoughts and comportment are no longer governed by the push and pull of attraction and aversion, and I no longer try to plot a path of liberation with reference to them. All things remain just as they are in their relative differentiation and diversity, but I am not buffeted about by that differentiation and diversity. The other constituents of the Eightfold Path follow a similar trifold formulation, and, through their exercise, guide the aspirant from the first kind of right view to the second in various situations.

The Eightfold Path is frequently referred to in the *Nikāyas* and elsewhere as the *Middle Way*. It is "middle," but not because it is a negotiated *mean* between extremes, which would still only belong to the first kind of right view and would involve, after all, an ongoing process of tinkering in search of some sweet spot among various conditions. Instead, it is "middle" in that it *goes beyond* oppositional thinking—pain versus pleasure, gain versus loss, right versus wrong, too much versus too little—together with the thorough abandonment of the notion of an *optimum state* between or among any of them. Each component of the Eightfold Path, if followed, helps the aspirant cut through the machinations of evaluation, assessment, and strategizing by offering a rather straightforward and uncomplicated alternative that is present in any situation whatsoever: cling or abandon clinging, adhere or set aside[26]—*and let the chips fall where*

25. Ñāṇamoli and Bodhi, *Middle Length Discourses*, 935.

26. Paul Fuller puts it this way concerning right view: "The notion of *diṭṭhi* has

they may. Depending on the choice one makes, one will either persist in dukkha or one will not, and on that score, at least, there is neither a middle nor a mean, however these are reckoned.

~

If the end of dukkha does not happen willy-nilly, it also does not happen overnight. Like any human practice, it begins haltingly and rather superficially, and guided training is required. When the Buddha was asked whether he offered a gradual training in the Dharma in much the same way that, say, brahmins, archers, and accountants use to train their novices and apprentices, the Buddha replied that he did indeed offer a gradual training. His, however, was not a program of skill acquisition as much a series of ever more subtly refined and intentional exercises whereby an aspirant is confronted with two clear and distinct paths—cling or abandon clinging, persist in dukkha or be free of it.

The Buddha compared the gradual training he offered to the kind of training a horse trainer uses in slowly breaking a horse.[27] Here, of course, we are dealing with a human being who voluntarily submits to the discipline, but otherwise the comparison is instructive. The untrained everyday person, having for so long been his or her own lord and master with nothing to show for it but dukkha, gets the vague sense that there might be something right about the Dharma as he or she has heard it. Seeing others who have pursued it and come to some measure of insight and release, that person entrusts him or herself to those more advanced in the discipline—handing over the reins, as it were—in order to be slowly guided into and tempered by this new way of life:

> The Dhamma is heard by a householder or a householder's son, or one reborn in some family or other. Having heard this Dhamma, he gains faith in the Tathāgata. Having gained faith, he reflects: "The household life is close and dusty, the homeless life is free as air. It is not easy living the household life, to live the fully-perfected holy life, purified and polished like a conch-shell. Suppose I were to go forth from the household life into homelessness!"[28]

---

less to do with truth and falsehood, than with craving and its cessation." Fuller, *Notion of* Diṭṭhi, 7. The same would be true of the other components of the Path as well.

27. Ñāṇamoli and Bodhi, *Middle Length Discourses*, 874.

28. Walshe, *Long Discourses*, 99.

This very first step in the Dharma already involves a tradeoff—setting aside the "householder way" of doing things in order to be trained in the "renunciant-contemplative way" of doing things.[29] This root tradeoff is referred to in the tradition as *taking refuge* in the Buddha, the Dharma and the Saṅgha, or the Three Jewels. Taking refuge is an act of faith, not in the sense of registering one's agreement with certain propositional content[30] but in the sense of entrusting oneself to something other than one's own preferred way of going about things, confident that that trust will not be in vain. Taking refuge is thus also at the same time an act of renunciation, a resolute setting aside of the blind, self-fancied autonomy of always following one's own inclinations, attachments, and aversions in favor of what needs to be done.[31]

We see this reflected already in the first stage in the training, which confirms in the aspirant the first form of right view and the basic distinction between virtuous and blameworthy actions: "Come, bhikkhu, be virtuous, restrained with the restraint of the Pātimokkha, be perfect in conduct and resort, and seeing fear in the slightest fault, train by undertaking the training precepts."[32] For a bhikkhu, this means submitting to the 227 training rules (311 for a bhikkhunī). For an upāsaka or upāsikā, this means conformity to at least the five root precepts, though more may be taken.[33] Whether as a monastic or as a layperson, the precepts or

29. Because so much of what the Buddha will describe in terms of the gradual training is no less applicable to non-monastics than to monastics, I would caution the reader against too quickly making a mental distinction between ordained and non-ordained here. At issue here is not exclusively (or even primarily) where and among whom I lie down to sleep at night as much as the cultivation of a way of living that, whether pursued as a monastic in robes or as a householder in street clothes, is distinguished from the common, undisciplined, everyday way of living in which everything gets reduced to some variation of "what I happen to want."

30. As the Noble Truths can only be seen into at the *end* of practice, a neophyte (or anyone shy of awakening for that matter) has no standing for either agreeing with *or* rejecting them.

31. Giuliano Giustarini has pointed out the integral connection between faith (*saddhā*) and renunciation (*nekkhamma*) in the pursuit of the Dharma. While his focus is on the early canonical sources, I would make the case that that dyad remains operative through all levels of the gradual training in any school of the Dharma that accords with the Noble Truths. Giustarini, "Faith and Renunciation," 161–79.

32. Ñāṇamoli and Bodhi, *Middle Length Discourses*, 874.

33. The five root precepts for the upāsakas and upāsikās were frequently augmented with further training precepts. On uposatha days of more dedicated practice the lay disciples took three additional precepts (against eating at the wrong time, against taking in entertainment, and against enjoying luxurious accommodations) as a way

training rules are *received* from another who is in a position to *give* them, and it is the aspirant's job simply to *follow* them.[34] Like an unbroken horse that only does what it wants to do and so chafes at the bit, the beginning aspirant is sure to find some of the precepts and training rules constricting and will push back on them:

> There are certain misguided men here who, when told by me "Abandon this," say: "What, such a mere trifle, such a little thing as this? This recluse is much too exacting!" And they do not abandon that and they show discourtesy towards me as well as towards those bhikkhus desirous of training. For them that thing becomes a strong, stout, tough, unrotting tether and a thick yoke.

But whether the rule is trifling or weighty does not depend on what the rule demands but the degree of resistance one maintains in the face of it:

> There are certain clansmen here who, when told by me "Abandon this," say: "What, such a mere trifle, such a little thing to be abandoned as this, the Blessed One tells us to abandon, the Sublime One tells us to relinquish." Yet they abandon that and do not show discourtesy towards me or towards those bhikkhus desirous of training. Having abandoned it, they live at ease, unruffled, subsisting on others' gifts, with mind [as aloof] as a wild deer's. For them that thing becomes a feeble, weak, rotting, coreless tether.[35]

As the Buddha points out, it is not the rule that is confining; both parties here agree that the matter at hand is a trifle. They part company on the issue of whether they are going to fight the rule or simply comply.

---

of further clearing the ground for more concerted meditation. In the Mahāyāna, the core precepts are ten in number, and, as captured in the *Brahmā's Net Sutra*, there are a further forty-eight minor precepts for upāsakas and upāsikās.

34. Such a description might strike one as formulaic at best or downright legalistic at worst, but the aim of the training is not simply to follow a rule because it is a rule, but to stick to the rule in order to suss out where one's points of ego-attachment still lie. One only need consider the various means that are employed when trying to skirt the plain truth that one did nor did not do what was required: denial ("I didn't do it"), gaslighting ("That's not what you saw"), justification ("I did it, but . . ."), deflecting responsibility ("She made me do it"), questioning the norms themselves ("Who says this is so bad?"), seeking an excuse in the lapses of others ("Everyone else does it"), and relativizing ("It's not like I *killed* somebody"). In each of these instances one detects the voice of a self that does not want to be called out for the plain fact of the matter that the rule either was followed or it was not.

35. Ñāṇamoli and Bodhi, *Middle Length Discourses*, 553.

This is not a blind compliance, for the novice aspirant has good grounds for following the rule as stipulated. It is the same rule followed by those who have gone forth before in the holy life, so if I am interested in knowing what they have come to know, I do well to do what they have done. Moreover, I should not be surprised at their disapproval if any act is committed that is not worthy of their company. "The first cause and condition that leads to obtaining the wisdom fundamental to the spiritual life when it has not been obtained and to its increase, maturation, and fulfilment by development after it has been obtained," the Buddha said, is "a keen sense of moral shame and moral dread" along with "affection and reverence" for those who have gone further on the path.[36] The affection and reverence are already implied in taking refuge and placing oneself under the guidance of a teacher or one more advanced in the holy life; moral shame (*hiri*) and moral dread (*ottappa*) together make up the compass by which the aspirant can sense whether a prospective course of action is worthy of one who would be counted among them, both in terms of one's own estimation and in the estimation of others.

If *hiri-ottappa*[37] provides a skillful disincentive by which to guide my actions, the fearlessness and freedom that come with following its counsel are an attractive incentive and actually facilitate further progress on the path. When I follow a rule or a precept, I am never driven to hide anything I do from others: "Bhikkhus, the Tathāgata is one whose bodily behavior . . . verbal behavior . . . mental behavior . . . [and] livelihood [are] purified. There is no [such] behavior on the part of the Tathāgata that he might need to hide, [thinking]: 'Let others not find this out about me.'"[38] This is a fearless freedom that is not at all on par with the liberty to do as one pleases, since that liberty will almost inevitably prompt everything from defensive rationalizations to outright hiding and evasion. Once my conduct is purified, I can look at myself in the mirror and my spiritual betters in the eye and not blink. If I fail, at least I fail honestly, and I am free to start over again.

The next step in the training builds upon this first one:

> When, brahmin, the bhikkhu is virtuous . . . and seeing fear in the slightest fault, trains by undertaking the training precepts,

36. Bodhi, *Numerical Discourses*, 1112.

37. Moral shame and moral dread are almost invariably conjoined as a unified disposition, *hiri-ottappa*, in the *Nikāyas* and commentarial sources.

38. Bodhi, *Numerical Discourses*, 1056–57.

> then the Tathāgata disciplines him further: "Come, bhikkhu, guard the doors of your sense faculties. On seeing a form with the eye, do not grasp at its signs and features. Since, if you were to leave the eye unguarded, evil unwholesome states of covetous and grief might invade you, practice the way of its restraint, guard the eye faculty, undertake the restraint of the eye faculty. On hearing a sound with the ear . . .[39]

What until now had been a matter of external compliance is now slowly being internalized. The precept indicates the bright line between stealing and not stealing, for instance, but it does not address what prompted me to entertain theft in the first place. For that, I need to examine my own disposition toward the things around me. How is it, I might wonder, that this object—out of all the ones around me—is so captivating that I simply *must* have it, even if it means surreptitiously depriving another of it. The teaching on the skandhas provides the answer.

Recall that the operation of the skandhas provides the sole basis of any possible experience. Now given the way some things are and given the way I happen to be constituted, some experiences cause pain, others bring pleasure, and some are neither painful nor pleasurable. If I am not careful, I can easily be carried away by those qualities and try to make sure that the phenomena that help bring them about become part of my support system, pursuing and holding on to them when pleasurable, or avoiding them and, when possible, eliminating them should I find them displeasurable. Because it is the nature of dharmas to be continuously changing, this is going to keep me rather busy, and I might come to find that I have inadvertently chained myself exclusively to the pursuit of pleasure and the avoidance of pain.[40] To become free of all that and come to some degree of equanimity, I need only see things as the unsatisfactory, impermanent dharmas that they are:

> Bhikkhus, conditioned phenomena are impermanent; conditioned phenomena are unstable; conditioned phenomena are unreliable. It is enough to become disenchanted with all

39. Ñāṇamoli and Bodhi, *Middle Length Discourses*, 875.

40. The Dharma stands squarely against all utilitarian views about humans and actions that are appropriate in light of it. What Jeremy Bentham or John Stuart Mill saw as utterly obvious about the human condition—chained, as Bentham put it, to nature's dual thrones of pain and pleasure—the Buddha saw as being yet another conditioned state of affairs, widely present in the population of course, but not, for all that, unassailably so. We will have occasion again to see how the Buddha breaks ranks with a utilitarian perspective in the discussion of justice below.

> conditioned phenomena, enough to become dispassionate toward them, enough to be liberated from them.[41]

While it may enough to see all phenomena dispassionately to be liberated from them, I am not likely to be firm in the conviction of the unsatisfactoriness of *all* of them until I have come to see directly *some* of them this way for myself. At this stage of the training, it is enough to begin with those individual things that are especially attractive or repulsive to me. Since we are not all affected by phenomena equally, and what to one person may be particularly pleasurable or painful might just as soon leave another person cold and indifferent to their pursuit or avoidance, the aspirant proceeds, at least for a while, by taking them up one by one:

> When a bhikkhu sees a form with the eye, there arises in him what is agreeable, there arises what is disagreeable, there arises what is both agreeable and disagreeable. He understands thus: "There has arisen in me what is agreeable, there has arisen what is disagreeable, there has arisen what is both agreeable and disagreeable. But that is conditioned, gross, dependently arisen; this is peaceful, this is sublime, that is, equanimity." The agreeable that arose, the disagreeable that arose, and the both agreeable and disagreeable that arose cease in him and equanimity is established.[42]

Guarding the doors of the sense faculties is a rather focused practice that is a far cry from *eliminating* the sense faculties altogether. If it were simply a matter of not being able to see, then the blind would be the most accomplished of all.[43]

41. Bodhi, *Numerical Discourses*, 1071.

42. Ñāṇamoli and Bodhi, *Middle Length Discourses*, 1148.

43. Ñāṇamoli and Bodhi, *Middle Length Discourses*, 1147. Those familiar with the Gospels will no doubt be reminded of the injunction, "If your right eye causes you to sin, tear it out and throw it away; it is better for you to lose one of your members than for your whole body to be thrown into hell" (Matt 5:29). Following the Buddha, there is no need to extract an organ but simply to guard what one does with respect to what that organ helps bring about, and this no doubt accords with most exegeses of this passage; there are few Christian congregants, if any, who would follow it literally, and few pastors who would seriously recommend it. Still, there are passages in the *Nikāyas* that parallel quite closely the verse in Matthew. Consider the following:

> It would be better, bhikkhus, for the eye faculty to be lacerated by a red-hot iron pin burning, blazing, and glowing, than for one to grasp the sign through the features in a form cognizable by the eye. For if consciousness should stand tied to gratification in the sign or in the features, and if one should die on that occasion, it is possible that one will go to one of two destinations: hell or the

Here, too, moral shame and moral dread come into play, and in the *Nikāyas* they are identified as the "proximate cause"[44] of sense restraint. It may not be immediately obvious to me why I shouldn't just go after what is pleasing and why I shouldn't shy away from what is not; it is what I have been doing rather unthinkingly all of my life, others around me do the same, and I have received plenty of positive reinforcement of that behavior in the way my friends and family respond to me. Others may have even laughed along when I said something like, "That cake was calling to me and I just *had* to answer" but beneath the witticism is an admission that I simply couldn't guard my sense faculties in the face of—of all things—a baked good. But now that I have set out on the path, I should be ashamed to have to admit something like that in the presence of those who have mustered the kind of self-discipline called for here, especially if I hope to consider myself part of their company.

Here we come upon a sound understanding of the role renunciation plays in the practice of the Dharma. As Bhikkhu Bodhi points out, "Real renunciation is not a matter of compelling ourselves to give up things still inwardly cherished, but of changing our perspective on them so that they no longer bind us."[45] One way the tradition has offered to facilitate that change is to consider the conditioned nature of the object in question. If one is attracted to someone, one is invited to reflect on the fact that bodies are made up of all kinds of things that, when taken individually, are not really all that attractive. If some object is at issue, one can consider its composite makeup, the various stages of growth and decay, rising and falling it goes through, and see that none of that is particularly gripping, either. That cake, after all, is nothing but some flour, sugar, eggs, oil, leavening, salt, and flavoring—none of which seem to exercise quite the hold on me that cake does. If it gets left out for another few days, it will dry out or get moldy, and I will just as soon be repulsed by it as I was attracted to it. In any case, the attraction and repulsion have nothing to do with the cake but only with my dependently arisen thoughts, and it is these that I abandon in the exercise of sense restraint. So when the Buddha stated that it is "impossible" that one still attached to sensual pleasures "could know, see or realize that which must be known through renunciation, seen through renunciation, attained through renunciation,

animal realm. Having seen this danger, I speak thus. Ñāṇamoli and Bodhi, *Middle Length Discourses*, 1234.

44. Bodhi, *Numerical Discourses*, 1070.

45. Bodhi, *Noble Eightfold Path*, 27.

[and] realized through renunciation,"[46] he was inviting the hearer to take aim at the attachment, not at things themselves. Of course, as I surrender the attachment and stop thinking in terms of "things I simply *must have* in order to be a certain kind of person," it will follow that I come to live more and more with less and less around me. In the end—and this point cannot be emphasized enough because of the misunderstandings surrounding renunciation—it is the discipline of the mind that is aimed at with renunciation, not some projected image of a life of penury:

> Bhikkhus, desire and lust for forms is a corruption of the mind. Desire and lust for sounds . . . for odours . . . for tastes . . . for tactile objects . . . for mental phenomena is a corruption of the mind. When a bhikkhu has abandoned the mental corruption in these six cases, his mind inclines to renunciation. A mind fortified by renunciation becomes wieldy in regard to those things that are to be realized by direct knowledge.[47]

Rendering the mind pliable facilitates further progress on the path; simply making oneself miserable does not.

Guarding the doors of the sense faculties is carried out with reference to percepts generally; the next step of the training cultivates that same kind of dispassion toward percepts as they relate particularly to my own embodiment:

> When, brahmin, the bhikkhu guards the doors of his sense faculties, then the Tathāgata disciplines him further: "Come, bhikkhu, be moderate in eating. Reflecting wisely you should take food neither for amusement nor for intoxication nor for the sake of physical beauty and attractiveness, but only for the endurance and continuance of this body, for ending discomfort, and for assisting the holy life, considering: "Thus I shall terminate old feelings without arousing new feelings, and I shall be healthy and blameless and shall live in comfort."[48]

Although only food is mentioned here, the other necessities of life—clothing, shelter, and medicinals—are intended as well. Together these are called the "four requisites," because they are the external causal grounds for the continuation of a human body. Once again, the exercise of hiri-ottappa is key to this level of training, since there is a form of

46. Ñāṇamoli and Bodhi, *Middle Length Discourses*, 990.

47. Bodhi, *Connected Discourses*, 1012.

48. Ñāṇamoli and Bodhi, *Middle Length Discourses*, 875.

blamelessness proper to using what one needs without luxury, posturing, or self-aggrandizement. No one will call me out for wearing clothing that conforms to standards of modesty and that keeps the body safe and protected, and no defense is required in such a case beyond a simple, "this is what a body needs." That I consume far more than my body needs, that I have four of something where one will do just as well, that I have a luxurious version where a plain one will suffice—all of these, when questioned, need explanation, and that explanation invariably returns to some version of "because I want it." Among the everyday run of people, that explanation may be convincing enough; I might even be honored for being particularly adept in satisfying my various wants. Among those who have set themselves to the cessation of tṛṣṇā, however, such a defense will always be found wanting and will command no respect.

Once disciplined in everyday livelihood[49] by renunciation, the aspirant is now able to press forward, turning the attention now to internal percepts related to one's bodily comportment generally in terms of walking, standing, sitting, and lying down.[50] The practice of mindfulness takes this general wakefulness to a much more granular level:

> When, brahmin, the bhikkhu is devoted to wakefulness, then the Tathāgata disciplines him further: "Come, bhikkhu, be possessed of mindfulness and full awareness. Act in full awareness when going forward and returning; act in full awareness when looking ahead and looking away; act in full awareness when flexing and extending your limbs; act in full awareness when wearing your robes and carrying your outer robe and bowl; act in full awareness when eating, drinking, consuming food, and tasting; act in full awareness when defecating and urinating; act in full awareness when walking, standing, sitting, falling asleep, waking up, talking, and keeping silent."[51]

This practice of mindfulness is not just a matter of noting the mechanics of these various bodily states (the Buddha did not counsel acting in full awareness *of* my body and what it is doing but acting in full awareness *when* my body is doing something) but a practice of opening oneself up to the unsatisfactoriness, impermanence, and conditioned nature of these

49. Discussions of right livelihood are often reduced to considerations about particular jobs or professions. *Livelihood* is much broader, encompassing not only the way in which I *earn* my keep but equally with how I *dispose of* my earnings.

50. Ñāṇamoli and Bodhi, *Middle Length Discourses*, 875.

51. Ñāṇamoli and Bodhi, *Middle Length Discourses*, 875–76.

actions *in order to become dispassionate towards them*. This is why, when the Buddha breaks down and expounds upon these various applications of full awareness, he adds after each, "As he abides thus diligent, ardent, and resolute, his memories and intentions based on the household life are abandoned; with their abandoning his mind becomes steadied internally, quieted, brought to singleness, and concentrated."[52] That expression, *memories and intentions based on the household life*, is used here and elsewhere in the *Nikāyas* as a shorthand way to describe the point of view that everything is to be evaluated in terms of gain and loss, pleasure and pain, right and wrong—precisely the oppositional pairs around which one develops one's self-concept. Acting "in full awareness" when grasping something with my hand, or when using the implements of my trade, or even when I am availing myself of the toilet, then, would be an exercise in noting how I turn what is going on with my body into assessments of agreeableness or disagreeableness that give rise to the exercise of tṛṣṇā—"I am because of this," "I may be because of this," "May I be because of this," etc. Sometimes movements are more agile, sometimes more graceless; sometimes digestions are easy and regular, sometimes sluggish or quick. The practice of mindfulness consists in watching the arising of this chain of thought, seeing its conditioned nature, and, through that, coming that much closer to the realization, "This is not mine, this I am not, this is not my self."[53]

In addition to keeping the precepts, the ethical component of the path encompasses all of the training stages to this point: "That a bhikkhu who does not guard the doors of the sense faculties, who is immoderate in eating, and who is not devoted to wakefulness will maintain all his life the complete and pure holy life—this is impossible."[54] These are the solid foundation of the practice of the Dharma, absent which nothing firm can be built.[55] Without having become firm in these practices it will certainly

52. Ñāṇamoli and Bodhi, *Middle Length Discourses*, 950–51.

53. Bodhi, *Connected Discourses*, 902.

54. Bodhi, *Connected Discourses*, 1193.

55. It is a commonplace in many Buddhist circles that keeping the precepts is the foundation for the practice of meditation and the attainment of wisdom. Here I am following the *Nikāyas* in suggesting that it is not *just* the keeping of the precepts but the conforming of everyday life toward the Dharma in all its aspects that is foundational. I may not have run afoul of the law or those around me, but my life can still be so governed by sense desire, immoderation, and a continuous misapprehension of what is going on with and around me that any clarity I might get through meditation practice will be quite dim and rather fleeting.

not be possible to engage in the further stages of the gradual training that involve the progressive training of the mind, the practice of meditation proper. Here, too, it is important to distinguish meditation practices generally understood from those that would be fitting as components of the Eightfold Path to liberation:

> The Blessed One, brahmin, did not praise every type of meditation, nor did he condemn every type of meditation. What kind of meditation did the Blessed One not praise? Here, brahmin, someone abides with his mind obsessed by sensual lust, a prey to sensual lust, and he does not understand as it actually is the escape from sensual lust. While he harbours sensual lust within, he meditates, premeditates, out-meditates, and mismeditates. He abides with his mind obsessed by ill will, a prey to ill will . . . with his mind obsessed by sloth and torpor, a prey to sloth and torpor . . . with his mind obsessed by restlessness and remorse, a prey to restlessness and remorse . . . with his mind obsessed by doubt, a prey to doubt and he does not understand as it actually is the escape from arisen doubt . . . The Blessed One did not praise this kind of meditation.[56]

In the *Māratajjaniya Sutta* that word string, "meditates, premeditates, out-meditates, and mismeditates," is used pejoratively to describe a kind of "meditation" in which one just sits silently and intently—not unlike a cat waiting out the mouse or a jackal by the side of the stream waiting for a fish, as the Buddha described it.[57] One is certainly quite still and focused and impervious to whatever else is going on, but missing is the penetrating investigation of one's own mind and the ever clearer awareness of one's own obsessively obstructive states, not to mention the requisite effort needed to abandon them.[58]

And one does need to abandon them. These five hindrances, the nīvaraṇas, are the last great strongholds of the self, and the tenacity of their grip is owed to nothing quite so much as the fear of letting them go. Even when I have come to some degree of dispassion toward the objects of the senses and of thought, I find that I still cling to the very *ability to cling*, whether that clinging be reserving the right to anger and retaliation

56. Ñāṇamoli and Bodhi, *Middle Length Discourses*, 885.

57. Ñāṇamoli and Bodhi, *Middle Length Discourses*, 433.

58. Here we have, I think, one of the brightest lines of demarcation between the many forms of meditation offered in the marketplace and meditation that accords with the Dharma or can in any way even be said to be "Buddhist" in its orientation.

toward those who do me harm (ill will), self-directedness enough to try to fix things in and around myself (restlessness and remorse), the option to just quit the practice altogether in the face of the tedium that it involves (sloth-torpor), or the liberty to withhold wholehearted commitment to the path by keeping my options open (doubt). For this reason, the Buddha was quite keen to single out the nīvaraṇas for special mention: "Bhikkhus, saying 'a heap of the unwholesome,' it is about these five hindrances that one could rightly say this. For these five hindrances are a complete heap of the unwholesome."[59] They are such a mess of unwholesomeness that, without having abandoned them, "it is impossible that a bhikkhu, with his powerless and feeble wisdom, might know his own good, the good of others, or the good of both, or realize superhuman distinction in knowledge and vision worthy of the noble ones."[60]

When the Buddha next directs the aspirant to the practice of seated meditation in solitude, then, it is with the understanding that the nīvaraṇas still need to be overcome and that a particular kind of concentrated awareness is the most skillful way of accomplishing it:

> When, brahmin, the bhikkhu possesses mindfulness and full awareness, then the Tathāgata disciplines him further: "Come, bhikkhu, resort to a secluded resting place: the forest, the root of a tree, a mountain, a ravine, a hillside cave, a charnel ground, a jungle thicket, an open space, a heap of straw."
>
> He resorts to a secluded resting place: the forest . . . a heap of straw. On returning from his almsround, after his meal he sits down, folding his legs crosswise, setting his body erect, and establishing mindfulness before him. Abandoning covetousness for the world, he abides with a mind free from covetousness. Abandoning ill will and hatred, he abides with a mind free from ill will, compassionate for the welfare of all living beings; he purifies his mind from ill will and hatred. Abandoning sloth and torpor, he abides free from sloth and torpor, percipient of light, mindful and fully aware; he purifies his mind from sloth and torpor. Abandoning restlessness and remorse, he abides unagitated with a mind inwardly peaceful; he purifies his mind from restlessness and remorse. Abandoning doubt, he abides having gone beyond doubt, unperplexed about wholesome states; he purifies his mind from doubt.[61]

59. Bodhi, *Numerical Discourses*, 681.

60. Bodhi, *Numerical Discourses*, 680.

61. Ñāṇamoli and Bodhi, *Middle Length Discourses*, 876.

This is a very *engaged* (for lack of a better word) meditative practice because one is still in the process of becoming untethered from these hindrances, and the *Nikāyas* and commentarial literature are keen to offer numerous directed strategies for working with them as a whole and individually precisely because of their cunning nature.[62]

Only once the nīvaraṇas have been overcome can one now—at long last—begin to taste the first fruits of this long and difficult practice:

> Having thus abandoned these five hindrances, imperfections of the mind that weaken wisdom, quite secluded from sensual pleasures, secluded from unwholesome states, he enters upon and abides in the first jhāna, which is accompanied by applied and sustained thought, with rapture and pleasure born of seclusion.[63]

The jhānas are the four ever-deepening stages of contemplative concentration or samādhi, each attained as certain of the hindrances are definitively abandoned. They are marked by the advent of pleasant mind states—"rapture and pleasure born of seclusion," "rapture and pleasure born of concentration," "pleasure divested of rapture," and finally "pure bright mind"[64]—but even these will, in turn, need to be abandoned if the mind is to become increasingly purified. This is because even these samādhi states are conditioned phenomena, and so the gradual training does not end without the Buddha pointing even further—beyond all four jhānas, past the supramundane awareness of the infinity of space, the infinity of consciousness, the awareness of nothingness, perception-and-non-perception, all the way to the final cessation, the ultimate cessation, nirvāṇa. Even at the level of the supramundane awarenesses shy of final liberation the root structure of practice—investigating and coming to see that no phenomenon, no matter how banal or sublime, is worth adhering to—guides the practitioner just as it did with respect to those first bumbling efforts at being restrained by the precepts.

62. The nīvaraṇas are sometimes included among the Hosts of Māra the Tempter, attesting—even if only mythically—both to the strength of their hold and to the crafty ways they keep the practitioner in their grip. On the psychologically symbolic and literal understandings of Māra and his armies in the Pāli texts and beyond, see Gethin, "Cosmology and Meditation," 189–91.

63. Ñāṇamoli and Bodhi, *Middle Length Discourses*, 876.

64. Ñāṇamoli and Bodhi, *Middle Length Discourses*, 367–69.

If I have here devoted significantly more attention to the initial stages of the gradual training than to subsequent ones, it is not without reason. This is the domain where most everyone who will take up the practice will find themselves—and for quite some time, one might add, perhaps even for the rest of their lives. As with any form of renunciant-contemplative training, there are no quick fixes and no empty promises. Not everyone who sets out to pursue the path will come to the fullness of its attainment,[65] and if there were a scant few "with little dust in their eyes" who had the wherewithal even to set out on the path, one can be quite certain that there will be even fewer who will muster the fearlessness and resolve to see it through to the end. Talk of attainment or realization, whether for oneself or for others, is therefore nothing if not recklessly premature for the vast majority of those who take up the path.

What is not at all premature is the concerted work that the path entails along with all the pitfalls and false starts one will inevitably encounter. These messy and rather tedious dimensions of practice need to be underscored here, because the Dharma is frequently criticized for being almost exclusively focused on the individual practitioner. The charge seems to run something like this: "How can you pursue nirvāṇa for yourself without also helping others attain it as well?" or "Who are you to be free of suffering while others continue to suffer?" Such questions are compelling only if nirvāṇa is viewed as something of a prize in a zero-sum game, in which case I would indeed be selfish for pursuing something so wonderful and precious while leaving others in the dust. But when one sees that nirvāṇa is simply the cessation of tṛṣṇā, that tṛṣṇā is only ever a product of my own doing, and that it can only be let go of when I give myself over to the arduous practice of identifying and surrendering the many manifestations of greed, anger, and delusion that keep it going, one can begin to appreciate why that is a groundless charge. It is simply the nature of the deeply personal work involved—not some misanthropic or egotistical bent—that makes this a solitary enterprise:

> I do not praise bonding with everyone whatsoever, nor do I praise bonding with no one at all. I do not praise bonding with householders and monastics, but I do praise bonding with quiet

65. Ñāṇamoli and Bodhi, *Middle Length Discourses*, 877.

> and noiseless lodgings far from the flurry of people, remote from human habitation, and suitable for seclusion.[66]

If through that work in seclusion there is some measure of freedom and release, it is not because I am better or more deserving than others; it is because I was willing and able to stop making all of this about me in the first place. Besides, the business I call *me* never attains nirvāṇa, so where could a line possibly be drawn between nirvāṇa *for me* and nirvāṇa *for others*?

Of course, others are implicated in pursuit of the path. All of my deluded mind states and unskillful actions have resulted in collateral damage to everyone around me. If I am truly concerned for the wellbeing of others, the very first thing I can do is my level best to stop being such a thorn in their sides, both directly in terms of my unskillful actions and indirectly in terms of the traces of attachment and aversion I litter about for them to have to deal with. Such a task lies wholly within my power, since all that is required is that I set aside my own deluded agenda. As long as I have failed to manage even that, however, any thoughts I might entertain of benefiting others will ring hollow. I may not have come to the end of the path, but I will at least have a sober sense of what needs to be done and how far I have yet to go.

That said, doing the utterly thankless work of slogging through the sketchy terrain of the gradual training (the Buddha likened it to passing through a dense thicket, followed by a marshy swamp, followed by a steep precipice before at long last finding "a delightful expanse of level ground"[67]) is already a form of benefit to others. The moral shame and moral dread that help guide the aspirant at each step of these early stages of training are called "the bright guardians of the world."[68] They guard the world from *me*. One of the most beloved texts of the Buddhist tradition, the *Mettā Sutra*, is nothing if not sweeping in its embrace of every being in lovingkindness, but the grandness of its vision is rooted firmly—already in its opening verses—in the very moral shame and moral dread that prompt and develop the renunciant-contemplative practice the Dharma prescribes from the first keeping of the precepts through to the elimination of the mental hindrances and beyond:

66. Bodhi, *Numerical Discourses*, 1061.

67. Bodhi, *Connected Discourses*, 930.

68. Bodhi, *Numerical Discourses*, 143; Ireland, *Udāna & Itivuttaka*, 132–33.

> This is what should be done by one skilled in the good,
> having made the breakthrough to that peaceful state:
> he should be able, upright and very upright,
> amenable to advice and gentle, without arrogance.
>
> [He should be] content and easily supported,
> of few duties and a frugal way of living;
> of peaceful faculties and judicious,
> courteous, without greed when among families.
>
> He should not do anything, however slight,
> because of which other wise people might criticize him.[69]

Even after crossing the threshold of awakening ("having made the breakthrough to that peaceful state," as the sutra puts it), moral shame and moral dread continue to govern and perfect the mind of loving-kindness, "a state of mind," it continues, "without boundaries—above, below, and across—unconfined, without enmity, without adversaries."[70]

There is simply no ground for claims that the early training stages, aimed as they are at breaking my idiosyncratic fetters and uprooting my own personal defilements, are in any way antithetical to concern for others or can be put off in the name of prioritizing lovingkindness or compassion. In fact, the matter at hand tacks in the very opposite direction, for the cultivation of lovingkindness itself directs one back to the patient practice of ever-increasing dispassion cultivated in each of the stages of the gradual training. This certainly was the understanding that Asaṅga, one of the most penetrating of the Mahāyāna scholar-monks, held when he expressly linked moral shame and moral dread to the life of renunciation and solitude that bodhisattvas, too, must lead if their concern for others is to have any traction:

> A bodhisattva . . . who has [developed] loving-kindness in his or her mind is willing to give up everything and is indifferent to possessions and remaining alive . . . He or she will feel shame and abasement if he or she should develop any of the mental afflictions. [A bodhisattva] who feels shame and abasement will not let him- or herself be controlled by the mental afflictions and will attain the power of firmness.[71]

69. Bodhi, *Suttanipāta*, 179.
70. Bodhi, *Suttanipāta*, 180.
71. Asaṅga, *Bodhisattva Path*, 598.

The first demonstration of lovingkindness is found already in submitting to the gradual training, following its counsel, becoming indifferent to everything else, surrendering all, and not doing anything, however slight, that would prove unworthy of the company of the Noble Ones.

Indeed, one who would claim to pursue the Dharma but does not follow the path of renunciation and solitude governed by moral shame and moral dread is, following the *Nikāyas*, no more a practitioner of the Dharma than a donkey is a cow:

> Bhikkhus, suppose a donkey was following right behind a herd of cattle, [thinking]: "I'm a cow too, I'm a cow too." But his appearance . . . braying . . . footprint would not be like that of the cows. Yet he follows right behind a herd of cattle, [thinking]: "I'm a cow too, I'm a cow too."
>
> So too, a bhikkhu might be following behind the Saṅgha of bhikkhus, [thinking]: "I'm a bhikkhu too, I'm a bhikkhu too." But his desire to undertake the training in the higher virtuous behavior . . . the higher mind . . . higher wisdom is not like that of the other bhikkhus. Yet he follows right behind the Saṅgha of bhikkhus, [thinking]: "I'm a bhikkhu too, I'm a bhikkhu too."[72]

Of course, all of this would apply to anyone who would pursue the Dharma, not just duly ordained bhikkhus and bhikkhunīs:

> Householders . . . you should not be content with merely this much, [thinking]: "We have presented robes, almsfood, lodgings and medicines and provisions for the sick to the Saṅgha of bhikkhus." Therefore, householders, you should train yourselves thus: "How can we from time to time enter and dwell in the rapture of solitude?" In such a way you should train yourselves.[73]

And lest one think this smacks a bit too much of a so-called "Hīnayāna" fastidiousness and exclusive concern for moral purity, Nāgārjuna, the towering philosopher-monk of the Mahāyāna, uses exactly the same language and supplies even more similes to bolster the point:

> A person who breaks the precepts is different from good people. It is just as when a donkey is present within a herd of cattle.
>
> When a person who breaks the precepts is present within the vigorous assembly, it is like when a weakling child is present among strong men.

72. Bodhi, *Numerical Discourses*, 315.

73. Bodhi, *Numerical Discourses*, 789.

> Although a person who breaks the precepts may look like a bhikkhu, he is like a corpse in the midst of a group of sleeping men.[74]

The purpose of such comparisons is not to be judgmental but simply to be clear about the lay of the land. They accord with the first kind of right view, the view that sets the stage for practice to begin with: here are cows, there are donkeys, and a cow is not a donkey; here are noble practitioners, there are everyday people, and the two are not the same. Aspiring to be the one necessarily involves surrendering being the other.

Such comparisons also serve to reinforce the broader observation that the Dharma is simply not for everyone, as the Buddha had realized already upon his own awakening:

> This Dhamma is for one with few desires, not for one with strong desires. This Dhamma is for one who is content, not for one who is discontent. This Dhamma is for one who resorts to solitude, not for one who delights in company. This Dhamma is for one who is energetic, not for one who is lazy. This Dhamma is for one with mindfulness established, not for one who is muddle-minded. This Dhamma is for one who is concentrated, not for one who is unconcentrated. This Dhamma is for one who is wise, not for one who is unwise.[75]

It is not for everyone, not because anyone is preemptively excluded from it, but because most will either resist it or simply fail to take seriously the nature of the work involved. The Buddha was swift to admit that it was not until his own heart leapt at the thought of sense restraint, renunciation, solitude, and the surrender of everything that he was able to pursue the path resolutely and come to liberation.[76] Knowing this about himself, he expressly distanced himself from those who would set great store by the widest possible spread of the Dharma and the liberation it offers:

> The Tathāgata has no concern whether the entire world will be emancipated, or half the world, or a third of the world. But he can be sure that all those who have been emancipated, or who are being emancipated, or who will be emancipated from the world first abandon the five hindrances, corruptions of the

74. Nāgārjuna, *Six Perfections*, 223. Nāgārjuna is here referring only to keeping the precepts, but since the subsequent training levels follow from them, it is not unwarranted to include his observations here.

75. Bodhi, *Numerical Discourses*, 1160.

76. Bodhi, *Numerical Discourses*, 1309–18.

> mind that weaken wisdom, and then, with their minds well established in the four establishments of mindfulness, develop correctly the seven factors of enlightenment. In this way they have been emancipated or are being emancipated or will be emancipated from the world.[77]

For every half of the world emancipated, there is another half not; for every third of the world emancipated, there is another two thirds not—and nothing in that indicates a flaw in the teaching. If anything, it attests to its soundness. Not everyone is of few desires, not everyone eagerly resorts to solitude, and not everyone will come to enjoy "the taste of liberation"[78] the Dharma offers.

If the call, "We must change the world," is beginning to sound somewhat out of step with all of this, it is not surprising. To understand more clearly why such a call is at odds with the teaching-and-discipline, we need to unpack the constituent elements of that call—the conditioned dharma called *the world* and the conditioned dharma of the *we*—a task that has been made all the easier for having set out so much here already in advance.

77. Bodhi, *Numerical Discourses*, 1471.

78. Ireland, *Udāna & Itivuttaka*, 66.

2

Taking Saṃsāra Seriously

The snippets of conversation I overhear at the table next to me in a restaurant, the half of the interchange I hear on the train as someone is talking on her cellphone, the fleeting gesture I catch out of the side of my eye as I pass a group of people in conversation, the person on the street who unwittingly steps into the frame of my selfie—all of these are reminders of the fact that those around me are by and large but background characters in my storyline, much as I am but a background character in most of theirs. Their stories, along with the scenarios they build, for the most part only lightly touch upon mine, if at all really, just as my story only lightly touches upon the vast majority of theirs. That light touch, should I consider it for a moment, offers but a momentary glimpse into some small aspect of another person's vast networks of ideas, assumptions, hopes, dreams, and fears—networks that condition and constitute that person's life in more ways than they or anyone can possibly imagine. We may walk past dozens of people on the street and in grocery stores, drive past hundreds and sometimes thousands on the road, and sit in stadiums filled with tens of thousands of fellow spectators and in so doing occupy the same physical *space*, but it cannot for all that be said that we share the same experiential *worlds*.

The Buddha's teaching antedates by millennia the now increasingly common realization that we simply do not have access to what might be called *the world as a whole*. Instead, each person constitutes a world (nay, worlds) for him- or herself in accordance with his or her own particular circumstances and tailored by his or her particular inclinations, desires, aversions, and ignorance. The canonical expression of this is found in the *Loka Sutta*:

> Dwelling at Savatthi. There the Blessed One addressed the monks: "I will teach you the origination of the world & the ending of the world. Listen & pay close attention. I will speak."
>
> "As you say, lord," the monks responded to the Blessed One.
>
> The Blessed One said: "And what is the origination of the world? Dependent on the eye & forms there arises eye-consciousness. The meeting of the three is contact. From contact as a requisite condition comes feeling. From feeling as a requisite condition comes craving. From craving as a requisite condition comes clinging/sustenance. From clinging/sustenance as a requisite condition comes becoming. From becoming as a requisite condition comes birth. From birth as a requisite condition, then aging & death, sorrow, lamentation, pain, distress & despair come into play. This is the origination of the world. [The same for ear, sounds, ear-consciousness, etc.][1]

As we can see, *world* here is not an astronomical, physical, or geographic term, and the process the Buddha described as the *origination* of the world is not a creation story about the beginnings of the cosmos. It is, rather, an account of the ongoing arising of the content-horizon of one's own experiential life on the basis of the working of the skandhas taken up and framed in accordance with attachment, aversion, and ignorance.[2]

From one moment to the next, as the operation of the skandhas continues, and as particular forms, sense-consciousness, feelings, and the like now come to the fore and recede, my content-horizon shifts and changes. Of course, these newly arisen forms do not last either, and so just as it is a characteristic of the world that it assumes this or that configuration in light of my self-understanding and activity, that shifting content-horizon undoes those world formations same as well:

> Then a certain bhikkhu approached the Blessed One . . . and said to him, "Venerable sir, it is said, 'the world, the world.' In what way, venerable sir, is it said 'the world'?"
>
> "It is disintegrating, bhikkhu, therefore it is called the world. And what is disintegrating? The eye, bhikkhu, is disintegrating,

1. Bodhi, *Connected Discourses*, 581.

2. It is not uncommon to refer to the *world* as a domain of human interest and activity, as in *Runner's World* magazine, "the world of the Baroque," and the like. Each of these worlds is born of a particular attachment, sustained by it, and ends when that attachment abates.

> forms are disintegrating, eye-consciousness is disintegrating, eye-contact is disintegrating, and whatever feeling arises with eye-contact as condition . . . that too is disintegrating. The ear is disintegrating . . . The mind is disintegrating . . . Whatever feeling arises with mind-contact as condition . . . that too is disintegrating. It is disintegrating, bhikkhu, therefore it is called the world."[3]

Stasis is not at all a quality of any phenomenon, yet out of the drive to keep things put or to move things along more quickly or at least in a different direction, I try to create for myself some stabilizing framework that allows me to direct the rising and the falling, the constitution and the dissolution of myself and everything around me. When that stability threatens to fail—as fail it will—I reach for yet another framework to take up the slack.

Saṃsāra is the name given to this continuous stream of rising and falling, intertwining and untangling world formations wrought under the sway of the kleśas. It is, according to the Buddha, the default condition of our lives. If there is to be an understanding of the social world that squares with the Dharma, then saṃsāra is the place to start.

At its root, saṃsāra means "perpetual wandering."[4] Other renderings, such as "cycle of existence"[5] or "the round of rebirth,"[6] while fitting enough on one level, have a tendency to be interpreted as the activity of some agent that is making its way through stations in an already-laid-out pattern, or who transmigrates somehow intact across discrete psycho-physical rebirths. Saṃsāra is oftentimes spoken of as if it were a place, a set of conditions, or something to that effect. Frequently heard locutions such as, "leaving saṃsāra and entering nirvāṇa," makes it seem as if saṃsāra and nirvāṇa were related to each other the way, say, Latvia is to Estonia; in leaving the one, one enters the other. Saṃsāra, however, is best understood as a *process*. It is the process by which an individual creates about him- or herself a concatenation of worlds that correspond to his or

3. Bodhi, *Connected Discourses*, 1162.
4. Nyanatiloka, *Buddhist Dictionary*, 165.
5. Rahula, *What the Buddha Taught*, 146.
6. Gethin, *Foundations of Buddhism*, 321.

her projected and fluctuating self-image. Nirvāṇa, as have seen, is simply the cessation of that particular process. It is not a second or alternative reality.

Recall that the teaching on the skandhas indicates that any perceptual awareness is constituted by the interplay of embodiment (*rūpa*), sensations (*vedanā*), apperception (*saññā*), volitional activities (*saṅkhāra*), and consciousness (*viññāṇa*). On the basis of these I develop a factual enough everyday account of the world and my relation to it. The operation of the skandhas is sufficient, for instance, for me to reach for the keys in my pocket, start the car, put it in gear, share the road with any number of cars and trucks and bicycles, discern a roadblock up ahead, figure out an alternative route, park the car, get out my cell phone to pay for parking on the app, see the door to the hardware store and reach for the handle to open it, and so on.

As I move through this sequence of events, I find I do not really hold on to much; in fact, most of the time I would be hard-pressed to account for every last one of my actions and for everything I happened to negotiate along the way. Sure, I navigated traffic, but the cars I passed, their makes and models, the numbers on their license plates, and the like all came and went without my keeping tabs on any of them. I passed by any number of buildings, trees, and fire hydrants, crossed a bridge or two, perhaps, and made countless adjustments to the accelerator, the brakes, the clutch, the gear stick, and the steering wheel, but I would be hard-pressed to recount all of that in exacting detail. Even this ensemble of activity I can lump together as "going to the hardware store" was just another thing on the to-do list, along with other, equally broad descriptors such as "filling up the gas tank," "stopping by the post office," and "picking up some groceries for dinner"—things I will soon enough forget about, perhaps even by the time the day is over.

What turns this ceaseless flow of experience into a samsaric world (or worlds) is the introduction of tṛṣṇā. On the basis of the play of attachment and aversion grounded in ignorance I begin to stitch together a narrative that demarcates this or that into things or situations that either advance or hinder my self-concept, or else that fulfill or disappoint my expectations of how the flow of experience should be. Now, not only does "this" happen, but it is cast as "I am, etc. because of this." To keep with the example, instead of simply navigating traffic, I add the internal monologue: "Those bicyclists think they own the road. They're supposed to follow the same rules the cars do. If I have to stop, they have to stop."

"I bought an electric car; what's with that gas guzzler over there? They are the reason for sea levels rising." "I'm going to be late if that car in front of me doesn't start moving faster. What's their problem?" In each of these cases the leap is made from what is the case (the cyclists violating the rules of the road, the kind of vehicle in question, one car in physical relation to another) to a fitting of what is the case within my own sense of what would be optimal (or at least less bad) for me at the time, or, at the very least, what marks me out as special in comparison to others.

As is often the case with such an internal monologue, these self-filled observations do not just end there but give rise to further implications, further observations, and further connections to other aspects of life. I hear someone on the radio who holds the same position I do, and I am pleased; I hear someone with the opposite view, and I question their judgment—or their motives. Noting the commercial sponsor of the broadcast, I might elect to stop buying their products; even though they may be selling quality widgets, I wouldn't want to be associated with *those* widgets, since I might come to be known as someone who also supports what the company that made them supports, and I simply cannot have people thinking *that* about me. I find myself soon enough falling in with or seeking out others who agree with me, and I come to view myself—and hope they view me—as a certain kind of person, one that, now as a matter of some principle, thinks and acts this way as opposed to that. In short, I fashion an *identity* that now further organizes the subsequent flow of experience into something like territories, creating structures that, so I hope, will help bring about or sustain exactly those conditions that make that kind of person I take myself to be feel more at ease and at home.

In addition to driving a car, I eat food, secure clothing and housing, and hold a job. I may find myself having certain abilities not widely shared, like having twenty-twenty vision, being a particularly fast swimmer, or having a knack for making a killer crème pâtissière. I may find myself lacking certain abilities that others have, like walking without assistance, speaking Urdu, or crocheting. Some of these I chose, some of these may have been present at birth, and some of these may be the result of my upbringing or social conditioning. It is a purely speculative question (and not a terribly relevant one) how any of these fall out on the nature/nurture spectrum, for no matter how I came by them, they are the present and only conditions of this business I now identify with and take to be me. The same is true for any interests I happen to have, the kinds of things I find meaningful or funny, or the kinds of commitments I am wont to make. Each of them is as good as any other upon which to construct an identity, and the many and varied identities we find humans adopting only underscores the relative arbitrariness of any one of them. They may make a certain kind of general sense given present circumstances (some options are rather modern, perhaps, others more historically perduring, and others are no longer available), but that I find myself to be the kind of person who is more interested in debugging computer software than ridding roses of aphids—or Greece of Persians more so than Lexington and Concord of redcoats—is pretty much the luck of the draw.

It is perhaps for this reason that the Buddha did not say much descriptively about saṃsāra except to indicate its existence as a process.[7] The "content," so to speak, of saṃsāra—the various dharmas on which I might ground my identity claims and the available structures by which I organize and give legs to that identity—is not particularly significant. No matter which identity I take up, it will always be marked with unsatisfactoriness as it rises and falls in relation to any of the others. No matter which one I take up, it will never quite measure up to the burden of selfhood I place on it. So no matter which one I take up, I will soon enough press on to another that, at least at the time, seems to hold some promise of keeping up the conceit. To be sure, as I guide my actions in light of them, samsaric worlds can be more or less harmful, more or less beneficial, more or less inclusive, more or less conducive to human flourishing and the like, but the Dharma is not a standard for evaluating the merits of various identities but a tool for cutting through to the very nature of the process itself—the ongoing drive to maintain a sense of self—in order to be liberated from *all* of them.

The one point that is consistently stressed in the *Nikāyas* is that the origin of saṃsāra is unknown: "Bhikkhus, this saṃsāra is without discoverable beginning. A first point is not discerned of beings roaming and wandering on hindered by ignorance and fettered by craving."[8] In the *Anamataggasaṃyutta Sutta* the Buddha employs any number of

7. Traditional schema such as the realms of gods, asuras, humans, hungry ghosts, animals, and hell beings that make up the "Wheel of Saṃsāra" are still somewhat broad and generalized designations of certain kinds of processes.

8. Bodhi, *Connected Discourses*, 651.

metaphors to drive home the inconceivability of any discernible first instance of this roaming, which is measureless according to space and time:

> Suppose, bhikkhus, a man would reduce this great earth to balls of clay the size of jujube kernels and put them down, saying [for each one]: "This is my father, this is my father's father." The sequence of that man's fathers and grandfathers would not come to an end yet this great earth would be used up and exhausted.[9]

Or again,

> "What do you think, bhikkhus, which is more: the mother's milk that you have drunk as you roamed and wandered on through this long course—this or the water in the four great oceans?"
>
> "As we understand the Dhamma taught by the Blessed One, venerable sir, the mother's milk that we have drunk as we roamed and wandered on through this long course—this alone is more than the water in the four great oceans."
>
> "Good, good, bhikkhus! It is good that you understand the Dhamma taught by me in such a way."[10]

These powerful metaphors and others like them are useful for freeing the mind from what would be a pointless search for a unique and discrete prime moment of saṃsāra for the purpose of constructing an etiology that would handily identify where things went awry from an original, pre-saṃsāra state.

The significance of this rejection of any lapsarian narrative should not be overlooked or underappreciated. On an individual level it means that I simply have no understanding of myself, no identity, except in terms of my samsaric formations. The postulate of a *tabula rasa* might be a helpful tool for solving certain epistemological problems, but it is not possible that I should ever know myself as one. No matter how far back I can remember, I can see that I have filtered experience through the lens of the self and created a corresponding world accordingly. In every stage of life, I have looked to my circumstances, my choices, and my interests as being somehow indicative of "who I really am." I might be able to stitch together a causal chain to explain certain limited aspects of my life today—"if I hadn't gone to the party I wouldn't have met the person I started dating, fell in love with, and married," on a positive note; "if I hadn't become friends with Sid I wouldn't have found myself drinking as

9. Bodhi, *Connected Discourses*, 652.

10. Bodhi, *Connected Discourses*, 653.

much as I did the night I crashed the car and ended up losing my leg," on a less positive one—but I can always take the story back further and further until the thread is lost in obscurity.

Even the very inclination to develop one particular storyline as opposed to another is itself colored by the aspect of my present self-understanding I feel most needs to be accounted for. One of the perduring marks of tṛṣṇā is the very drive to identify some particular event or set of external conditions as the precipitating cause of my current situation ("I am because of *this*," I am just so because of *this*," "What made things turn out like *this*?" etc.), absent which, so I fancy, I would have remained in some kind of pure, or possibly better, and in any case assuredly different, condition. It comes as no surprise that many will try to figure out what they did to "deserve" cancer or come up with some explanation of why their child, and not someone else's, died of SIDS. Many, too, will try just as hard to find some clear root cause for their prodigious talents or uncommon success. If the everyday mind, which tends to get disoriented when presented with the prospect of an infinite regress, oftentimes ends the account of the causal chain by postulating an ultimate origin in God, it has not for all that *explained* the causal network's particular lineup of causes but has simply *named* its obscure, mysterious, and ultimately incognizable source—*quod omnes* dicunt *deum*, which all *call* God, as Aquinas put it at the end of his argument for God's existence as the prime source of all causality.

On the social level, saṃsāra's lack of discoverable beginning means there are no grounds for postulating an ur-state from which humanity as a whole might have fallen and to which it might yet hope to be restored. No matter how far back the historical record goes, it too emerges out of the deepest obscurity. We can know of no common Eden, no one shared first transgression, and so we have no sense at all of what a restoration of all things (*apokatástasis*) to their primal state would entail, to borrow Christian language for a moment. But this is not merely a theological issue, and there are many who have cast aside all religious origin stories only to replace them with sociological, historical or political variants. "Things were better before the advent of industrialization," the neo-agrarian might offer, and push for a more land-based economy. "We ate better before the dawn of agriculture," the advocate of a paleo diet might claim, and advocate for the elimination of complex carbohydrates from the pantry. "We have failed Reconstruction to blame for the current state of race relations in the United States," someone concerned with present-day racism might opine, and speak in favor of restorations. The beginninglessness of saṃsāra means that we simply have no control state to use either as a benchmark to determine just how far things are off course from some first normative ordering *or* as a beacon to indicate the way back. Any moment that might be identified as decisive for making sense of present circumstances will itself have been conditioned by antecedent circumstances.

Most importantly, none of these personal or social narratives can account for the origin of my *ongoing* samsaric formations, because they place the cause of that wandering on a state of affairs over which I had no control or in which I never even took part. I did not smoke the cigarettes my mother did that resulted in my low birth weight and subsequent health issues, nor did I get my father the job that landed me along with the rest of the family in Pie Town, New Mexico, yet here I am framing my world by bemoaning my fate as an asthmatic who cannot get decent medical care deep in the Southwest and is bored out of his wits there besides. I also did not mechanize production, domesticate cattle, vote to end Reconstruction, or develop satellite communication technology, yet here I am in a sea of mass-produced items eating feed-lot beef that many cannot even access because of the structural racism that creates the presence of food deserts in cities. If any of these circumstances are the source of my dukkha, it is difficult to discern how I might be free of them. I cannot turn back time, and even if I were to press on with the intention of undoing or changing them, I do well to consider that not one of them was the production of a demiurge; they are simply what happened to fall out after countless numbers of men and women, each pursuing their own world formations, acted in accordance with their own greed, anger, and delusion in response to antecedent conditions. "For such a long time, bhikkhus, you have experienced suffering, anguish, and disaster, and swelled the cemetery,"[11] the Buddha said at the conclusion of each description of saṃsāra's beginninglessness. He could have just as well spoken of swelling the *landfill*, since the historical record is filled with remnants of the samsaric formations of previous generations, some of which are still taken up and so populate the present landscape. That my current personal or social environment is a tangled conditioned *mess* that could, perhaps, have turned out differently but, in any case, did not

11. Bodhi, *Connected Discourses*, 651–61.

simply goes without saying. That I now have to navigate *this* mess and not some other one also goes without saying.

Although there is no discernible single phenomenon or set of phenomena that can be identified as the origin of the river of saṃsāra—or even of the particular eddies and subcurrents within it—there is, the Buddha offered, a knowable causal ground for its *ongoing arising*, and that causal ground is my own ignorance:

> Thus have I heard. On one occasion the Blessed One was dwelling among the Vajjis at Bhaṇḍagāma. There the Blessed One addressed the bhikkhus: "Bhikkhus!"
>
> "Venerable sir!" those bhikkhus replied. The Blessed One said this: "Bhikkhus, it is because of not understanding and penetrating four things that you and I have roamed and wandered for such a long stretch of time. Which four?
>
> "It is, bhikkhus, because of not understanding and penetrating noble virtuous behavior, noble concentration, noble wisdom, and noble liberation that you and I have roamed and wandered for such a long stretch of time."[12]

It is simply because I have taken dharmas to be otherwise than they are that I have found myself adrift. It is not that anything in the world has ever been out of place; it is that I have failed to see that the self has no place anywhere within it.

One of the most disconcerting aspects of saṃsāra is that it never manifests itself as one, but as a conglomeration of various world formations that I engage in depending on what aspect of my presumed selfhood I focus on—and they never seem to quite agree with one another. I might find that my career does not square with my religion, my religion with my sexual orientation, my sexual orientation with my intended family structure, my family structure with the availability of social services in my zip code, and so on and on and back around again. I can modify my expectations and behavior in light of any of them, or I can try to modify any of them in light of my expectations and behavior, but in so doing I am simply continuing the ongoing arising of saṃsāra. If I privilege my religion over my gender identity, I will be disappointed just as if I privilege my gender identity over my religion. If I privilege my career over my family, I will be disappointed just as if I privilege my family over the prospects of my upward mobility in the workplace. There is no Archimedean

12. Bodhi, *Numerical Discourses*, 387.

point among samsaric worlds from which to calibrate and order the rest of the lot.

But since the causal ground of saṃsāra itself is knowable, the way to have done with the whole process is also knowable. Because the root cause of all of my samsaric formations is the same, I can put an end to the ceaseless negotiation I feel compelled to carry out among them by coming to see *all* of them as equally misguided and illusory. The Buddha concluded each of the metaphors concerning the beginninglessness of saṃsāra with the comment about the swelled cemetery and then went on to add, "It is enough to experience revulsion towards all formations, enough to become dispassionate towards them, enough to be liberated from them."[13] This revulsion arises from the dawning realization that *none* of these samsaric worlds are me. My career world is not me. My preferred pastimes are not me. My family world is not me. My resume, tax return, credit score, or zip code are also not me. My religious or political expression are not me. My sexual orientation, gender identity, age, or ability level are not me, either, and neither is my status, privileged or not, in currently obtaining social or economic structures. This revulsion is simply a consequence of coming to see the non-identity of self and circumstances:

> Therefore, bhikkhus, any kind of form [feeling, perception, volitional formations, or consciousness] whatever, whether past, future, or present, internal or external, gross or subtle, inferior or superior, far or near, all [these] should be seen as [they] really [are] with correct wisdom thus: "This is not mine, this I am not, this is not my self."
>
> Seeing thus, bhikkhus, the instructed noble disciple experiences revulsion towards form, revulsion towards feeling, revulsion towards perception, revulsion towards volitional formations, revulsion towards consciousness.[14]

If talk of *revulsion* strikes modern ears as a bit harsh, one can equally well substitute *divestment*. When I find that none of these are worth adhering to, I find that I am no longer interested in investing in them.

Samsaric worlds require nutrition to keep them going, and cutting off their food supply by divesting in them is of a piece with bringing to an end the dukkha they give rise to:

13. Bodhi, *Connected Discourses*, 651–61.

14. Bodhi, *Connected Discourses*, 902–3.

> With the arising of craving there is the arising of nutriment. With the cessation of craving there is the cessation of nutriment. . . .
>
> When a noble disciple has thus understood nutriment, the origin of nutriment, the cessation of nutriment, and the way leading to the cessation of nutriment, he entirely abandons the underlying tendency to greed, he abolishes the underlying tendency to aversion, he extirpates the underlying tendency to the view and conceit "I am," and by abandoning ignorance and arousing true knowledge he here and now makes an end of suffering.[15]

It is no accident that the path outlined by the Dharma is marked with a spirit of renunciation from start to finish and that each stage of the gradual training invites the aspirant to abandon, abolish, and extirpate anything that might serve as food for the conceit of the self—from its most trivial and everyday manifestations to its most supramundane and sublime forms. The training that begins with guarding the sense faculties, which may have seemed overly fastidious and exacting at the outset, shows its skillfulness when I find that I am no longer propelled by conditions and can, instead, see them as they are:

> Herein, Bāhiya, you should train yourself thus: "In the seen will be merely what is seen; in the heard will be merely what is heard; in the sensed will be merely what is sensed; in the cognized will be merely what is cognized." In this way you should train yourself, Bāhiya.
>
> When, Bāhiya, for you in the seen is merely what is seen . . . in the cognized is merely what is cognized, then, Bāhiya, you will not be "with that." When, Bāhiya, you are not "with that," then, Bāhiya, you will not be "in that." When, Bāhiya, you are not "in that," then, Bāhiya, you will be neither here nor beyond nor in between the two. Just this is the end of suffering.[16]

There will be *just this*, but the tṛṣṇā that insists on adding "I am because of this," will have lost its toehold.

The realization of my own emptiness with respect to conditions is coextensive with the realization of the world's emptiness as well:

> Then the Venerable Ānanda approached the Blessed One . . . and said to him: "Venerable sir, it is said, 'Empty is the world,

15. Ñāṇamoli and Bodhi, *Middle Length Discourses*, 134.

16. Ireland, *Udāna & Itivuttaka*, 18.

> empty is the world.' In what way, venerable sir, is it said, 'Empty is the world'?"
>
> "It is, Ānanda, because it is empty of self and of what belongs to self that it is said, 'Empty is the world.' And what is empty of self and of what belongs to self? The eye, Ānanda, is empty of self and of what belongs to self. Forms are empty of self and of what belongs to self. Eye-consciousness is empty of self and of what belongs to self. Eye-contact is empty of self and of what belongs to self . . . Whatever feeling arises with mind-contact as condition—whether pleasant or painful or neither-painful-nor-pleasant—that too is empty of self and of what belongs to self.
>
> "It is, Ānanda, because it is empty of self and of what belongs to self that it is said, 'Empty is the world.'"[17]

The skandhas will continue or not in accordance with conditions, but any inkling of identity or the self among them will be nowhere to be found.

A misunderstanding of the emptiness of the world has given rise to the not-uncommon charge that the Dharma is *world-denying*, and in a certain sense it is, but not in the way frequently imagined. If one understands that "the world" is nothing but my own churning rounds of samsaric projections, and that what is produced as far as worlds go is fleeting, subject to change, uncertain, and occasions of dukkha given their stickiness, then one might counter the world-denying charge by asking what there is, exactly, to deny—*or* affirm. There is nothing in the Dharmic account of saṃsāra that can lead to the conclusion that the world exists or does not exist, any more than that any particular phenomenon does or does not exist. Those are the kind of metaphysical claims the Buddha was resolutely silent about, since they are extraneous to the task of seeing into the process that gives them rise and how that process might be brought to an end. No thing, no dharma, is denied here at all. What is emphasized instead is the conditioned and non-abiding nature of dharmas and the ultimate futility of building much that is abiding upon them. Despite my best efforts to pin down some dharma and try to ensure its continuation for the sake of myself and those people and things I hold dear, the world consistently proves itself to be otherwise. The burden would then be on the world-affirmer to show that dharmas are *not* like this.

Behind the accusation that the Dharma is world-denying lurks the assumption that there is a commonly shared world—the one to which the accuser belongs, one can suppose—that binds us all and that the aspirant

17. Bodhi, *Connected Discourses*, 1163–64.

is somehow turning her back on it. In order for any samsaric world to do what I expect of it, namely that it bolster my self-conceit, it requires the cooperation of others to play along with the ruse. In order to "be a master pianist," I need to be affirmed as one by others who share a conception of what being a master pianist entails. In order to "be a spiritual adept," I need to be recognized as one by those who share my understanding of what that means. In realizing the emptiness of *all* identities and the worlds they create the pursuer of the Dharma is not in a position to offer that kind of affirmation to anyone at all, since, as we have seen, "Nothing is worth adhering to."[18] From this perspective it is hard not to see in the charge that the Dharma is world-denying something along the lines of "dukkha loves company."[19]

It is one of the most distinctive teachings of the Buddha that our troubles are not solved by the maintenance, alteration, or dismantling of particular worlds but by seeing the emptiness of the process of world-formation itself. So just as the realization of the emptiness of the world puts to rest any charge of affirming or denying it, it also sets to the side any discussion of *changing* it:

> Subhuti, if a bodhisattva should thus claim, "I shall bring about the transformation of a world," such a claim would be untrue. And how so? The transformation of a world, Subhuti, the "transformation of a world" is said by the Tathagata to be no transformation. Thus it is called the "transformation of a world."[20]

It is no transformation, because what it produces is yet another samsaric world. Modifications in one samsaric formation undertaken out of attachment, aversion, and delusion simply give rise to other samsaric formations. Everything is already in the process of change, since change is a condition of every dharma whatsoever. Because of that, concerted

18. Ñāṇamoli and Bodhi, *Middle Length Discourses*, 347.

19. The Dharma of the Buddha is not alone in being subject to this kind of charge—and for very similar reasons. We find echoes of it in Christianity as well. Consider this passage from Matt 11:16–19:

> But to what will I compare this generation? It is like children sitting in the marketplaces and calling to one another, "We played the flute for you, and you did not dance; we wailed, and you did not mourn." For John came neither eating nor drinking, and they say, "He has a demon"; the Son of Man came eating and drinking, and they say, "Look, a glutton and a drunkard, a friend of tax collectors and sinners!" Yet wisdom is vindicated by her deeds.

20. Pine, *Diamond Sutra*, 19.

attempts to *change* the world are, despite what the words would indicate, actually further attempts to *arrest* the ceaseless flow of cause and effect, to see that it conduces to outcomes that are more pleasing to or supportive of me than others. Besides, when I set down the burden of samsaric creating by becoming dispassionate towards *all* samsaric world formations, as the Dharma suggests I do, why—or even how—could I now take any one of them up again for transformative reworking? "Bodhisattvas," it has been pointed out, "cannot find any self to sacrifice, much less a world to transform."[21]

The Buddha taught neither the denying nor the changing of the world but its *ending*, the cessation of every tṛṣṇā-driven construction and arrangement:

> And what is the ending of the world? Dependent on the eye & forms there arises eye-consciousness. The meeting of the three is contact. From contact as a requisite condition comes feeling. From feeling as a requisite condition comes craving. Now, from the remainderless cessation & fading away of that very craving comes the cessation of clinging/sustenance. From the cessation of clinging/sustenance comes the cessation of becoming. From the cessation of becoming comes the cessation of birth. From the cessation of birth, then aging & death, sorrow, lamentation, pain, distress, & despair all cease. Such is the cessation of this entire mass of stress and suffering. This is the ending of the world.[22]

Talk of ending the worlds of saṃsāra might sound rather dramatic, but it need not be thought of as cataclysmic. Anyone who has made it to adulthood has already seen the end of most of the world-formations of his or her childhood. Those things that seemed so pressing to me in third grade, the angst felt by my fourteen-year-old self, the desperate need to fit into this or that group in high school, the image of myself and its future I relied on in picking a major in college all just simply ceased as I stopped feeding them or as conditions changed. As they went, the worlds I gave rise to went as well. I no longer define myself by whether I am invited to Mary Beth's ninth birthday party, have to wear hand-me-downs from the neighbor kid, or am denied the keys to the family car on Friday night to go to a friend's party with my high school sweetheart. It is one of the signs of maturity and everyday wisdom that I can gracefully surrender

21. Pine, *Diamond Sutra*, 304.

22. Bodhi, *Connected Discourses*, 581.

the things of youth. I would not be the kind of person I am today without them, but they did their work, and now there is no good reason to cling to them and every good reason not to—the longer I hold on to them, the more I feed them from my present state, the longer I am still held in their sway. But one need not simply wait for time to move on or for conditions to change for samsaric worlds to end; one can become dispassionate toward one's samsaric formations, see them for what they are, and actively surrender them now. If this were not the case, then the whole of the Noble Path and the gradual training outlined by the Buddha would be mistaken to the core, and we would be fooling ourselves to think that liberation is at all possible among conditions such as they are.

For those inured to their own ignorance of the matter, talk of worlds ending is no doubt a disconcerting proposition. Again, it need not be. The things around me do not "disappear" in realizing the emptiness of the world any more than I "disappear" with the dawn of insight into the emptiness of the self. Buildings and trees, television programs and antibiotics remain after as before, just as my arms and lungs, left-handedness and taste for well-made Semmelknödel remain after as before. There will be, as the Buddha told Bāhiya, only the seen in the seen, the tasted in the tasted, but once I come to see that none of these are constitutive of an identity but are rather simply the products of causes and conditions that rise and fall, I am free to engage with them just as they are without at the same time using them as props for—or fearing them as threats to—a purported selfhood. I am free from birth and death when I am no longer bound up with their fate. What might seem from the point of view of the self like being thrown into an unfamiliar abyss is, in point of fact, nothing other than becoming finally free of my self-built enclosure:

> Through many births
> I have wandered on and on,
> Searching for, but never finding,
> The builder of [this] house.
> To be born again and again is suffering.
>
> House-builder, you are seen!
> You will not build a house again!
> All the rafters are broken,
> The ridgepole destroyed;
> The mind, gone to the Unconstructed,
> Has reached the end of craving![23]

23. Fronsdal, *Dhammapada*, 40–41.

If it had been a matter of changing the world, the Buddha would have characterized his quest as the search for a blueprint for a better house. Instead, he sought the builder of the house, tṛṣṇā, and, having seen that builder for exactly what it is, watched the house fall down around him without any plans for further construction projects whatsoever. The creation of a *better* world, according to the Dharma, is never as skillful as the non-creation of *any* world.

Taking saṃsāra seriously means, in the first place, that I will begin take myself and my own projections of the world far *less* seriously. When I begin to see clearly how my worlds rise and fall, I can begin to understand just how non-abiding they really are. I can start to see that they are products of so many moments of my attachment, aversion, and ignorance—so much so that I would be hard-pressed to think of any of them as being particularly important or weighty, when all is said and done. I can even be somewhat amused at the bizarre concatenation of worlds I've pieced together once I begin to exercise dispassion with respect to them. How curious, I might reflect, that I took up paintball *and* subscribed to *The Economist* in the same week, or added Dvořák *and* Nickelback to my playlist around the same time. I might even see the sheer fluke in having heard of the Dharma at all and being intrigued enough to take up practice at the local temple, even while I was (or maybe still am) bar hopping on the weekend *and* giving up whiskey for the forty days of Lent.[24] I could drive myself to utter madness trying to make sense of it all, but there is no need to. Nothing in that mishmash requires justification so much as dispassionate awareness, and a robust measure of self-effacing humor when it comes to that mishmash is as good a place as any—and better than most—to start in cultivating that dispassion.

Taking saṃsāra seriously, I can also see that although something might happen to fit rather nicely into my own created world, it may not fit quite so nicely—or even at all—in someone else's. If I am sometimes

24. Much ink has been spilt on the matter of Buddhist-Christian "dual belonging." But if one understands that *being a Buddhist* and *being a Christian* are each a matter of samsaric world formations, and if one understands that samsaric world formations are products of one's own attachments and aversions, then one can set aside the task of trying to fit them together into a coherent description of what that kind of dual selfhood might entail.

baffled by others' particular ensembles of samsaric worlds, I can be quite sure they are just as baffled by mine. Because of the sheer diversity and differentiation of samsaric worlds in play at any given time, I will understand that I have no grounds for demanding that others and the worlds they fashion accord with or actively accommodate mine. The insistence that my identity (or, more accurately, my many *identities*) be recognized, affirmed, and supported by others is just as kleśa-driven and dukkha-laden an enterprise as holding fast to and supporting it (or them) myself. It is simply not the job of others to abet me in my delusions, and I should not be at all surprised to encounter either their indifference or rejection when it comes to them. Since even otherwise neutral material conditions continuously prove unsatisfactory for maintaining my sense of self and its attendant world-formations, by what stretch of the imagination would I expect that the people around me, who have their own agendas afoot, prove to be any different? People are simply of a nature to disappoint when it comes to my expectations. If saṃsāra were not like this, it would not be saṃsāra.

On the other hand, taking saṃsāra seriously means that I will begin to take others' projections of their worlds far *more* seriously—not in terms of their particular content necessarily (who knows what countless variations there are?) but at least in terms of understanding just how deeply they are held and how pervasive are the attachment, aversion, and ignorance that give them rise. Once I am able to see just how thoroughly and consistently I have been hoodwinked by phenomena due to my own ignorance of their true nature and mine, I can appreciate just how much most everyone around me has been and continues to be hoodwinked as well. Seeing that, I will not be surprised at the tenacity with which others hold on to their worlds, given the tenacity with which I have held on to mine. I will understand that seeing into and surrendering worlds is no easy task and that putting too much pressure on a person to change or abandon his or her world is more often than not going to be met with resistance in equal or greater measure. If one finds oneself flabbergasted as to how someone can so doggedly hold on to his or her views and how deeply intrenched that person can be in the worlds those views give rise to, one need only reflect—if one can—on one's own dogged insistence on maintaining one's own.

From this perspective taking saṃsāra seriously also means that I need not be scandalized by the seemingly discordant worlds that a person might create and move among. The sense of shock that ensues when, say, a person of who has taken a vow of celibacy is also discovered to be engaging in illicit sex, or when an elected official who ran on an anti-corruption campaign is found to be taking kickbacks from powerful corporations, is proportionate to the degree to which one either sees these as just more instances of samsaric wandering or as contradictions within an otherwise unified self. I might be absolutely dumbfounded at how a person can manage to move among her various worlds, since they seem at times to be so at odds with one another, but I can understand that, for her, this is just another day in the life, and about *that* I certainly need not be vexed.

Similarly, I need not be thrown off or distressed by the messy state of a social environment made up of not just one, or even a thousand, but *billions* of such samsaric world-makers, each of whom is busy creating worlds for him or herself in light of his or her self-understanding. If I find that my own actions have turned out to be a mixed bag of the skillful and the unskillful, given my ignorance and delusion, I cannot but expect that others' actions prove to be the same. And just as those around me have had to deal with the fallout of my delusions in ways that may not even be apparent to me, I cannot but expect to have to deal with the fallout from all of theirs. If anything, I might even take some small consolation that things hang together as passably as they do from one day to the next. It is no small matter that food finds its way from field to table, that a plane taking off in Buenos Aires will have air traffic control ready for it in Miami, or that even in the largest cities most everyone's flush is conveyed to the waste treatment facility. I might be relieved that I do not have to carry those burdens completely on my own, even if it means dealing with the unseemly or harmful actions those who make all of that possible also happen to engage in.

Indeed, with ever deepening insight I might even come to find that I am *grateful* for every last one of those billions of people that make all that possible—and for every last one of their samsaric shenanigans along with it. This, at least, is the spirit in which Torei Enji, Hakuin's dharma heir, approached the whole tangled mess:

> When I regard the true nature of all things and all living creatures, I find them to be the sacred forms of the Tathagatha's never-failing essence. Each particle of matter, each moment, is no other than the Tathagatha's inexpressible radiance.
>
> With this realization, our noble ancestors gave tender care to beasts and birds, with compassionate minds and hearts.

> Among us, in our own daily lives, who is not reverently grateful for the protections of life: food, drink and clothing! Though they are inanimate things, that are nonetheless the warm flesh and blood, the merciful incarnations of Buddha.
>
> All the more, we can be especially understanding and affectionate with foolish people, particularly with someone who becomes a sworn enemy and persecutes us with abusive language. That very abuse conveys the Buddha's boundless loving-kindness. It is a compassionate device to liberate us entirely from the mean spirited delusions we have built up with our wrongful conduct from the beginningless past.
>
> With our open response to such abuse we completely relinquish ourselves, and the most profound and pure faith arises. At the peak of each thought a lotus flower opens, and on each flower there is revealed a Buddha. Everywhere is the Pure Land in its beauty. We see fully the Tathagata's radiant light right where we are.
>
> May we retain this mind and extend it throughout the world so that we and all beings become mature in Buddha's wisdom.[25]

The whole kit and caboodle down to the very last dharma is nothing but the manifestation of the Buddha's radiant light, but to see that requires relinquishing the childishness of self-attachment, and becoming, as Torei put it, *mature* with respect to my assessment of the world. The tradition frequently refers to the dawning of insight as a kind of *waking up*. It may be just as appropriate—and perhaps even more compelling—to cast it as a kind of *growing up*, of coming not to expect more of people and things than they are capable of offering, and instead developing the mind that has "great realization of delusion,"[26] as Dōgen put it, no matter how pervasive and widely-shared those delusions are.

For all of these reasons (and more, as we will see in subsequent chapters), taking saṃsāra seriously means being deeply suspicious of anything that would present the teaching of the Buddha as underwriting calls to "change the world." From beginningless time saṃsāra has been *nothing but* an ongoing process of trying to change the world carried out by persons afire with the defilements, as it is put in the *Ādittapariyāya Sutta*,[27] and it has resulted in the tangled and checkered human environment we now find ourselves in. It makes little sense, within the context of

25. See "Torei Zenji's Bodhisattvas' Vow."

26. Dōgen, *Moon in a Dewdrop*, 69.

27. Bodhi, *Connected Discourses*, 1143.

the path that leads to the quenching of the flames, to advocate throwing even more fuel onto the fire. The teaching-and-discipline of the Buddha is no more a technique for *changing the world* than it is for *changing myself.* Instead, it offers liberation from all world- and self-formations, not a guideline for refashioning those currently obtaining or developing new ones in light of what I or even a number of people might think would be something much better. There is no quarter in the Dharma for a second or alternative reality—or society. In an environment in which many religious systems see fit to offer just that in one way or another, it is understandable that some might think it important that Buddhism take its place among them, put forth its own distinctive version of a better world, describe the mechanisms for achieving it, and advocate action to make it all come to pass. The gift of the Dharma lies elsewhere.

3

The *Nos* Delusion

UNLIKE THE ABRAHAMIC RELIGIONS, which focused on the formation of a *people,* the Dharma has never been first and foremost about the creation and maintenance of a corporate body as the locus of salvific action. Here there is no people of God entered into a covenant with YHWH, no church (*ekklēsia*) of a people called forth and set apart to be the living body of Christ on earth. There is nothing resembling a tithe or zakat to support the religious body as a whole, and there are no congregation-sustaining requirements that married couples be co-religionists, for instance, or that parents promise to raise or educate their children in a certain way. Here one finds no forum for the adjudication of disputes among everyday practitioners, nor a panel of decision-makers to determine whether or not a social convention or custom is authentically "Buddhist" in the way that, say, a decision by a diocesan marriage tribunal considering the sacramentality of a marriage or a rabbinic determination whether a particular foodstuff is kashrut would be. Male bodies are not made physically identifiable as part of the religious body along the lines of a bris, nor is there even anything like the equivalent of having one's membership permanently documented with a baptismal certificate. One would be hard-pressed indeed to prove (or have it proven) that one is *a Buddhist,* because the standard marks by which one is made part of a corporate religious body are in large measure lacking.

There are reasons internal to the teaching of the Buddha for this dearth of collective identity-forming structures. First—and primary—among them would be that the soteriological aim of the Dharma can only be realized by oneself; there is no collective coming to the end of one's ego attachment, no redemption by association. While we are all bound by the kleśas of attachment, aversion, and ignorance, we are not each of us bound by them in the same ways. Each of us created the particular conditions of our fetters, and it is up to each of us as individuals to abandon them. Time and again throughout the canon and beyond the responsibility for one's own liberation is placed squarely at one's own feet, and whether that individual finds herself alone or in the presence of others makes little difference, ultimately, for accomplishing that task.[1] As Jay Garfield has pointed out, "there is no explicit assertion in classical Indian Buddhist literature or in Tibetan commentarial literature that virtue arises from the appreciation of community membership, or of interpersonal, or of inter-sentient being connection."[2]

Moreover, identity-forming structures, whether they aim to fashion an individual or a group, are themselves just so many variations of the myriad worlds otherwise created out of attachment, aversion, and ignorance. Like all the other worlds of saṃsāra, they ride the waves of birth and death. Cultures, civilizations, organizations, religions, states, social clubs, educational institutions, and professional guilds all share this much in common: they come into being, and they pass away. Etruscans and Aztecs and Whigs and Shakers and Donatists and Achaemenids all had their day, and the days of any presently existing social group are numbered as well, as difficult as that may be, at present, to imagine. The Buddha himself was fully aware that even the teaching-and-discipline would be eclipsed and eventually disappear from the world as a counterfeit of the Dharma (with a lack of reverence and deference toward the Teacher, the Dharma, the Saṅgha, the training, and even the reality of awakening itself) would rise.[3] Few other religious systems—if *any*—have their own sure historical demise so soberly and fearlessly in view.

1. Rita Gross makes the point that "community is far more central in Buddhism and far more crucial to achieving Buddhism's goal of liberation from suffering that is commonly perceived either by Buddhists or non-Buddhists" (Gross, "'I Go for Refuge," 230). Her argument is that an overemphasis on aloneness runs the risk of psychological discomfort that poses an obstacle to one's achieving the aims of practice. My point is not that we do not benefit from the kindness and support of fellow travelers but simply that the creation of a community for its own sake is not crucial to the pursuit of the Dharma and, if too much value is placed on it, it becomes an obstacle in its own right.

2. Garfield, "What Is It Like," 341.

3. Bodhi, *Connected Discourses*, 681.

Finally, the Dharma was never attended with the rule of law as the Abrahamic religions were. There was no pretense that any of the Buddha's teachings were to function either as temporal or divine ordinances, and, absent the likes of mitzvot, canons, and sharia, the life of an upāsaka or upāsikā was governed exclusively by the law of the land.[4] The Pātimokkha training rules were reserved for the bhikkhus and bhikkhunīs alone, and while expulsion from the ranks of the ordained was possible, an offending bhikkhu or bhikkhunī was not for all that excommunicated from the broader Dharmic community as well. Among the upāsakas and upāsikās, if one were to fall short of maintaining a precept, there was no absolution to receive, no rites or sacraments to be barred from, and no anathema to endure.

While some may decry the lack of an express social bond inherent in the core teachings or try to find ways to make the Dharma more communitarian than it is, there is a good reason to take seriously the brakes the tradition has put on any attempt to forge coherent collective identities, Buddhist or otherwise. The conceit of a *plural* self, a "we," bears all the same marks as the conceit of the *singular* self, the "I": anattā, anicca, and dukkha, and while one may have a sense that "the cause of our sorrow is ego delusion," as Hakuin put it,[5] one is not at all freed from that sorrow by the substitution of a *nos*, a "we," in its place. The root delusion is the same in either case, and so too is its attendant sorrow. The conceit of a plural self, like the conceit of an individual self, must also be seen into and abandoned along the path to liberation.

This makes any alignment of the Dharma with social and political thought problematic from the outset. Jean-François Lyotard has suggested that modern politics is distinctive in that it aims primarily at "the manufacture of a subject that is authorized to say 'we.'"[6] Whether that "we" is in some way always already operative in a people, as Rousseau suggested with the *volonté générale*; whether it is constructed out of the agreement of otherwise discrete individuals as in Hobbes or Locke, or whether it is established on the basis of the common material interest of a determinate group as in Marx makes little difference to the aim of the

4. The case of Aśoka the Mauryan emperor of the Indian subcontinent (ca. 304–232 BCE) is often proffered as a case of "Buddhist" governance. Though he may well have adopted certain principles of Buddhism and supported the establishment of monasteries and the like, Aśoka was still acting *as an emperor*, not *as a religious leader*.

5. Hakuin, "Master Hakuin's Chant," 34.

6. Lyotard and Thébaud, *Just Gaming*, 81.

exercise—the establishment of a collective unified subject, a *body politic*. If the Dharma stands apart from all of this in pointing to the emptiness of any "we" formation, it is bound to run, if not counter to, then certainly quite independent of, not only politics but the concerns of other collective associations and social movements as well.

The institution of the saṅgha would seem to stand as a counterexample to these observations, and some have attempted to construct a social theory on the basis of it, seeing in the saṅgha a model of collective belonging and transformative agency. Sulak Sivaraksa, the Thai social activist, put it quite baldly: "One prototypical form of the emerging counter-civilization is the Buddhist sangha,"[7] and he is far from alone. Before addressing the *nos* delusion directly, then, we first need to take a closer look at saṅgha, its functions, and its limits.

The conventional use of *saṅgha* in the tradition refers to ordained male (*bhikkhu*) and female (*bhikkhunī*) renunciants, those who have made the realization of the Dharma the focus of their life and who live in accordance with the Vinaya, the code of discipline. These are distinguished from lay male disciples (*upāsaka*) and lay female disciples (*upāsikā*), who, living in ways that accord with their responsibilities as layfolk, also take refuge in the Three Jewels of Buddha, Dharma, and Saṅgha, and strive to uphold the five precepts. While both ordained and lay disciples are fully capable of realization, the ordained function as the guides in the teaching-and-discipline, and their lives are to be lived in a way commensurate with that task.

The Buddha portrayed entering the ordained life as a matter of "going forth," away from the constraints of everyday life. The aspirant was freeing himself from something much more than he was placing himself under the aegis of a new social structure. He was leaving the householder world for homelessness, in both its literal and figurative sense—the lack of a stable environment for his daily life and the lack of a haven for his ego. As much as the life of the householder was "close and dusty" and the homeless life "free as air," living as a homeleaver was not without its

7. Sivaraksa, *Seeds of Peace*, 102. Here Sivaraksa is following his Hegelian-Marxian frame of reference. An historical materialist conception of history requires the identification of a material causal agent of change.

difficulties; in fact, it exposed the aspirant ever more glaringly to the vicissitudes of life.

In the *Anagata-bhayani Sutta* the Buddha enumerates the many kinds of perils a bhikkhu faces upon entering into renunciant life. In addition to the expected run of such things as snake bites, scorpion stings, falls, and hoodlums to be faced, the Buddha exhorts a bhikkhu to remind himself that he is as yet young, healthy, well-fed, and living in a locality where people are at ease. However, there will come a time when he is old, the food scarce, and when penury leads the people of the region to focus on the necessities of life so much that they forget spiritual practice and the support of the bhikkhus. Even though there was a form of tacit agreement that the householders would support the homeleavers, and the homeleavers, in turn, would live and preach the Dharma, this was far from some kind of fixed arrangement on the basis of which a bhikkhu could assert some *right* to support. The *four requisites* that set the limits on what a bhikkhu may accept were nothing close to *four guarantees*.[8] Bhikkhus were prohibited from making their needs known directly to the laity, and they were expressly forbidden from outright begging except as a last resort, and even then the begging could prove fruitless. Having surrendered the guaranteed support of kin and the ability to ply a trade, in the end the homeleaver could not even count on the broader community for sustenance and material assistance. Because of this, the Buddha counseled, the bhikkhu should resolve to practice diligently under the current favorable conditions, so that when adversity comes, as come it will, he will "dwell at ease."[9]

Though personal and social conditions might prove troublesome, the immediate assembly of renunciants was no sure point of refuge on the path, either. The Buddha invites a bhikkhu to further reflect:

> The Saṅgha is now dwelling at ease—in concord, harmoniously, without disputes, with a single recitation. But there will come a time when there will be a schism in the Saṅgha. Now when there is a schism in the Saṅgha, it is not easy to attend to the Buddha's teaching, it is not easy to resort to remote lodgings

8. David Loy reads into the four requisites the basis for a theory of a guaranteed social minimum (Loy, *Great Awakening*, 32). This does not seem warranted either by the textual tradition or by sound reasoning. To say that a body needs nutrition is one thing; to say that someone has a *right* to sound nutrition or is in a position to *demand* that it be supplied by another is something else entirely.

9. Bodhi, *Numerical Discourses*, 711.

> in forests and jungle groves. Before that unwished for, undesirable, disagreeable condition comes upon me, let me in advance arouse energy for the attainment of the as-yet-unattained, for the achievement of the as-yet-unachieved, for the realization of the as-yet-unrealized. Thus when I am in that condition, I will dwell at ease even though there is a schism in the Saṅgha.[10]

Even if it does not come to outright schism, the Buddha reminds the homeleaver, "there will be bhikkhus who are undeveloped in body, virtuous behavior, mind, and wisdom." They will ordain others but not be able to guide them; they will fall into a "dark Dhamma" but not be able to discern that they have; they will not incline to hearing or understanding the Tathāgata's teaching but be taken in by poetry and pleasing words; they will bond with women, or become fond of luxury, or disinclined to solitude. In sum, these bhikkhus will corrupt the Dharma and the discipline even from their position of seniority in the saṅgha.[11]

The Buddha was under no illusion that the assembly of bhikkhus was going to run into difficulties; a community of those still bound by tṛṣṇā is nothing to take refuge in. Humans shy of being firmly established on the path to awakening—and this would include pretty much all of the rank and file (and most likely many among the upper-ups as well) of the saṅgha's members—are of a nature to disappoint. Only the most starry-eyed would assume that simply because someone has donned robes and submitted to the discipline they have thereby freed themselves of the kleśas, and only the most undiscerning would place their trust unreservedly in the guidance of an all-too-human fellow traveler—or group of them.

It is particularly telling that Buddha does not instruct a bhikkhu to work for the reformation of the schismatic or heretical in order to save the saṅgha, either. The training rules were there, and if during the fortnightly confession of faults a bhikkhu did not admit to an infraction, or if the assembly was inclined not to censure the one who had, that was the end of the affair. If unanimity was not reached on matters requiring it, and if the minority refused to abide by the majority's decision, there was no further place to take the issue; the Buddha had set up no provision for an ultimate authority figure to strong-arm a recalcitrant bhikkhu or

10. Bodhi, *Numerical Discourses*, 712.

11. The many financial and sexual scandals at Buddhist temples and monasteries—not to mention the many attempts to render the Dharma socially and aesthetically pleasing that are nothing short of legion—should come as absolutely no surprise.

group of bhikkhus into compliance. When pressed to appoint a successor before he died, the Buddha retorted:

> But, Ānanda, what does the order of monks expect of me? I have taught the Dhamma, Ānanda, making no "inner" and "outer": the Tathāgata has no "teacher's fist" in respect of doctrines. If there is anyone who thinks: "I shall take charge of the order," or "The order should refer to me," let him make some statement about the order, but the Tathāgata does not think in such terms . . .
>
> Therefore, Ānanda, you should live as islands unto yourselves, being your own refuge, with no one else as your refuge, with the Dhamma as an island, with the Dhamma as your refuge, with no other refuge.[12]

The Buddha counseled that in response to the shadow of schism and inept bhikkhus, "it is enough for a bhikkhu to dwell heedful, ardent, and resolute" to attain what has not yet been attained, alone—*as an island*—if need be. A bhikkhu's task would simply be to "recognize" and "make an effort to abandon" these practice-defeating circumstances should he encounter them.[13]

Even the teacher-student relationship, the very backbone of training in the Dharma, ultimately falls short as a point of refuge: "Bhikkhus, this holy life is lived without students and without a teacher. A bhikkhu who has students and a teacher dwells in suffering, not in comfort. A bhikkhu who has no students and no teacher dwells happily, in comfort."[14] The Buddha used this as a metaphor for the fetters and how they bind one within (student) and without (teacher), but the strength of the metaphor is derived from taking what would seem to be a perfectly reasonable assumption, namely that there should be students and there should be teachers and that having students and teachers is a good and happy thing, and turning it on its head. "Having a student" is binding; a competent Dharma teacher knows that, ultimately, there are no students and no teachers. The teacher gives nothing to the student the student does not already have and imparts no wisdom that is not already the student's birthright. "Having a teacher" is binding; the student, from her side, must eventually realize that pursuing the Dharma is not a matter of chasing

12. Walshe, *Long Discourses*, 245, also Bodhi, *Connected Discourses*, 882–83.

13. Bodhi, *Numerical Discourses*, 712–13.

14. Bodhi, *Connected Discourses*, 1213.

down some teacher attempting to "get" something special; awakening is her true nature, not a boon bestowed by another.

All of this helps explain why there is no Dharmic equivalent to the Christian *extra ecclesiam nulla salus*, no salvation outside the church, and why there is no inherent pressure to increase membership in the saṅgha because it would somehow be "good for people" to join it. The closest Dharmic approximation of the Christian "Great Commission"[15] is the Buddha's exhortation to the bhikkhus:

> Wander abroad, monks, for the good of the many, for the happiness of the many, out of compassion for the world, for the welfare and happiness of devas and humans. Do not go two together, monks, but teach the Dhamma that is lovely in its beginning, lovely in its middle, and lovely in its ending, both in the letter and in the spirit, and display the holy life fully complete and perfect. There are beings with little dust in their eyes who are perishing through not hearing Dhamma: they will become knowers of Dhamma.[16]

The Buddha described this as giving them *permission* to go out into the world; it was not a mandate, and it certainly was not for the purpose of bringing all nations into a common fold or making the world a better place, but simply to make available to those few with little dust in their eyes, wherever they may be found, the resource they need to break through to liberation. Even in wandering abroad in this way the bhikkhus did not constitute a strategically effective united front, and the qualification, "not going two together," was a caution against the establishment of a concerted missionary or proselytizing force.

From any number of angles, then, it is hard to make the case that the saṅgha, understood in sociologically describable terms, could serve as a secure haven of refuge much less as the blueprint of the new society. From the outset, and true to its nature as a loose association of renunciants, the saṅgha was understood to stand at the periphery of the established social order—not contributing to its population, adding nothing to its production of goods and services, and sharing not at all in its governance.[17] It was also most assuredly not a latent society-in-the-

15. "Go therefore and make disciples of all nations, baptizing them in the name of the Father and of the Son and of the Holy Spirit, and teaching them to obey everything that I have commanded you" (Matt 28:19–20).

16. Walshe, *Long Discourses*, 217–18.

17. To be sure, the historical record is replete with accounts of land-holding (and

making, or prototype of the world to come, since nothing in a Dharmic understanding of the world could possibly underwrite such ideas. The attractiveness of homeleaving for the aspirant lay, in part, precisely in the fact that he was setting all that business aside, with all of the occasions for the free reign of the kleśas that come with it. Should the saṅgha then become itself a playground for attachment and aversion, a wise bhikkhu would know simply to leave that to the side as well.

~

There is in the tradition another understanding of saṅgha, however, one that does not fall prey to the vicissitudes of samsaric ups and downs. Already in the canonical formulations, it is clear that the saṅgha in which one takes refuge is not at all the association of those who simply have some affinity towards or affiliation with the Dharma, nor is it even straightforwardly equated with those who happen to be ordained. Instead, the saṅgha that is intended is what is often referred to as the *āryasaṅgha*—the *noble* saṅgha—the saṅgha of those firmly on the path of awakening. Frequently in the *Nikāyas* we find references to the "four pairs and eight types" that make up this saṅgha:

> The Saṅgha of the Blessed One's disciples is practising the good way, practising the straight way, practising the true way, practising the proper way; that is, the four pairs of persons, the eight types of individuals—this Saṅgha of the Blessed One's disciples is worthy of gifts, worthy of hospitality, worthy of offerings, worthy of reverential salutation, the unsurpassed field of merit for the world.[18]

The four pairs and eight types are those on the path to stream-entry and those who have realized the fruit of stream-entry, those who are on the path to once-returning and those who have realized the fruit of once-returning, those who are on the path to non-returning and those who

even slave-holding) monasteries, periodic collusions between rulers and monastic heads, and the like. My point here is to indicate that even when and where that was the case, it was not the institutional structure of the saṅgha that was pressed into service for social organization—which would have included structures and stipulations for everything from marriage to commercial relations, from provisions for the common defense to the adjudication of legal disputes—but the demands of the prevailing social forces on a monastic life that otherwise stood more or less outside them.

18. Bodhi, *Connected Discourses*, 320.

have realized the fruit of non-returning, and, finally, those on the path to becoming arhats and those who have realized the fruit of arhatship. To the four pairs and eight types the Mahāyāna adds the bodhisattvas. When Śāntideva in the *Śikṣā-Samuccaya* takes up the saṅgha under the recollection of the Three Jewels, he describes bodhisattvas, their attainments, and their activity,[19] and in the *Bodhicaryāvatāra*, it is the Conquerors and Bodhisattvas in whom he takes refuge:

> Right now I go for refuge to the mighty Protectors of the world, who have undertaken the care of the world, the Conquerors who remove all fear.
>
> I also go whole-heartedly for refuge to the Dharma they have realized, which destroys the danger of cyclic existence, and to the assembly of Bodhisattvas.[20]

All of these have come to some degree of realization; the threshold of awakening has been crossed, and for some more definitively than for others.

Although they share with one another some level of attainment, the members of the āryasaṅgha do not constitute a corporate body in their own right. They are united (if one can even speak of *unity* here) in awakening, not in fraternal solidarity. They do not rely on each other, nor do they band together in order to accomplish some end. They are not a mutual aid society, and they certainly do not constitute an economic community. This saṅgha is not even delimited by space and time, and its members occupy something of a position, as it were, of "timeless simultaneity."[21] They simply practice, wherever and whenever they are found, "the good way, . . . the straight way, . . . the true way, . . . the proper way," each on his or her own, and in so doing constitute an "unsurpassed field of merit for the world" that is unbounded by space and time.

While not exhibiting a collective "we" structure, these āryas and bodhisattvas, because they have done what needed to be done or are doing what needs doing, are nevertheless still capable of functioning as rallying points for practice by offering the particular kind of friendship the Buddha said constituted "the whole of the holy life":

19. Śāntideva, *Training Anthology*, 302–22.

20. Śāntideva, *Bodhicaryāvatāra*, 18.

21. The locution is Nietzsche's. He employs it when referring to "individuals who constitute a kind of bridge across the wild stream of becoming. These do not, as it were, continue a process but live in timeless simultaneity" (Nietzsche, *Advantage and Disadvantage*, 53).

> On one occasion the Blessed One was dwelling among the Sakyans where there was a town of the Sakyans named Nāgaraka. Then the Venerable Ānanda approached the Blessed One. Having approached, he paid homage to the Blessed One, sat down to one said, and said to him:
>
> "Venerable sir, this is half of the holy life, that is good friendship, good companionship, good comradeship."
>
> "Not so, Ānanda! Not so, Ānanda! This is the entire holy life, Ānanda, that is, good friendship, good companionship, good comradeship.

If one were to stop reading the passage there, one might be led to the conclusion that the Buddha was referring to some kind of shared fellowship, thereby offering a pretext for community-forming initiatives and the like. But being a *good friend* in the holy life is not at all a matter of being a *good buddy*:

> When a bhikkhu has a good friend, a good companion, a good comrade, it is to be expected that he will develop and cultivate the Noble Eightfold Path.
>
> "And how, Ānanda, does a bhikkhu who has a good friend, a good companion, a good comrade, develop and cultivate the Noble Eightfold Path? Here, Ānanda, a bhikkhu develops right view, which is based upon seclusion, dispassion, and cessation, maturing in release. [The same for the remaining seven.] It is in this way, Ānanda, that a bhikkhu who has a good friend, a good companion, a good comrade, develops and cultivates the Noble Eightfold Path."[22]

A good Dharma friend is simply one toward whom I feel a degree of respect that then allows me to develop moral shame and moral dread—the disposition of hiri-ottappa that, as we saw, is "the first cause and condition that leads to obtaining the wisdom fundamental to the spiritual life."[23] If good friendship is the whole of the holy life, it is not because it is important that we all hang out together but because the presence of such noble ones serves as the proximate cause for me to muster the wherewithal to develop and cultivate the path for myself.

Indeed, as fine a spiritual companion as any one of them might be, what makes the āryas and bodhisattvas helpful in the end has less to do

22. Bodhi, *Connected Discourses*, 1524.

23. Bodhi, *Numerical Discourses*, 1112.

with anything *they* can do and everything to do with *me* and what I am able to accomplish. The *Dhammapada* puts it this way:

> A fool associating with a sage,
> Even if for a lifetime,
> Will no more perceive the Dharma
> Than a spoon will perceive the taste of soup.
>
> A discerning person who associates with a sage,
> Even if for a brief moment,
> Will quickly perceive the Dharma
> As the tongue perceives the taste of soup.[24]

Just as the spoon cannot rely on the soup, the aspirant cannot expect to be carried along the path by the āryas. It is simply not their responsibility, as Ānanda himself elsewhere pointed out: "It is not the worthy ones that make us act; it is the Dhamma that makes us act."[25] This is perhaps why the saṅgha is the last of the Three Refuges. Unlike the Christian profession of faith in the Father, the Son, and the Holy Spirit (which, though three, are one co-equal Godhead, "not three Gods, but one God," as formulated in the Athanasian Creed), there is something of a lexical order to be detected in taking refuge in Buddha, the Dharma, and the Saṅgha:

> Bhikkhus, I say this: If you have gone to a forest or to the foot of a tree or to an empty hut, and fear or trepidation or terror should arise in you, on that occasion you should recollect me thus: "The Blessed One is an arahant, perfectly enlightened, accomplished in true knowledge and conduct, fortunate, knower of the world, unsurpassed leader of persons to be tamed, teacher of devas and humans, the Enlightened One, the Blessed One." For when you recollect me, bhikkhus, whatever fear or trepidation or terror you may have will be abandoned.
>
> If you cannot recollect me, then you should recollect the Dhamma thus: "The Dhamma is well expounded by the Blessed One, directly visible, immediate, inviting one to come and see, applicable, to be personally experienced by the wise." For when you recollect the Dhamma, bhikkhus, whatever fear or trepidation or terror you may have will be abandoned.
>
> If you cannot recollect the Dhamma, then you should recollect the Saṅgha thus: "The Saṅgha of the Blessed One's disciples is practicing the good way, practising the straight

24. Fronsdal, *Dhammapada*, 17.
25. Ñāṇamoli and Bodhi, *Middle Length Discourses*, 882.

> way, practising the true way, practising the proper way; that is, the four pairs of persons, the eight types of individuals—this Saṅgha of the Blessed One's disciples is worthy of gifts, worthy of hospitality worthy of offerings, worthy of reverential salutation, the unsurpassed field of merit for the world." For when you recollect the Saṅgha, bhikkhus, whatever fear or trepidation or terror you have will be abandoned.[26]

It is to the Dharma that the Buddha awakened, and it is because of the Buddha's awakening to the Dharma that the Dharma is expounded, and it is in response to the Dharma that men and women take up, pursue, and attain the Great Way. In the *Mahāparinibbāna Sutta* it is put this way:

> In whatever Dhamma and discipline the Noble Eightfold Path is not found, no ascetic is found of the first, the second, or the third or the fourth grade. But such ascetics can be found, of the first, second, third and fourth grade in a Dhamma and discipline where the Noble Eightfold Path is found.[27]

In other words, the saṅgha of the noble ones emerges with the dhamma-vinaya as its condition; it is not the case that the dhamma-vinaya emerges with the saṅgha of the noble ones as its condition.

This understanding of the saṅgha as the assembly of the Noble Ones helps dispel certain views about the kind of association best found among those who would pursue the Dharma. To begin with, by making the āryas and bodhisattvas the frame of reference, any simple ordained versus lay differentiation is already set to the side. Without wishing in any way to diminish the particularly effective training ground the homeleaver life provides, there is nothing in this formulation that indicates that a stream-enterer or any of the others must come *only* from the ranks of the bhikkhus and bhikkhunīs. Instead, what is emphasized is the threshold between delusion and awakening; some have made the crossing, and others have not yet, regardless of station. In the *Sotāpattisaṃyutta Sutra* the Buddha underscores this point by reminding his listeners that if the upāsaka or upāsikā has confirmed confidence in the Three Jewels and can progressively withdraw from anxiety concerning family relations, the five fetters, and supramundane awarenesses, then, upon attaining surrendering the self he or she is no different from a monastic who has done the same:

26. Bodhi, *Connected Discourses*, 319–20.

27. Walshe, *Long Discourses*, 268.

> If he says, "My mind has been withdrawn from the brahmā world and; I have directed my mind to the cessation of identity," then, Mahānāma, I say there is no difference between a lay follower who is thus liberated in mind and a bhikkhu what has been liberated in mind for a hundred years, that is, between one liberation and the other.[28]

As one so liberated, the upāsaka or upāsikā becomes part of the boundless field of merit as well.

This understanding of saṅgha also undercuts any move to get overly expansive or overly restrictive with just who (or what) is included (or excluded) under its head. Forming an "eco-saṅgha" of all beings is perhaps a bit too sloppy in scope; I may find the squirrels nesting outside my window entertaining and pleasant, and I may even understand that they and I are "not-two," but it is hard to get the sense that they can be for me or I for them the kind of "good friend" the Buddha described. Establishing a "persons of color saṅgha," or a "women's saṅgha," or a "youth saṅgha," or a "queer saṅgha" or a "saṅgha of social action" (to name just a few currently out there) is no doubt a bit too narrow: How much "of color" must I be to join? When do I age out of the youth saṅgha? And what then? Just where on the Kinsey scale would I have to fall to belong to the queer saṅgha? And how much of an agenda must I subscribe to in order to be welcomed into the saṅgha of social action?

While these groups may be mind-broadening for some and a source of sharing and support for others, not one of them quite captures the *nobility* the saṅgha of the Noble Ones entails, because they are based upon, and take as their principle of association, conditioned dharmas like race, age, gender, social perspectives, and the like. As we saw, the path of the gradual training leads me to see that I am *not* my place in the biota, *not* my race, *not* my gender identity, *not* my age, *not* my politics, and *not* my sexual or gender expression. That being the case, I have no good reason to make of any of them a base upon which to build a collective association through which I, together with others who share with me such a distinctive identity, can pursue the Dharma. To be clear: while it is understandable that like-minded and similarly-situated people will no doubt be drawn to one another and find solidarity for their practice as a result of such associations, when all is said and done it is the individual's

28. Bodhi, *Connected Discourses*, 1836.

realization that is aspired to, not the establishment of a community based on shared interests and identity.

Up to this point we have been looking at the saṅgha with a particular aim in mind, namely to show that the saṅgha cannot be employed as the basis for a conception of social relations broadly; whatever else it is, it is not a blueprint for social structures, nor does it seem that it was ever intended to be. As with so much else we have had a chance to look at, the issue here is whether that absence of a social frame of reference is a lack that needs to be filled or whether it speaks to something distinct and liberating about the Dharma.

Recall the description of tṛṣṇā we looked at in chapter 1, where it was cast in terms of "currents of craving" captured in the series of "I" statements ("I am," "May I be," "May I be otherwise," etc.). As we saw, dukkha arises when these kinds of statements fail to square (as they inevitably do) with the ceaseless flow of dependently originating conditions. Thinking that some of these conditions speak to the existence of a "self," I attach to them but then become frustrated as they change, forcing me either to undo, and then recreate, my self-understanding, or else to seek to control conditions in order to make them fit it. Suppose now that "we" is substituted for "I" in the passage:

> There are, bhikkhus, these eighteen currents of craving related to the internal and eighteen currents of craving related to the external.
>
> And what are the eighteen currents of craving related to the internal? When there is [the notion] "We are," there are [the notions] "We are thus," "We are just so," "We are otherwise," "We are lasting," "We are evanescent," "We may be," "We may be thus," "We may be just so," "We may be otherwise," "May we be," "May we be thus," "May we be just so," "May we be otherwise," "We shall be," "We shall be thus," "We shall be just so," "We shall be otherwise." These are the eighteen currents of craving related to the internal.
>
> And what are the eighteen currents of craving related to the external? When there is [the notion], "We are because of this," there are [the notions]: "We are thus because of this," "We are just so because of this," "We are otherwise because of this," "We are lasting because of this," "We are evanescent because of

> this," "We may be because of this," "We may be thus because of this," "We may be just so because of this," "We may be otherwise because of this," "May we be because of this," "May we be thus because of this," "May we be just so because of this," "May we be otherwise because of this," "We shall be because of this," "We shall be thus because of this," "We shall be just so because of this," "We shall be otherwise because of this." These are the eighteen currents of craving related to the external.

It is not at all difficult to read in these lines much of the fret and worry that beleaguers communitarians of every stripe and social activists of one kind or another, the fret and worry over the existence or annihilation of a human (or perhaps, by extension, biotic[29]) collective, which is, of course, the same kind of fret and worry that plagues me as an individual when I attempt to cling to my own self-concept.

Just as there are myriad conceptions of self and a concomitant number of worlds for the single individual, there is no shortage of the variety of attempts to fashion a "we" from among groups of individuals, either. Sometimes these are made by appeal to some shared characteristic: "we women," "we gays," "we victims of Ankylosing Spondylitis," or "we Kurds." Sometimes they are made by appeal to a common project, as Chögyam Trungpa (rather cheekily) pointed out:

> We should discover wisdom and share it with others. Or we should create a better political order, reinforcing democracy so that all men are equal and everyone has a right to do whatever he wants within the limits of mutual responsibility. Perhaps we should raise the level of our civilization to the highest point so that our world becomes a fantastic place, a seat of wisdom, of enlightenment, of learning and the highest technological developments. There should be plenty to eat, pleasant houses, amiable company. We should become sophisticated, rich and happy, without quarrels, war or poverty, with tremendously powerful intellects that know all the answers, the scientific explanations of how the jellyfish began and how the cosmos operates.[30]

And of course one cannot in this connection fail to mention the religious "we" formations of "we Zen Buddhists," "we members of the Anglican Communion," or "we Shia." Debates on the relative merits of any of

29. See, for example, the collection of essays in Tucker and Williams, *Buddhism and Ecology*.

30. Trungpa, *Myth of Freedom*, 8.

these projects or associations can take place (and perhaps they should in certain contexts) without hitting upon the fundamental point that each serves as a locus around which to center the conceit of a collective selfhood. As such, they are so many projections of samsaric world-formation and further occasions of dukkha, each striving to situate and maintain itself and its project in the face of ever shifting conditions.[31]

Now as we saw, one of the reasons to take saṃsāra seriously as endless concatenations of worlds on the part of each individual is to counter the idea that all of course share in a common world and to recall that even more limited samsaric worlds are not shared in the same way by any two individuals. It is one of the distinctive features of the Dharma that individuals are to be met on their own terms. The bhikkhus were not to teach unless they were expressly asked to, which meant it was up to an individual to initiate the interchange when she felt the time was right and was prepared to listen respectfully. Moreover, anyone who taught the Dharma was to tailor it to the abilities and aspiration of the hearer, since what might be said to one person may not be at all appropriate for another to hear. In the *Vanasaṃyutta Sutta* we find a bhikkhu expressly upbraided for trying to teach the Dharma to someone who had neither asked for it nor was particularly ready to hear it:

> On one occasion the Venerable Kassapagotta was dwelling among the Kosalans in a certain woodland thicket. Now on that occasion, when he had gone for the day's abiding, the Venerable Kassapagotta exhorted a certain hunter. Then the devatā that inhabited that woodland thicket, having compassion for the Venerable Kassapagotta, desiring his good, desiring to stir up a sense of urgency in him, approached him and addressed him in verses:
>
> "The bhikkhu strikes me as a dolt
> Who out of season exhorts a hunter
> Roaming in the rugged mountains
> With little wisdom, devoid of sense.
>
> "He listens but does not understand
> He looks but does not see;
> Though the Dhamma is being spoken,
> The fool does not grasp the meaning.

31. None of this goes so far as to say that they are pointless; like all conditioned phenomena they have their relative utility. This is simply an observation that focusing on their preservation for the mere sake of their preservation runs counter to their nature as conditioned, selfless, and—yes—ultimately unsatisfactory formations.

> Even if you would bring ten lamps
> [Into his presence], Kassapa,
> Still he would not see forms,
> For he does not have eyes to see."

> Then the Venerable Kassapagotta, stirred up by that devatā, acquired a sense of urgency.[32]

The devatā, unlike the bhikkhu, knew exactly what right speech entailed in such a situation. Right speech is not only true speech; it is also skillfully deployed true speech, and the measure of that skillfulness is not whether it would be conducive to a particular outcome but whether it meets with a hearer exactly as she happens to be in the context of his or her samsaric formations. Noble silence is preferable to ill-timed discourse, no matter how true it may very well be.

One might be inclined to excuse the bhikkhu Kassapagotta, "dolt" that he was, for his zeal, even while appreciating the devatā's instruction; it is all too easy to slip from *what has been helpful for me* to *what must be helpful for others*. There is a difference in someone's well-meaning, though unconsidered, enthusiasm for the Dharma, though, and forging such zeal into a program of collective action. The one reflects an ongoing personal attachment to outcomes, something anyone aspiring to the Dharma has to work on and abandon; the other elevates such attachment to the level of a communal rallying cry on the order of, "We must change the world, we must change ourselves, and we must change ourselves in order to change the world,"[33] and it becomes even more problematic when that cry is cast as a high expression of the Dharma. Above we saw the difficulties a Dharmic understanding of *the world* poses for a program of social transformation; at issue here is the nature of the *we* doing the transforming.

As with all such charges, it is never entirely clear who the "we" initiating the change here is. Is it everyone? Such a broad net is hard to cast in a world of over seven billion people without losing sight of their samsaric particularities in some universal abstraction that could not possibly square with fluctuating conditions on the ground. Buddhists generally? That seems like a tall order, too, and for precisely the same reasons. Engaged Buddhists in particular? Perhaps. This is not to be peevish; the identification of a collective agent of social change has been a perennial sticking point in all theories of social transformation over the past few hundred years. For Marx and others, it was the proletariat. For many in

32. Bodhi, *Connected Discourses*, 296.

33. Kraft, *Wheel of Engaged Buddhism*, 10.

the 1960s it was the students. There was even speculation at one point that the peasants of the world might be the ones to do the job.[34] And of course any number of religious and political groups have put themselves forward as the ones called to the task of being exactly the salt the world needs. When one of them fails to deliver, as it inevitably does, the search is on for a new agent that, this time, might prove up to the challenge.

Whether in its secularized or religious form, there are echoes here of a *remnant theology*, developed in the Hebrew Prophets and carried into the New Testament—the idea that out of catastrophe there will be a faithful few who will function as the leaven for a transformed socio-religious order.[35] These few, steadfast in their vocation or enlightened beyond their peers, are called to the task of making known to the lax and benighted their errors and hearkening them back to their commitments and responsibilities. Within the context of the Abrahamic religions, which from the outset were understood to be constitutive of a people, the presence of such a prophetic voice is an important one. Since the salvation of every member requires that the ship of faith be on course, someone needs to step up and take charge of the navigation. If most everyone on board is impervious to the ship's bearings, then the job falls to the one who can best read the instruments and the sea in addition to having a clear sense of the destination. Liberation theologians could therefore draw on both the prophetic tradition in the Christian scriptures and the demands of revolutionary social agency in assuming for themselves something of this guiding role in relation to society. Although the content of their message is different, conservative Evangelicals who attempt to influence social policy understand themselves to be fulfilling the same kind of prophetic function as well.

Rita Gross has noted that such a prophetic voice is a missing element in Buddhism, and she and others[36] have sought to fill in that gap by emulating the Christian theologians and fashioning a Buddhist equivalent. On her view, "we [Buddhist scholar-theologians] have responsibilities to use our knowledge to address problems, rather than to leave troubling issues of social and environmental justice to those less knowledgeable, with less respect and good will for diverse and alternative world views."[37]

34. Harris, "Revolutionary Role of the Peasants."

35. For a discussion of the continuity of the use of "the remnant" from the Prophets through Paul's letters, see Sheinfeld, "Righteous Remnant," 33–50.

36. Strain, "Is a Buddhist Praxis Possible?," 71–101.

37. Gross, "Buddhist Theology?," 55–56.

Even setting aside the hubris of a claimed superior knowledge, respect, and good will for a moment, there are issues with the job description as written within a Dharmic context. If the Buddha himself was unconcerned whether the whole world or even a third of it should be liberated, and if he felt no particular need to commandeer the saṅgha, either on his own authority or by designating authority to others, whence the *responsibilities* of social guardianship that Gross sees needing to be fulfilled? And who, exactly, is the *we* that should be *so keen* to bear that responsibility?

In the Abrahamic religions a prophet was granted his or her authority from God. In theistic (as opposed to deistic) systems, God cares for his creation and his people, and, in order to guide them and correct them in their ways, he commissions spokespersons to communicate his will to them from time to time. When a prophet spoke, it was understood not to be in the prophet's own voice—which would have constituted a form of idolatry by setting oneself in the place of God—but in God's. Prophethood is not something to be claimed for oneself, and doing so has always been sufficient grounds for standing out as a false prophet. As if to emphasize the point, the Hebrew scriptures go to great lengths to describe a true prophet's personal resistance to the call, and time and again we are reminded of the fact that a prophet is in no hurry to take up the mantle. Moses asked, "Why me?" (Exodus 3:11) and further protested that he was not terribly eloquent (Exodus 4:10); Isaiah pointed out that his lips were unclean (Isaiah 6:5); Jeremiah objected that he was still too young (Jeremiah 1:6); and Jonah even tried skipping town to dodge the call to convey God's message to Nineveh (Jonah 1:3).

The Dharma, of course, makes no use of a concept of God in its expression, so that avenue is closed off here. One way that responsibility for the whole has been claimed by Engaged Buddhist has been on the basis that the teaching on dependent co-arising (*pratītyasamutpāda*), either on its own or in its metaphorical description as the "Net of Indra," actually demands a concern for the well-being of a *nos*. The argument seems to be essentially this. As every dharma is conditioned and without abiding self, it arises only in conjunction with other dharmas that are themselves likewise conditioned. Those who do not recognize that mutual conditionality will engage in activity that runs counter to it in order to maintain their presumed individual selfhood through attachment or aversion. That attachment and aversion will set into motion modifications in every other conditioned dharma, causing a ripple effect throughout the whole network. In order to maintain the network in as felicitous a state as possible, it is therefore incumbent upon individual members to come to see the delusion of their presumed separateness and to engage in actions that foster rather than hinder other members. Those who have seen through that delusion have the responsibility to teach those who have not, to point out the error of their ways, and to work to create safeguards for mitigating their harmful actions—in other words, to exercise the prophetic function that Gross calls for.

As with all of the Buddha's teachings, however, dependent co-arising can be either skillfully or unskillfully grasped. "I am not separate" is a vague recognition that might arise in conjunction with the dawning awareness of the mutually conditioning nature of dharmas. "We are all interconnected," is not. The one claims just a little too much (there is still an "I" involved, at least provisionally, even as emptiness is beginning to be seen into); the other claims far too much. No programmatic conclusions can be drawn from the realization of emptiness, whereas the assertion of the interconnectedness of all carries with it the overtones of a major premise in a syllogism from which particular conclusions may be (and often are) drawn. Because we are all interconnected, one might argue, then any and all acts are appropriate that—well, *what*? *Whatever* anyone does, and *whatever* happens or does not happen as a result, it's all interconnected all the same. Whether nuclear Armageddon occurs or whether sea levels rise, the simple fact of dependent co-arising would still obtain as much as if nuclear warheads were eliminated or atmospheric carbon brought down to sustainable levels.

Dependent co-arising, the plain observation that "this is like this, because that is like that," is a sober recognition that no present configuration of dharmas is awry or amiss and that none of them can presently be otherwise than they are. As a description of the nature and relationship of dharmas, dependent co-arising carries with it no normative orientation—one is invited to *see* it and *become dispassionate* toward it, not to *evaluate* and then *change* or *redirect* it. Buddhadāsa Bhikkhu referred to the *unconcoctability* (*atammayatā*) that arises in conjunction with insight into dependent co-arising. With this insight, he notes, "there is nothing taken or regarded as positive or negative such that it can affect, condition, or concoct thought, moods, or reactions in mind."[38] Insight into dependent co-arising thus calls for the cultivation of equanimity and non-attachment, not selection and targeting, because as soon as the

38. Buddhadāsa, *Under the Bodhi Tree*, 29.

move is made from a full-throated "Just *this*" to "More of that, please" or "Less of that, thank you," the move has been made away from the path to insight, tṛṣṇā has entered the picture, another samsaric world has arisen, and dukkha is its altogether not unexpected result.

A related heuristic, the concept of the *Net of Indra*, is frequently invoked in engaged Buddhist circles as a basis for a normative social order and particularly for an ecological ethic.[39] It does not provide much support for a prophetic function, either. It is helpful to recall just what, exactly, the metaphor states:

> Far away in the heavenly abode of the great god Indra, there is a wonderful net which has been hung by some cunning artificer in such a manner that it stretches out infinitely in all directions. In accordance with the extravagant tastes of deities, the artificer has hung a single glittering jewel in each "eye" of the net, and since the net itself is infinite in dimension, the jewels are infinite in number. There hang the jewels, glittering like stars of the first magnitude, a wonderful sight to behold. If we now arbitrarily select one of those jewels for inspection and look closely at it, we will discover that in its polished surface there are reflected *all* the other jewels in the net, infinite in number. Not only that, but each of the jewels reflected in this one jewel is also reflecting all the other jewels, so that there is an infinite reflecting process occurring.[40]

The operative word throughout this description is *infinite*. The aim of Huayan Buddhist thought, which takes its cue from the Net of Indra metaphor, is not only to point to dependent co-arising but also at the same time to frustrate the mind in its attempt to lay grasp of the whole of it. The key Huayan text, the *Avataṃsaka Sutra*, with its extravagant and lavish imagery, seemingly endless lists, and multi-factored exponential numbers, skillfully cultivates in the reader the disposition to surrender any attempt to circumscribe the limits of reality already in the very structure of the text; its prose and verse are so thoroughly *exhausting* that one is practically driven to give up hope of ever finishing *reading* it without succumbing to utter fatigue. But that is exactly the point of the exercise—to realize that any attempt to circumscribe the whole (or lesser wholes within it) reveals a lack of patience with and understanding of the true nature of reality (*dharmadātu*). One would become utterly spent long

39. Gary Snyder led the pack on this; see Barnhill, "Great Earth *Saṅgha*," 187–217.

40. Cook, *Hua-Yen Buddhism*, 2.

before coming remotely close to the limits of any of it, if there even were any such limits to begin with.

The Net of Indra metaphor is helpful for getting an intuitive sense of the interpenetration of dharmas, but it rightly says nothing particular about the measureless (save that it is, indeed, measureless), so it loses traction when employed in the direction of discernible social structures within it. Ken Jones's claim that "from the standpoint of an engaged Buddhism the net [of Indra] is valuable as a working ideal for society and its organizations, in which we are brothers and sisters in mutuality,"[41] has to be read with some good measure of skepticism. There will be more to say on the inability of the boundless to ground determinate action in the following chapter, where we look at a Dharmic understanding of karuṇā, that boundless and immeasurable compassion. For the moment, though, it can be said that, whatever else there is to say about dependent co-arising or the Net of Indra, they neither translate into the establishment of a collective selfhood out of many discrete actors any more than the co-arising bundle of the skandhas establishes individual selfhood, nor do they lay out the parameters of a workable field of action for such a presumptive social self the way samsaric world formations do. All things are indeed interconnected, but they are not interconnected as a determinate, definable, unified, and perduring *one*.

Gross was quite right to say that a prophetic voice is missing from the Dharma, but I would suggest that its absence is by design and consistent with the core teaching, not something that needs to be added. A prophetic function works within the confines of a determinate group of people with a clearly prescribed communal task. When the prophets rose in Israel, it was not primarily for the purpose of transforming the surrounding nations but of calling the Jewish people back to the terms of their covenant. As we have seen, it is one of the distinctive marks of the practice of the Dharma that it is understood precisely *not* to serve this function. Whether internally with respect to divisions within the saṅgha or externally with the relation of the saṅgha to the rest of society, there is no claim that the pursuit of the Dharma will "make the world a better place" or that one should take it up and use it in order to achieve that or some similar end. If the Buddha was unwilling to strong-arm erring bhikkhus into compliance, and if Kassapagotta was remiss in preaching the Dharma "out of season," then it is not clear that the prophetic

41. Jones, *Social Face of Buddhism*, 17.

function as portrayed here can find much of a toehold, because it relies on assumptions concerning individual actors as being bound in a kind of unified body—a *we*—that the saṅgha, any other social group, or even reality as a whole can never be.

There is no need to fear the loss of *nos* delusion in the light of the Dharma any more than one need fear the loss of *ego* delusion, because seeing into the emptiness of the *nos* no more annihilates the conventional social interactions we have with one another any more than seeing into the emptiness of the *ego* annihilates my everyday, conventional personhood. Food has to find its way from field to table, requiring some collective economic and logistical agreement. An individual is well served knowing both the reach and the limits of her legally enforced responsibilities toward others and their responsibilities (or lack of them) toward her within a given polity. If some measure of literacy is required for modern social and economic life, then a discussion might well take place concerning the nature and funding of public schools in the community. In an uncertain world, provision for the common defense and internal policing will be forthcoming. All of the above require roads and vehicles and fuel and regulations and enforcers of regulations and provisions for breakdowns and accidents and natural disasters—and so much more. There is nothing amiss in any of this, none of this requires purportedly *Buddhist* arguments in order to make it all happen, and there is no particularly *Dharmic* take on it, save that, in the end, these will always turn out to be unsatisfactory. This is just how sentient beings, at any given state of their samsaric formations, cobble together a life with one another with all of its ups and downs, agreements and disagreements, joys and pains. The most the Dharma can do is serve as a reminder (again, for those who have eyes to see and ears to hear) that any and all of these social processes rise and fall as conditions warrant, that none of them are satisfactory, that attachment or aversion with respect to them leads inexorably to dukkha, and that one should not be at all surprised at the messy fallout that endlessly dogs their pursuit. Any individual or group that would arrogate to itself the responsibility for steering all of that in one direction or another might indeed be exercising a prophetic function, but it would be that of a false prophet at best.

II

Alone in the World

4

A Distinctive Compassion

One day some bhikkhus ventured into a nearby town in order to make the alms round. Finding it still too early in the day for begging, they decided to pay a visit to a park where some mendicants of other sects gathered. After exchanging pleasantries, the followers of the other sects, who appear to have had some knowledge of the Buddha's teaching, began to talk shop with the bhikkhus. As far as they were concerned, what the Buddha taught was not all that different from what their schools taught as well, so they pressed the bhikkhus to explain the difference between the Buddha's teaching and theirs:

> We, too, friends, teach the Dhamma to our disciples thus: "Come, friends, abandon the five hindrances . . . dwell pervading the entire world with a mind imbued with lovingkindness . . . compassion . . . altruistic joy . . . equanimity . . . without ill will." So, friends, what here is the distinction, the disparity, the difference between the ascetic Gotama and us, that is, regarding the one Dhamma teaching and the other, regarding the one manner of instruction and the other?[1]

The bhikkhus did not respond, since they themselves were not at all clear on the issue, and they went back to the Buddha to get his take on the matter at hand.

It is easy to understand their hesitation. There is a general similarity to the renunciant-contemplative strands in many religious traditions in that they call upon their aspirants to overcome those things that obscure them and to develop the broadmindedness and even temper that

1. Bodhi, *Connected Discourses*, 1608.

characterize ongoing ego-attrition. This was true of the other śramaṇic schools around the time of the Buddha, as we see here, and we find it in non-Buddhist renunciant-contemplative traditions as well.[2] One would be quite wide of the mark in claiming that any one of these schools has exclusive claim on any of these exercises, as all of them attest to the real work of clearing the ground of spiritual practice that is anyone's to do simply by virtue of a shared humanity.

One would be equally wide of the mark, however, in claiming that the double-edged process of overcoming obstructive mind states and cultivating the mind advanced by these various traditions all have the same end in view. This is the gist of what the Buddha told the bhikkhus who did not know how to answer the mendicants of the other sects:

> Bhikkhus, when wanderers of other sects speak thus, they should be asked: "Friends, how is the liberation of the mind by lovingkindness developed? What does it have as its destination, its culmination, its fruit, its final goal? How is the liberation of the mind by compassion developed? What does it have as its destination, its culmination, its fruit, its final goal? How is the liberation of the mind by altruistic joy developed? What does it have as its destination, its culmination, its fruit, its final goal? How is the liberation of the mind by equanimity developed? What does it have as its destination, its culmination, its fruit, its final goal?" Being asked thus, those wanderers would not be able to reply and, further, they would meet with vexation. For what reason? Because that would not be within their domain.[3]

The Buddha continued that no one—not Māra, not Brahmā, no other ascetic or brahmin, no deva or human—could provide a satisfying answer to these questions except he, the Tathāgata. This is because he, unlike the rest, understood the place of cultivating these sublime abodes (*brahmavihāras*) within the framework of the path to the cessation of dukkha in nirvāṇa as captured by the Four Noble Truths.

We do well to keep this exchange in mind when addressing the issue of compassion and its relation to practice. Compassion that accords with the Dharma is never removed from the core teaching of the Noble Truths

2. There are, for instance, rather clear parallels between the training sequence in the Dharma and the training sequence we find in Evagrius, one of the early Christian Desert Elders.

3. Bodhi, *Connected Discourses*, 1609.

and their realization,[4] and if the sutras and the subsequent tradition have gone to some lengths to differentiate Dharmic from non-Dharmic understandings of compassion, it is not without reason: the idea of compassion has an immediate popular appeal to it that, taken at face value, can all too easily obscure both what it consists in and what role it plays in the development of one on the path to awakening.

This is especially important to keep in mind when one considers the Dharmic teaching on compassion within a Christian cultural horizon. The New Testament is replete with accounts of Jesus and his disciples curing the blind, the lame, and the lepers, dispelling demons, and even raising the dead. Moreover, the Gospels offer direct injunctions to feed the hungry, clothe the naked, visit the prisoner and the like, failing which one cannot claim a share in the life of Christ (Matt 25:31–46). Finally, the Gospel parables in which the rich or well-stationed are directly called out for their lack of material concern for the poor and the suffering are numerous and have been frequently recalled in the culture and represented in the arts; despite its origin in a parable of Jesus, being a "good Samaritan" is now an everyday—quite secular—trope.

Contrast that ensemble with the account of the Buddha's response to a certain Gotami in the *Therīgāthā*. It seems that Gotami's young son had died suddenly and unexpectedly while out playing:

> Then the madness of grief arose in her . . . Because of her madness from grief, she went from door to door of the houses in the village with the dead body fastened to her hip, saying "Give me medicine for my son." The people treated her with contempt, saying, "What good is medicine?" She did not understand what they said.
>
> Then a certain wise man thought, "She has become mentally deranged through grief for her son. Only the [Buddha] knows the medicine for her." And he said, "Mother, go to the Fully and Perfectly Awakened One to ask for medicine for your son."
>
> She went to the monastery at the time for the discourse on the Doctrine by the Teacher and said, "O Blessed One, give me medicine for my son." . . .

4. Bhikkhu Anālayo makes this point when considering compassion in the canonical sources: "Compassionate activity should ideally be based on the perspective afforded by the four noble truths . . . This is what makes compassion become thoroughly Buddhist, namely by way of being combined with the wisdom of the four noble truths." Anālayo, *Compassion and Emptiness*, 12.

> "Go, enter the town," he said, "and bring some white mustard seed from any house where there has never been any death."
>
> "Very well, sir," she said. Pleased, she entered the town, and at the first house she said, "The Teacher has told me to bring white mustard seed as medicine for my son. If this house has never had a death, give me white mustard seed."
>
> "Who can count the dead people here?" they replied.
>
> Going to the second and third houses, she thought, "What use is white mustard seed?" Through the power of the Buddha, her madness went away, and established in her normal mind, she thought, "This will be true for the whole town. The Blessed One, who is friendly and sympathetic, saw this would be so."
>
> She became profoundly stirred, went out and threw away her son in the cemetery.[5]

When Mary and Martha informed Jesus of the death of their brother, Lazarus, Jesus joined in their sorrow to the point of weeping and then called forth Lazarus, four days dead, from the tomb (John 11:32–44). When Gotami pleaded with the Buddha, the Buddha did not cry, and she did not get her dead son back; instead, she became free of her sorrow through insight into the nature of conditioned existence:

> Then she offered this verse:
>
> This is not doctrine for a village, the doctrine of a town, nor the doctrine of a family. This is the Doctrine for the whole world of [men] and devas: all of this is impermanent.
>
> Then having said this, she went back to the Teacher. Then the Teacher asked her, "Did you obtain white mustard seed, Gotami?"
>
> "The task of the white mustard seed is finished, sir," she said. "Be my support." Then the teacher said this verse to her:
>
> Death takes away a man possessed with longing, intoxicated by children and cattle, like a great flood [takes away] a sleeping village.
>
> At the end of the verse, just as she was standing there, she stood firm in the fruition state of Stream-Entry, and she asked to go forth. Then the teacher gave permission for her to go forth. She [went around] the Teacher three times, keeping him on the right, paid homage, and went to the bhikkhunīs' monastery. She went forth and then received the full ordination.[6]

5. Dhammapāla, *Commentary on Verses of the Therīs*, 223–24.
6. Dhammapāla, *Commentary on Verses of the Therīs*, 224.

The compassion of the Buddha is exercised by serving as an occasion whereby a person might come to the end of her dukkha for herself.[7]

We have here then a distinctive understanding of the exercise of compassion, one that—like the Dharma itself—is oftentimes "deep, hard to see, subtle, going against the stream."[8] It does not deny the merit of responding to and striving to alleviate the material hardship of others; many and wide-ranging are the passages in the canon and in the tradition where the Buddha or a Dharma ancestor enjoins a hearer, particularly one well-stationed in society, to attend to the needs of the everyday penury of others. What it does do is indicate is that such activity cannot simply be the point of one's aspiration or taken to be the fullness of the path. More importantly, as we will see, it also shows that such attention to and involvement in another's hardship can actually get in the way of one's further progress as the *near enemy* of compassion if it is not first grounded in the discipline and fruits of the Dharma.

In the *Nikāyas*, compassion, or karuṇā, is usually taken up in conjunction with the other *brahmavihāras*, the "abodes of Brahmā" or "divine abodes": lovingkindness (*mettā*), sympathetic joy (*muditā*), and equanimity (*upekkhā*). They are also called *appamañña*, boundless states, because they transcend the boundaries I have hitherto maintained between myself and others and extend infinitely. The brahmavihāras were not unique to the teaching of the Buddha; as we saw above, they were part of the practice of other sects at the time. What is unique to the Dharma are the answers to the questions the Buddha himself posed: How are they developed? What do they have as their destination, their culmination, their fruit, their final goal?

7. This idea will be more fully developed in chapter 5. To be fair, one finds similar activity in the Gospels as well. When the hungry crowd looks for a miracle of manna, Jesus offers himself as the bread of life which will never leave them hungry again (John 6:31–35); when he encounters the woman fetching water at the well, Jesus offers himself as the living water which will never leave her thirsty again (John 4:11–13). These passages, which are distinctively Johannine and point to something much more than giving someone a bit of bread or something to drink, tend to be eclipsed by the discussions of everyday compassionate action such as we find in the Synoptics.

8. Bodhi, *Connected Discourses*, 232.

The *Tevijja Sutra* outlines where the brahmavihāras fit within the aspirant's development. The sutra begins with two local Brahmins, Vāseṭṭha and Bhāradvāja, disputing the right path to follow in leading to union with Brahmā, and to settle the debate they agree that they will abide by what the Buddha says on the matter. The Buddha starts off by prompting them to admit that none of the various paths taught by the various Brahmins are trustworthy, since none of them have actually seen Brahmā (they lack insight), and all of them see the sun and moon just as other people do (they are still bound to their samsaric worlds). Since they do not know where they are heading, instruction from them would be as stupid and baseless as the talk of a man saying he was off to meet a beautiful girl without knowing her caste, her name, her height, her appearance, or her home town. Moreover, since they do not act differently from anyone else in that they "neglect what a Brahmin should do," all their prayers and supplications will no more get them to union with Brahmā than if a man were to try to reach the far shore of a river by begging and imploring the bank of the far shore to come to him. A different form of practice is required.

At this point, the discussion shifts, and the Buddha begins to lay out the right path for a Brahmin to take. First, he states that no one can enter into Brahmā's abode who is still bound by the fetters of sense-desire, the attachment to forms that are "agreeable, loved, charming, attractive, pleasurable, [and] arousing desire" whether by the eye, ear, nose, tongue, or body:

> But that such Brahmins learned in the Three Vedas, who persistently neglect what a Brahmins should do, . . . who are enslaved by these five strands of sense-desire . . . knowing no way out, should attain after death, at the breaking-up of the body, to union with Brahmā—that is just not possible.[9]

The first step, then, is to discipline oneself in non-attachment to the desires of the senses in order to break one's chains to the nearer shore. Next, the Buddha points out that a person wishing to cross the river cannot do it if he were "to lie down on this bank, covering his head with a shawl." He continues,

> In the same way, Vāseṭṭha, in the Ariyan discipline these five hindrances are called obstacles, hindrances, coverings-up, envelopings. Which five? The hindrance of sensuality, of ill-will,

9. Walshe, *Long Discourses*, 191.

> of sloth-and-torpor, of worry-and-flurry, of doubt. These five are called obstacles, hindrances, coverings-up, envelopings. And these Brahmins learned in the Three Vedas are caught up, hemmed in, obstructed, entangled in these five hindrances.[10]

Without overcoming the five hindrances, union with Brahmā is, again, not possible. What is more, if one is in any way encumbered, be it with hate, ill-will, impurity, lack of discipline, wives, and wealth, it is also impossible to be united with "the unencumbered" Brahmā.

The five hindrances are labeled as such because of their capacity for "obstructing and hindering and concealing [reality] from consciousness"[11] (hence the shawl metaphor above). They conceal the aspirant from reality by casting a veneer of independence and solidity and worthiness on to the plain and sober truth that all conditioned things are marked by impermanence and non-self and are not worthy of attachment. They are particularly vexing and difficult to work through, since they are the last strong attempts of the mind to remain with what is familiar and comforting. The hindrances all have an element of fear about them (hence *covering oneself* with the shawl) that keeps the practitioner from pressing on in the direction of the hitherto unknown shore. As we saw in conjunction with the gradual training, it is only when the nīvaraṇas have been overcome that one enters into the practice of the jhānas and the attainment of ever-deepening samādhi. The aspirant has now attained a state of concentrated, meditative absorption, undistracted by the push and pull of the senses and various mind states.

The *Tevijja Sutra* indicates that only when the first jhāna has been obtained does the aspirant begin the practice of the four immeasurables:

> *A disciple goes forth, practices the moralities, attains the first jhāna.*
>
> Then, with his heart filled with loving-kindness, [compassion, etc.], he dwells suffusing one quarter, the second, the third, the fourth. Thus he dwells suffusing the whole world upwards, downwards, across, everywhere, always with a heart filled with loving-kindness, [compassion, etc.], abundant, unbounded, without hate or ill-will.
>
> Just as if a mighty trumpeter were with little difficulty to make a proclamation to the four quarters, so by this meditation, Vāseṭṭha, by this liberation of the heart through loving-kindness,

10. Walshe, *Long Discourses*, 191–92.
11. Buddhaghosa and Ñāṇamoli, *Path of Purification*, 714.

> [compassion, etc.], he leaves nothing untouched, nothing unaffected in the sensuous sphere. This, Vāseṭṭha, is the way to union with Brahma.[12]

That ability to suffuse the whole world with loving-kindness, compassion, sympathetic joy, and equanimity is simply not possible for one still tied to the senses, not yet restrained by the precepts, living without mindfulness, and unwilling to pull back the covers of obstructive mind states. This explains why at the end of a discussion on how the practice of the brahmavihāras mutually reinforce one another the Buddha did not fail to add that the development of any and all of them was "based upon seclusion, dispassion and cessation":

> And how, bhikkhus is the liberation of the mind by compassion developed? What does it have as its destination, its culmination, its fruit, its final goal? Here, bhikkhus, a bhikkhu develops the enlightenment factor of mindfulness accompanied by compassion, the enlightenment factor of lovingkindness accompanied by compassion, the enlightenment factor of equanimity accompanied by compassion, based upon seclusion, dispassion and cessation, maturing in release.[13]

That qualifier succinctly sums up the whole trajectory we have just been looking at, reinforcing the idea that he brahmavihāras are not capable of being entertained, let alone practiced, before one has abandoned one's own obstructive hindrances.

Understanding the place of karuṇā and the other brahmavihāras in the gradual training allows us to see already some things about the nature of a Dharmic understanding of compassion that might not have otherwise been apparent at the outset. To begin with, there is no presumption that karuṇā is an everyday disposition. The Golden Rule may be widely shared across cultures, but extending to another what I want for myself or not inflicting on another what I would not want inflicted on myself still takes the self as the benchmark and still operates according to the dictates of pleasure and pain, gain and loss. It certainly belongs to the first kind of right view, and there is no reason to dismiss it outright. But because karuṇā's orientation is nothing if not universal, one would be hard-pressed to see in it such an everyday preoccupation with determinate individuals. The brahmavihāras are all of them characterized

12. Walshe, *Long Discourses*, 194; italics in the original.

13. Bodhi, *Connected Discourses*, 1610.

by their *boundlessness*: "above, below, across, and everywhere," as we just saw, and this is true of karuṇā, which has as its base the infinity of space:

> With the complete transcendence of perceptions of forms, with the passing away of perceptions of sensory impingement, with nonattention to perceptions of diversity, aware that "space is infinite," he enters and dwells in the base of the infinity of space. Bhikkhus, the liberation of the mind by compassion has the base of the infinity of space as its culmination, I say, for a wise bhikkhu here who has not penetrated to a superior liberation.[14]

The compassion captured by karuṇā is *simply vast*, but this vastness is not like some universal from which a particular can be derived; I cannot take "compassion for Sarah" as an instance of "boundless compassion" or "compassion for all beings," for example. To do so would involve taking into account her nexus of relationships and the content of her particular forms of saṃsāra—precisely the percepts that karuṇā does *not* take into account, since it presupposes that the desire to see them turn out one way or another has been cast aside.

To see just how this is so, we can rephrase the "currents of craving" that are the hallmarks of tṛṣṇā, now with reference to others and their condition:

> There is [the notion] "You are," there are [the notions] "You are thus," "You are just so," "You are otherwise," "You are lasting," "You are evanescent," "You may be," "You may be thus," "You may be just so," "You may be otherwise," "May you be," "May you be thus," "May you be just so," "May you be otherwise," "You shall be," "You shall be thus," "You shall be just so," "You shall be otherwise." These are the eighteen currents of craving related to the internal."
>
> And what are the eighteen currents of craving related to the external? When there is [the notion], "You are because of this," there are [the notions]: "You are thus because of this," "You are just so because of this," "You are otherwise because of this," "You are lasting because of this," "You are evanescent because of this," "You may be because of this," "You may be thus because of this," "You may be just so because of this," "You may be otherwise because of this," "May you be because of this," "May you be thus because of this," "May you be just so because of this," "May you be otherwise because of this," "You shall be because of this,"

14. Bodhi, *Connected Discourses*, 1610.

> "You shall be thus because of this," "You shall be just so because of this," "You shall be otherwise because of this."

As with the "I" and the "we" above, the "you" here—and one could, of course, include "he" or "she" or "they" as well—becomes a percept, a mental object, another conditioned dharma among others that I hope or fear will turn out a certain way based on the activity of other dharmas (". . . because of this").

In wishing for the particular success of one individual in his or her samsaric concatenation of worlds, I am also implying that other beings should arrange their actions accordingly. That the poor should have more means the rich should (be made to) have less. That the powerless should have a voice means that those currently enjoying a position of privilege should (be made to) pipe down. Indeed, it is one thing to say, "We are all in the same boat"; it is another to provide a detailed passenger manifest with a seating chart to show just who and in what specific way each is on board, and then to determine an optimal arrangement on that basis. Even "We are all in the same boat" is not as straight to the point as realizing, simply, "There is dukkha."

The brahmavihāras all reflect an awareness that the self is not to be singled out from of the vastness of all beings, and the training stages will have successively required the ever-further breakdown of the purported line that separates me from others. In this way, the lovingkindness, compassion, sympathetic joy, and equanimity developed is understood in such a way that it applies to all, myself included:

> Again, some person dwells pervading one quarter [of the world] with a mind imbued with compassion . . . altruistic joy . . . equanimity, likewise the second quarter, the third quarter, and the fourth quarter. Thus above, below, across, and everywhere, and *to all as to himself*, he dwells pervading the entire world with a mind imbued with equanimity, vast, exalted, measureless, without enmity, without ill will.[15]

This non-separation reveals another aspect of the brahmavihāras in their relationship to the full path, namely that they still, however subtly, retain an aspect of self to them. To be sure, the brahmavihāras's orientation is to expand one's awareness beyond the limited confines of the individual *ego*; but—and this appears to be the key point where the Buddha takes leave of the Brahmanic underpinnings of the brahmavihāras—if the self

15. Bodhi, *Numerical Discourses*, 510; italics mine.

(*ātman*) is simply *expanded*, then the nature of the self as *empty* has not yet been realized, and dukkha has still not found its cessation. Obliterating the line between self and other without realizing the emptiness of each leads to painting others with the same brush with which I have been painting myself; I may have seen the limitations of separating myself from others but I now run the danger of seeing them as more *me*,[16] with all the attendant taints that come with that self-concept.

The textual sources bear out the incompleteness of the brahmavihāras in conducing toward the end of the path. In the *Cūḷa-Assapura Sutra*, for instance, we see this in the distinction between "one who practices the way proper to the recluse" and "being a recluse." After enumerating many practices that align with the way of the recluse, including overcoming covetousness and the rest, the Buddha continues:

> Bhikkhus, if anyone from a clan of nobles [or a clan of brahmins, a clan of merchants, a clan of workers, or any clan] goes forth from the home life into homelessness, and after encountering the Dhamma and Discipline proclaimed by the Tathagata, develops loving-kindness, compassion, appreciative joy, and equanimity, and thereby gains internal peace, then because of that internal peace he practices the way proper to the recluse, I say.[17]

This is the last in the list of ways proper to the recluse. The Buddha then goes on to describe a further level of attainment:

> Bhikkhus, if anyone from a clan of nobles [or a clan of brahmins, a clan of merchants, a clan of workers, or any clan] goes forth from the home life into homelessness, and by realising for himself with direct knowledge here and now enters upon and abides in the deliverance of the mind and deliverance of wisdom that are taintless with the destruction of taints, then he is already a recluse because of the destruction of the taints.[18]

16. Loy relies on the non-separation of self and other as a basis for "Buddhist social engagement," but when he cites Joanna Macy on this point, it still reads more as an *expanded* self rather than an *empty* self: "A liberated person naturally wants to help the world, because he or she does not feel separate from it. This point is essential because it also provides the foundation for Buddhist social engagement. As Joanna Macy puts it, there is no need to ask why you take care of your own body." Loy, *Great Awakening*, 31.

17. Ñāṇamoli and Bodhi, *Middle Length Discourses*, 374–75.

18. Ñāṇamoli and Bodhi, *Middle Length Discourses*, 375.

This point is echoed in the *Aṅguttara Nikāya*. There the practice of the brahmavihāras is cast in such a way that it is best read as propaedeutic to the work of coming to insight into the emptiness of the skandhas:

> Again, some person dwells pervading one quarter [of the world] with a mind imbued with compassion . . . altruistic joy . . . equanimity, likewise the second quarter, the third quarter, and the fourth quarter. Thus above, below, across, and everywhere, and to all as to himself, he dwells pervading the entire world with a mind imbued with equanimity, vast, exalted, measureless, without enmity, without ill will. He [then] contemplates whatever phenomena there pertaining to form, feeling, perception, volitional activities, and consciousness as impermanent, as suffering, as a disease, as a boil, as a dart, as misery, as an affliction, as alien, as disintegrating, as empty, as non-self.[19]

Hence for a wise bhikkhu (or anyone else) who has not yet "penetrated to a superior liberation" the practice of the brahmavihāras is certainly an excellent training tool.[20] It does not of itself, however, conduce toward the fullness of awakening without further development,[21] and it certainly cannot simply be *equated* with awakening.

~

This differentiation of the boundless from the determinate, the perceptless from the percept-laden, that characterizes karuṇā in the *Nikāyas* set the framework for what would be developed in the commentarial sources as the demarcation of compassion and the other brahmavihāras from their *near enemies*, those states that bear a family resemblance to the brahmavihāras, but, upon closer inspection, reveal their lingering ties to the kleśas and a lack of understanding concerning the marks of conditioned existence.

Jack Kornfield has taken up the matter of the near enemies, and his formulation of the distinction has been widely cited in Buddhist circles

19. Bodhi, *Numerical Discourses*, 510.

20. See the discussion in Anālayo, *Compassion and Emptiness*, 70–72.

21. The *Bojjhaṅgasaṃyutta Sutra* continues the discussion of what separates the practice of the Buddha from the other sects by discussing the cultivation of the *bojjhaṅgā*, the seven factors of awakening, that are the next step in the training.

and beyond.[22] He regularly casts the distinction between compassion and its near enemy as the distinction between compassion and pity:

> The near enemy of compassion is pity. Instead of feeling the openness of compassion, pity says, "Oh that poor person. I feel sorry for people like that." Pity sees them as different from ourselves. It sets up a separation between ourselves and others, a sense of distance and remoteness from the suffering of others that is affirming and gratifying to the self. Compassion, on the other hand, recognizes the suffering of another as a reflection of our own pain: "I understand this; I suffer in the same way." It is empathetic, a mutual connection with the pain and sorrow of life. Compassion is shared suffering.[23]

Earlier he phrased it this way:

> The near enemy of compassion is pity, and this also separates us. Pity feels sorry for "that poor person over there," as if he were somehow different from us, whereas true compassion . . . is the resonance of our heart with the suffering of another. "Yes, I, too, together with you, share in the sorrows of life."[24]

Kornfield's differentiation of compassion from its near enemy rests squarely on the distinction between separation and connection: compassion is sharing another's sorrow as one's own, the near enemy perceives the other's sorrow, but does not share it. In popular parlance, for instance, one hears the expression, "There but for the grace of God go I," and, following Kornfield's lead, this would be a fine enough example of the near enemy; one sees the suffering of another, but one also considers oneself somehow exempt from actually sharing in it. A fuller sense of compassion, following Kornfield, would be reflected in saying something more like, "There go I." That person's suffering is mine as well, for she and I are not separate from each other. Again, even that is saying too much, for *There is dukkha*, without implicating any I or you, captures all that needs to be said.

Kornfield is right to direct our attention to the lingering attachment to the personal self that the near enemies reflect, and he is right to point out that compassion cannot manifest as long as that attachment is still in

22. It has been taken up quite eagerly by writers in clinical practices such as psychotherapy and the health professions, for example.

23. Kornfield, *Bringing Home the Dharma*, 103.

24. Kornfield, *Path with Heart*, 191.

tow. All the same, there are several points where Kornfield's differentiation of compassion from its near enemy fails to capture key aspects of karuṇā. To begin with, one finds in Kornfield's account no sense of the simple *vastness* of karuṇā. In casting the differentiation between compassion and its near enemy in terms of the quality of an interaction one person has with another, it seems that one only need to have extended one's concern to some one person who has come into view, or perhaps a group of people. The result is that compassion becomes psychologized, and the process of discerning compassion from its near enemy is turned into one of inventorying feelings on the spot. "Do I feel separate from this person? Then it must be pity." "Do I feel connected? Then it could be compassion." Of course, condescension cannot be viewed as reflecting compassion in any way, but one would be hard-pressed indeed to find any aspect of the aim of the Dharma being addressed as if it rises and falls simply on particular *feelings*.[25]

More importantly, Kornfield's distinction does not address what the "mutual connection" or "resonance of the heart" is *about*, nor why I should even worry about the near enemies except for perhaps wanting to be a more empathetic person or more effective in my interpersonal relations. Here one could well rehearse the question the Buddha raised concerning compassion as understood by the mendicants of the non-Buddhist sects in the park: "What does it have as its destination, its culmination, its fruit, its final goal?" One does not need to have heard the Dharma to hit upon the distinction such as Kornfield has cast it, and, as Kornfield has cast compassion, one need not aspire to awakening to cultivate it. The widespread popular appeal of his compassion/near enemy distinction no doubt lies to some extent in its serviceability in everyday settings free of any reference to Buddhism, the Dharma, or the like. All the same, it is ultimately insufficient for orienting practice.

Kornfield's depiction stands in sharp contrast to the way the near enemies have been understood by others in the tradition. One of the earliest mentions of the near enemies is found in Buddhaghosa's fifth century *Visuddhimagga* (*Path of Purification*), an extended systematic compendium of the core teaching of the *Tripiṭaka* and its commentaries.

25. One cannot, it seems to me, build a high enough firewall between the liberation offered by the Dharma and all attempts to *psychologize* it. Anything one could take up as an object of psychological analysis would still be but a conditioned phenomenon, an aspect of the skandhas. The cessation of tṛṣṇā in nirvāṇa is not a dharma, and the unshakable deliverance of mind is not something comparable to mental well-being.

In it Buddhaghosa identifies the near enemy of compassion as "grief based on the home life":

> Compassion has grief based on the home life as its near enemy, since both share in seeing failure. Such grief has been described in the way beginning, "When a man either regards as privation failure to obtain visible objects cognizable with the eye that are sought after, desired, agreeable, gratifying and associated with worldliness, or when he recalls those formerly obtained that are past, ceased and changed, then grief arises in him. Such grief as this is called grief based on the home life."[26]

Buddhaghosa is here quoting the *Saḷāyatanavibhanga Sutta*, where, among other matters, the contrast between the grief and joy of the everyday person and the grief and joy of the renunciant is taken up. To get a sense of what he is aiming at, it is helpful to recall what the sutra identifies as the grief of the renunciant:

> When, by knowing the impermanence, change, fading away, and cessation of forms, one sees it as it actually is with proper wisdom that forms both formerly and now are all impermanent, suffering, and subject to change, one generates a longing for the supreme liberations thus: "When shall I enter upon and abide in that base that the noble ones now enter upon and abide in?" In one who generates thus a longing for the supreme liberations, grief arises with that longing as condition. Such grief as this is called grief based on renunciation.[27]

Clearly there is much more than an issue of connection versus separation going on here.

Buddhaghosa draws a rather clear line between a kind of empathetic everyday concern for one's or others' manifest welfare and compassion as the keen awareness of the self-inflicted dukkha of all due to their tṛṣṇā, my own in the first place. Because the householder frets about the gain and loss of everyday things and states of affairs, his grief is tied up with the common person's assessment of what is good and bad and with what constitutes a successful life according to prevailing conceptions. To the extent that those around him share these samsaric worlds, his compassion towards others' misfortunes is framed accordingly. Contracting an illness, losing a home, a loved one, a job, failure to achieve one's ambitions

26. Buddhaghosa and Ñāṇamoli, *Path of Purification*, 313.

27. Ñāṇamoli and Bodhi, *Middle Length Discourses*, 1069.

or to secure one's happiness, or being unable to enjoy a life in relative ease and comfort—these are some of the situations that might prompt the householder's concern for others. He "gets" others' pain in these matters, because he, too, has perhaps experienced similar pain in conjunction with them.

By contrast, the grief of the renunciant arises in response to her initial seeing into the marks of conditioned existence and her eagerness to be free of tṛṣṇā at last. Beginning to realize that all samsaric forms are empty, her "grief in seeing failure" stems from the awareness that she still has a long way to go before at last being freed of the fetters altogether. Knowing this for herself, she is able to see that the proper end to dukkha, whether her own or that of anyone else, does not lie in getting a job or having one's health restored or getting recognized in school but, as the Buddha had put it, in "making the breakthrough to [the] Four Noble Truths as they really are."[28] The aspirant's compassion directs her toward the work of deepening that insight, and rightly so, for without first seeing clearly for herself, she could be in no position of assistance to others in making that breakthrough for themselves.[29]

The *Visuddhimagga* was intended as a training manual for the use of Buddhaghosa's fellow monks. It is not surprising, then, that he would have illustrated his point with the language of the householder/renunciant distinction. At bottom, however, what distinguishes the brahmavihāras from their near enemies here is not that the ones are practiced by monks and nuns and the others by shopkeepers and farmworkers; that would be a little too facile. Rather, it is more accurate to say that compassion is practiced by those with (at least some measure of) insight into the cause and end of dukkha while the near enemy is practiced by those without. For one without insight, the myriad ups and downs of day-to-day life seem preeminently real, significant, and demanding of attention, and one's response to their loss or changes in them will be guided by all the attraction, aversion, and ignorance that otherwise prompt one's everyday, tṛṣṇā-bound actions. Put somewhat differently, compassion's near enemy corresponds to the first kind of right view; it proceeds from the fact that there is right and wrong, better and worse, gain and loss. It is still affected by the taints, so it is still itself a cause of some dukkha. Compassion

28. Bodhi, *Connected Discourses*, 1855.

29. If, as Kornfield puts it, she is truly *sharing* another's suffering, it is not clear how she can be of assistance in *overcoming* suffering. It is a handicapped physician indeed who is just as sick as the patient.

itself, however, reflects the second kind of right view—proceeding from wisdom, noble, supramundane, a factor of the path to the end of dukkha with the cessation of tṛṣṇā.

However *near*, the near enemies are *enemies* all the same, because they lull one into easing off the path to ever-fuller awakening. From the standpoint of one not yet possessed of some degree of insight, they might bear enough of a family resemblance to count as the real thing. Avoiding patent cruelty (compassion's far enemy) is relatively easy; most people do not need much convincing not to murder or steal, and most have a general sense that it is better to be kind to others than not. But abandoning attachment to comely, satisfying, and seemingly noble attitudes and actions, particularly when faced with examples of real cruelty and hardship among those around us, is much harder indeed. Still, this too must be set to the side as just another exercise in tṛṣṇā. As Buddhadāsa Bhikkhu points out,

> The fact that if one grasps and clings, even to goodness, that is *dukkha*. In this sense, that which the world assumes to be goodness is actually false or evil. Goodness is still *dukkha*; it has the *dukkha* appropriate to it because it's not yet void; it's still busy and disturbed. Only when there is *suññatā*, and one is beyond goodness, can there be freedom from *dukkha*.[30]

Without abandoning the everyday concern for the material, psychological, and social well-being of myself and others (in the sense outlined), further progress on the path is not possible.

And this is not just a so-called "Hinayāna" attitude, a narrow focus on my own realization to the exclusion of all others; it is also a characteristic of bodhisattvic aspiration in the Mahāyāna. We see this reflected, for instance, in the *Vimalakīrti Sutra* with respect to Mahākāśyapa, one of the Buddha's foremost disciples. When the Buddha asked for volunteers to visit the Layman Vimalakīrti, Mahākāśyapa begs off. Seems Vimalakīrti had at one time upbraided him about the way he thought compassion should be exercised. Mahākāśyapa had made a point of begging from the poor in order that they, and not the rich, might accrue merit, and it was his "preferential option for the poor" that Vimalakīrti found wanting:

> Lord, I am indeed reluctant to go to the Licchavi Vimalakīrti to inquire about his illness. Why? I remember one day, when I was in the street of the poor begging for my food, the Licchavi

30. Buddhadāsa, *Heartwood of the Bodhi Tree*, 40.

> Vimalakīrti came along and said to me, "Reverend Mahākāśyapa, to avoid the houses of the wealthy, and to favor the houses of the poor—this is partiality in benevolence.[31]

In his partiality for the poor Mahākāśyapa revealed his lack of understanding that *poor* and *rich* capture nothing essential about beings. His presumptive compassion did not yet adequately reflect insight into emptiness. Mahākāśyapa is singled out here, but the mistake is a broader one. The line between karuṇā and its near enemy as described here is so subtle that it is said to be "most hard"[32] even for bodhisattvas to keep from crossing, yet keep from crossing it they must if they are to come to the fullness of awakening—and compassion—to which they aspire.

There is no question but that one of the most endearing features of the bodhisattva in popular imagination is her boundless compassion, but it cannot be forgotten (as it often is) that hers is a compassion that is never at any remove from her aspiration to the fullest insight. Bodhisattvas are not so named because they are "beings devoted to compassion"; they are so named because they are "beings devoted to enlightenment." In fact, however, their enlightenment and their compassion are inseparable; neither precedes the other but both are cultivated together as bodhicitta, the incomparable mind proceeding toward Buddhahood.

One of the greatest stumbling blocks to an appreciation of the importance of insight for the exercise of compassion is the commonplace, as frequently as it is uncritically repeated, that a bodhisattva *defers* or *renounces* her full awakening in order to remain in saṃsāra to aid sentient beings out of compassion for them. Taigen Daniel Leighton, for example, puts it this way: "A bodhisattva, as distinct from a buddha, vows not to personally settle into the salvation of final buddhahood until she or he can assist all of the beings throughout the vast reaches of time and space to fully realize this liberated experience."[33] Such language of deferral gives the impression that the bodhisattva chooses to forgo complete Buddhahood until all beings attain Buddhahood in the same way that one

31. Thurman, *Holy Teaching of Vimalakīrti*, 26.

32. Conze, *Perfection of Wisdom*, 259; see also Conze, *Large Sutra on Perfect Wisdom*, 462.

33. Leighton, *Bodhisattva Archetypes*, 25.

chooses to forego dessert until all of one's dinner has been eaten. This is hardly accurate. What the bodhisattva forgoes is remaining at the level of an arhat or a *pratyekabuddha*, opting instead to set her sights higher, namely the attainment of full Buddhahood. An arhat or pratyekabuddha is enlightened, but she does not possess the power to liberate all beings; that power belongs only to Buddhas. Out of her great compassion for sentient beings a bodhisattva strives for Buddhahood so that her enlightenment may be liberating for others as well. As Nāgārjuna put it:

> Once I have succeeded in making my way across, I shall endeavor to bring beings across as well. Once I have gained liberation, I shall then liberate these beings as well. Once I have succeeded in gaining peace, I shall see that beings are then established in peacefulness as well.[34]

Nāgārjuna is here completely in accord with the teaching in the *Nikāyas* that compassion follows upon awakening and not the other way around:

> If one is not tamed oneself and wishes to tame someone else who is untamed, that is impossible. [If] one is drowning oneself and wishes to rescue someone else who is drowning, that is impossible. [If] one has not extinguished one's own [defilements] and wishes to make someone else with unextinguished [defilements] extinguish them, that is impossible[35]

Indeed, without having myself first crossed to the other shore, how could I in any way assist others in navigating the waters—or even know for myself that there even *is* the other shore to help others cross over to?

John Makransky has shown that already in early Mahāyāna sources the deferment model was found to be unsatisfactory because it rested on conceptions of saṃsāra and nirvāṇa that, if correct, would render not only bodhisattvas, but Buddhas as well, powerless in the world.[36] As long as nirvāṇa was conceived of as the cessation of all twelve *nidānas* (*dvādasanidānāni*) or "links" of dependent origination (*paṭiccasamuppāda*), the mere fact of having a bodily form in a world posed an obvious roadblock on the path to awakening; one could not attain nirvāṇa except with the complete abandonment of that embodied form (*parinirvāṇa*). On this model, it makes sense to think that, if a bodhisattva were to abide among sentient beings, she would have to forgo

34. Nāgārjuna, *Generating the Resolve*, 23.
35. Ñāṇamoli and Bodhi, *Middle Length Discourses*, 130.
36. Makransky, *Buddhahood Embodied*, 93–96.

the highest levels of attainment and remain in embodied form until all other sentient beings, too, were able to shed their embodied forms. But this assumes that the mere fact of embodiment, and not tṛṣṇā itself, is what needs to find its cessation. Here it is helpful to recall the progression of the nidānas:

> Ānanda, mind-and-body conditions consciousness and consciousness conditions mind-and-body, mind-and-body conditions contact, contact conditions feeling, feeling conditions craving, craving conditions clinging, clinging conditions becoming, becoming conditions birth, birth conditions ageing-and-death, sorrow, lamentation, pain, grief and distress.[37]

If one is able to see into the emptiness of all dharmas, then one can well enough perceive them, but tṛṣṇā would not arise in conjunction with that kind of perception—mind-and-body, consciousness, contact, feeling would still be operative, but, overcoming ignorance by knowing that they are devoid of self, no attachment or aversion would arise.[38] As nirvāṇa is simply the cessation of tṛṣṇā which gives rise to samsaric worlds, this state of activity free of tṛṣṇā yet still very much alive and well was called nonabiding nirvāṇa (*apratiṣṭhita nirvāṇa*):

> A common term for Buddhahood in classical Mahāyāna literature is *apratiṣṭhita nirvāṇa* (nonabiding nirvāṇa) meaning that a Buddha is restricted neither by the uncontrolled suffering of saṃsāra nor by a quiescent state of liberation that would have him powerless to help beings in saṃsāra. Buddhahood is a state that is free from the power of worldly conditions (*dharma* and *kleśa*) without standing apart from the world.[39]

Nāgārjuna put it like this: "The magnanimous [bodhisattvas] do not abide in nirvāṇa or saṃsāra. Therefore the Buddhas have spoken of this as 'the non-abiding nirvāṇa.'"[40]

Here we need not get into some of the thornier issues that nonabiding nirvāṇa raises for other aspects of the Dharma nor need we consider its implications for the full range of practice. For present purposes I would like to draw attention to Vasubandhu's take on nonabiding nirvāṇa

37. Walshe, *Long Discourses*, 223–24.

38. It is to the realization of this that the exercise of guarding the doors of the sense faculties was directed.

39. Makransky, *Buddhahood Embodied*, 85.

40. Lindtner, *Master of Wisdom*, 67.

because of his express linking of compassion to it. Vasubandhu glosses on *apratiṣṭhita nirvāṇa* this way:

> 32. The compassionate best genius understands that everything included in the life-cycle is naturally both suffering and also selfless, and so neither becomes disgusted nor damaged by any faults.
>
> Having thoroughly understood all of the life-cycle [=samsara] as it is in reality, the bodhisattva, due to compassion, does not become disgusted, and, due to extreme intelligence, is not damaged by any faults. Thus he does not dwell either in Nirvana nor in the life-cycle, respectively.
>
> One verse on the thorough knowledge of the life-cycle:
>
> 33. When she observes the natural suffering of the world, the loving (bodhisattva) suffers; yet she knows just what it is as well as the means to avoid it, and so she does not become exhausted.
>
> "She suffers" means that she feels compassion. "She knows what it is" means that she knows suffering just as it is, and the "means to avoid suffering" means that she knows that by which it is destroyed. Thus, knowing the suffering of the cyclic life just as it is and (also knowing) the means of renouncing it, the bodhisattva does not become exhausted thanks to her distinctive compassion.[41]

It is not that the bodhisattva is unaware of the world around her in all its misery; she still has eyes and ears, so she knows full well what is transpiring. Unlike the common person, however, she does not read anything in the world as intrinsically good or bad, or of itself conducive to dukkha (or nirvāṇa for that matter); empty, selfless, and conditioned dharmas are powerless to make that happen. Her lack of "disgust" with respect to them allows her to move among sentient beings still shrouded by ignorance and still acting out on the basis of their defilements. She herself does not join them in that enterprise (to do so would be to engage in what Buddhaghosa identified as compassion's near enemy), but instead practices even more diligently in the direction of Buddhahood. Her distinctive, non-exhausting compassion consists precisely in manifesting the possibility of being freed from dukkha, even as she lives and breathes among those still quite inured to their own.

This is not an easy task, nor does one quickly come to possess the wherewithal to make it happen. It has been widely acknowledged

41. Maitreyanātha/Āryāsaṅga, *Universal Vehicle Discourse*, 233.

throughout the Mahāyāna that the attainment of Buddhahood takes countless eons. Across those many eons, the bodhisattva practices the *pāramitās*, the various perfections, and in so doing *comes to be* of benefit for sentient beings. This is different from saying she remains in saṃsāra *in order to be* of benefit for sentient beings, at least in the utilitarian way benefit is often understood. True to their name, bodhisattvas are "beings devoted to enlightenment," not beings that say, "No, thank you, I'll take my enlightenment later; I'm busy now saving others." Far from choosing to forgo realization, a bodhisattva never gives off the aspiration toward full awakening for a second. Coursing ever more deeply in wisdom, she comes to realize something along the lines of "All beings awaken with me," which has a much different ring to it than saying, "I will awaken only when all other beings awaken first with my assistance."

All of this helps make sense of the claim, frequently made in Mahāyāna sources, that a bodhisattva who even gives rise to a conception of a being to be liberated is in fact no bodhisattva at all. *The Diamond Sutra* puts it this way:

> The Buddha said to him, "Subhuti, those who would now set forth on the bodhisattva path should thus give birth to this thought: 'However many beings there are in whatever realms of being might exist, whether they are born from an egg or born from a womb, born from the water or born from the air, whether they have form or no form, whether they have perception or no perception or neither perception nor no perception, in whatever conceivable realm of being one might conceive of beings, in the realm of complete nirvana I shall liberate them all. And though I thus liberate countless beings, not a single being is liberated.'
>
> And why not? Subhuti, a bodhisattva who creates the perception of a being cannot be called a 'bodhisattva.' And why not? Subhuti, no one can be called a bodhisattva who creates the perception of a self or who creates the perception of a being, a life, or a soul."[42]

This point is driven home as well in *The Perfection of Wisdom in Eight Thousand Lines*:

> Wise Bodhisattvas, coursing thus, reflect on non-production,
> And yet, while doing so, engender in themselves the great compassion,
> Which is, however, free from any notion of a being.
> Thereby they practice wisdom, the highest perfection.

42. Pine, *Diamond Sutra*, 2–3.

> But when the notion of suffering and beings leads him to think
> "Suffering I shall remove, the weal of the world I shall work!"
> Beings are then imagined, a self is imagined,
> The practice of wisdom, the highest perfection, is lacking.[43]

As we can see, this is not at all a departure from the core teaching on compassion in the canon; imagining beings and imagining self were from the outset eclipsed by the vastness of karuṇā, and karuṇā is perfected through the realization of emptiness. The bodhisattva sees no self-possessed beings but knows them to be the tṛṣṇā-driven, skandha-constituted forms they are. Her insight into emptiness is precisely what separates her compassion from compassion's near enemy.[44]

I have drawn this exploration of the distinctiveness of Dharmic compassion from a range of sources. One need not have a Buddhist library at one's disposal to cobble together a coherent picture, however, since the key points of this understanding of compassion are all illustrated in one place, namely in the account of Avalokiteśvara, the Bodhisattva of Compassion, in the *Lotus Sutra*, to which we now turn.

43. Conze, *Perfection of Wisdom*, 11–12.

44. Ludovic Viévard has pointed out that insight into emptiness is the line that, at least formally, distinguishes everyday compassion from *mahākaruṇā*, or the "great compassion" of the bodhisattvas (Viévard, *Vacuité et compassion*, 233). While he rightfully questions just how strictly one can hold to that without losing the tie between the two, I think it is nevertheless fair to say that it is the dawning realization of emptiness itself that allows one to see for oneself the bright line between compassion and its near enemy.

5

The Bodhisattva of Compassion neither Plots nor Schemes

Chapter 25 of the *Lotus Sutra*, "The Universal Gateway of the Bodhisattva Perceiver of the World's Sounds," provides one of the most concise descriptions of Avolekiteśvara, the Bodhisattva of Compassion. In the narrative form of the sutra, the key points of the exercise of karuṇā we have just been looking at are addressed, providing much clearer insight into the distinctiveness of bodhisattvic compassion.

The chapter begins with a question put to the Buddha by the Bodhisattva Inexhaustible Intent: "World-Honored One, this Bodhisattva Perceiver of the World's Sounds—why is he called Perceiver of the World's sounds?" The Buddha responds,

> Good man, suppose there are immeasurable hundreds, thousands, ten thousands, millions of living beings who are undergoing various trials and suffering. If they hear of this Bodhisattva Perceiver of the World's Sounds and single-mindedly call his name, then at once he will perceive the sound of their voices and they will all gain deliverance from their trials.[1]

For those who hold fast to or call the name Perceiver of the World's Sounds, the sutra continues, fire will not burn them, tempests at sea will not waylay them, demons will not torment them, bandits will not steal their goods should they be merchants, those who want to give birth to a male child will bear a boy, those who wish to give birth to a female child will bear a girl, and so on.

1. Watson, *Lotus Sutra*, 298–99.

Avolekiteśvara is here portrayed as the universal granter of wishes, and other Mahāyāna sutras and popular accounts paint a similar picture. Chun-Fang Yü, in her exhaustive study of the historical transformation of Avolekiteśvara into Guanyin, points out that such miracle stories were part and parcel of the assimilation of Avolekiteśvara into Chinese culture.[2] As part of a larger genre known as *zhiguai*, or "anomaly accounts," we find such fifth and sixth century texts as *Guangshiyin yingyan ji* (Records of Proofs of Guangshiyin's Responses), *Xu Guangshiyin yingyan ji* (Continued Records of Proofs of Guangshiyin's Responses), and the *Xi Guangshiyin yingyan ji* (Further Records of Proofs of Guangshiyin's Responses). As Jeffrey Rice observes, while the *zhiguai* genre is not distinctively Buddhist but existed at the margins of Confucian and Daoist as well as Buddhist literatures, these accounts of Guanyin's activity are distinctly Buddhist in that they expressly "provide a narrative explication of the *Lotus Sutra* to convince the reader of the efficacy of the bodhisattva and the sutra itself."[3] It is perhaps no accident, then, that this chapter of the *Lotus* begins with such a crowd-pleasing description of the Bodhisattva as a way to draw the hearer in.

The focus in the *Lotus* quickly turns, however, from the origin of the Bodhisattva's name to an explanation of the Bodhisattva's action, and Inexhaustible Intent's next query of the Buddha gets to the heart of the matter with a very specifically formulated set of questions: "World-Honored One, Bodhisattva Perceiver of the World's Sounds—how does he come and go in this saha world? How does he preach the Law for the sake of living beings? How does the power of expedient means apply in his case?"[4] The first question here is a crucial one. To ask how a bodhisattva comes and goes in this sahā world is to ask how a bodhisattva, who is free of the tṛṣṇā that gives rise to worlds, can act in and through the myriad tṛṣṇā-driven worlds of sentient beings.

The Buddha's answer now shifts attention away from the wondrous boons of the Bodhisattva with which the sutra began towards the business of awakening. Here, the Bodhisattva does not give supplicants what they happen to *want*, as in the case of bearing baby girls or the ability to walk through a smelting furnace unsinged; to do so would be precisely to be caught up in attachment to their samsaric world-horizons

2. Yü, *Kuan-Yin*, 151–94.

3. Rice, "Records of Witness of Responses," 10.

4. Watson, *Lotus Sutra*, 301. The *saha world* is another appellation for saṃsāra.

and taking them seriously as the real source of their troubles. Instead, the Bodhisattva gives them what they *need* in order to be liberated from their dukkha, namely the Dharma. He does this, however, not by producing some alternate state of affairs, or even by furnishing them with doctrine, but simply by selflessly manifesting in a form that bears witness to the essential emptiness of all dharmas:

> The Buddha said to Bodhisattva Inexhaustible Intent: "Good man, if there are living beings in the land who need someone in the body of a Buddha in order to be saved, Bodhisattva Perceiver of the World's Sounds immediately manifests himself in a Buddha body and preaches the Law for them. If they need someone in a pratyekabuddha's body in order to be saved, immediately he manifests a pratyekabuddha's body and preaches the Law to them."[5]

The list of possible manifestations goes on. If they need a voice-hearer, King Brahmā, the lord Śakra, the heavenly being Freedom, the heavenly being Great Freedom, a general of heaven, Vaiśravana, a petty king, a rich man, a householder, a chief minister, a Brahman, a monk, a nun, a layman or laywoman, the wife of a rich man, a young boy or girl, a heavenly being, a dragon, a yakṣa, a gandharva, an asura, a garuda, a kimnara, a mahoraga, a human or a nonhuman vajra-bearing god—as any of these are needed, the Bodhisattva manifests as such. The *Śūraṅgama Sūtra* echoes the *Lotus* in providing a similar list of the many manifestations of the Bodhisattva:

> It is my command that after my nirvana, in the time of the Dharma's ending, the Bodhisattvas and the Arhats will appear before beings in whatever bodily form may be appropriate for rescuing them from the cycle of death and rebirth. The Bodhisattvas and Arhats may appear as elder monks or nuns, or as white-robed laity, or as kings, as high officials, as pure youths or maidens, or even as courtesans, widows, libertines, thieves, slaughterers, or traffickers in stolen goods.[6]

In the *Kāraṇḍavyūha Sūtra* we even find Avalokiteśvara manifesting as a bee.[7]

5. Watson, *Lotus Sutra*, 301.
6. Buddhist Text Translation Society, *Śūraṅgama Sutra*, 275.
7. Roberts and Yeshi, *Āryakāraṇḍavyūhanāmamahāyānasūtra*.

Here we stumble upon an underappreciated aspect of Mahāyāna teaching, that of the *trikāya*, or three bodies of Buddha: the *dharmakāya* (truth or reality body), the *nirmāṇakāya* (apparition body), and the *saṃbhogakāya* (bliss body). Concerning the Bodhisattva's activity in the *Lotus*, the focus is on the nirmāṇakāya, the countless ways in which an awakened or awakening one appears in the world. Oftentimes *incarnation* is used to render *nirmāṇa* into English.[8] If one felt compelled to reach into the religious lexicon for an equivalent, *epiphany* would be more accurate. It is not that the bodhisattva is some kind of spiritual being that, so to speak, dons a cloak of matter or assumes a disguised form; that language belongs to a metaphysics in which spirit and matter are set at odds with one another and which, in any case, does not map on to the dynamics of experience as discovered by the Buddha. Instead, *nirmāṇa* is best understood as *the activity of a person-like vehicle of the Dharma as perceived by one as yet unawakened.*[9]

Recall that the discussions of tṛṣṇā and saṃsāra above both pointed to the fact that all perceiving prior to awakening is a *perceiving as*. Tṛṣṇā leads to a perceiving as that involves the self, and saṃsāra is the product of surrounding oneself with dharmas that have particular relevance to the self. One who is still governed by tṛṣṇā can only begin to open up to the Dharma within the framework of her self-centered samsaric horizon. The various forms in which the bodhisattva appears are therefore "determined," so to speak, by those perceiving the Bodhisattva, not by the Bodhisattva himself. Because the sutra has just enumerated a long list of very different kinds of nirmāṇas the Bodhisattva manifests in accordance with the many different kinds of samsaric needs sentient being have, it may at first appear as though the Bodhisattva is somehow morphing into the form they require. A more accurate reading would be to say that the action of the Bodhisattva is so empty of self-nature that by simply appearing within the supplicant's world-horizon, the supplicant finds the Bodhisattva to be just the kind of person she needs at that moment.

It may be helpful to illustrate how this works in instances where non-person-like dharmas are involved. In the Zen kōan collections there are any number of cases in which someone comes to awakening in conjunction with a common situation in his or her everyday world—a turn of phrase, a raised flower or finger, a blown-out candle, a swat with a

8. Keenan, "Mahāyāna Theology of Emptiness," 15.

9. *Person-like* need not be taken as *human*; in the Jātaka tales, for example, the Buddha-to-be was seen as various creatures while still a bodhisattva.

stick, slipping into a bath, and the like. It is understood that while such circumstances are part of the particular precipitating moment of awakening, they are so only because of the readiness of the person in question. No one would suggest that *the bath*, for instance, is of itself effecting a moment of insight on the part of the bather or that bathwater possessed some sort of transformative power. If slipping into a bath were the *cause* of awakening, then any time anyone slipped into a bath, he or she would experience yet another degree of awakening. It is only when the person has come to some measure of readiness to drop the attachment to ego that that threshold might, completely unexpectedly, be crossed in conjunction with an event as quotidian as slipping into a warm tub. For that person to then go on about the enlightenment-producing properties of baths would be silly, as silly as it would be for her now to promote bath taking as a form of spiritual practice for others. In fact, the next time she gets in the tub she will likely find that it is just another evening bath with nothing remotely connected to insight about it. Since there is nothing enlightening about the circumstances surrounding insight in and of themselves, there is nothing to be gained by singling them out and making them the point of focus.[10] Particular dharmas, in other words, do not *produce* the cessation of tṛṣṇā in nirvāṇa, but may be *occasions* for it.

In the case of nirmāṇas, what is involved in the precipitating moment of awakening is not an object or state of affairs but the perception of

10. The mistake of treating the circumstances surrounding awakening as the efficient causes that produce it is one that is made often enough. Consider this passage:

> [Dōgen] goes on to discuss two other cases of sudden enlightenment in natural settings. A monk named Xiangyan, after practicing for many years, built himself a hut in the mountains and planted bamboo beside it "for company." One day, he was sweeping the path when a pebble flew up and struck a bamboo, triggering instant awakening. . . . As Dōgen remarks, there are many such stories in the Zen tradition; and while some of them involve artifacts such as the broom Xiangyan was using, these are all made of natural materials. Working with today's tools is less likely to conduce to satori: the roar of a motorized leaf-blower would render the sound of a pebble striking bamboo inaudible. (Parkes, "Kūkai and Dōgen," 77–78.)

One can agree that a gas-powered leaf blower will drown out the sound of a pebble hitting bamboo, but today's practitioner might well come to awakening while pulling the start cord on the contraption and hearing its deafening roar. There is nothing separating a *natural* from an *artificial* dharma that could warrant the claim that in a mechanized world satori is "less likely," since all dharmas are equally empty and hence can all equally serve as possible gates to liberation. We see here yet another case in which an activist—here environmentalist—bent can obscure key elements of the Dharma.

a person's activity. Just as the bathwater is only ever H_2O, the bodhisattva is only ever exactly as she appears and is seen to do only ever what she is seen to do. She is, effectively, just another dharma within the perceiver's world-horizon, and she is no more special, as far as dharmas go, than the water that happened to make it from the treatment facility, through the pipes, and to the tub on a given day. Since she knows she is no more capable of producing insight in others than the bath is, so she does not engage in the conceit of intentionally formulating a plan of action or developing an agenda in order to accomplish just that. Nevertheless—or precisely *because* of this kind of self-emptiness—the bodhisattva can appear to another as salvific in the context of that other person's coming to awakening.

There is ample ground for shying away from intentional, goal-directed agency on the part of a bodhisattva, because this kind of non-intentional activity is similar to the way the activity of the Buddha has long come to be understood:

> Buddha's nonconceptual gnosis . . . is not an intentional agent of activity, since an intentional agent requires discursive thought considering options and intending to do something. Rather, intransitive verbs are used to express the passivity and automatic nature of [the Buddha's] actions. The actions "arise" or "come forth" (*'byung ba, sambhava*) in dependence upon the various karmic capacities and conditions of sentient beings.[11]

Put even more directly, "Buddhahood remains an active part of samsara by appearing to beings within the phenomenological worlds of *their* conceptual construction."[12] The *Śūraṃgamasamādhisūtra* describes this as "action based on the absence of a base":

> *The devaputra*: Kalaputra, what do you think of this (*tat kiṃ manyase*)? On what do the imaginary beings created by the Tathāgata (*tathāgatanirmitanirmāṇa*) base themselves in order to speak?
>
> *Dṛḍhamati*: They base themselves on the supportive power (*adhiṣṭhāna*) of the Buddha, and then they can speak.
>
> *The devaputra*: And the Buddha, on what does he base himself in order to create those imaginary beings?

11. Makransky, *Buddhahood Embodied*, 95.

12. Makransky, *Buddhahood Embodied*, 4.

> *Dṛḍhamati*: The Buddha bases himself on the knowledge of non-duality (*advayābhijñā*) in order to create those imaginary beings.
>
> *The devaputra*: Just as the Tathāgata bases himself on the "absence of a base" (*apratiṣṭhāna*) in order to create those imaginary beings, so those imaginary beings base themselves on the absence of a base in order to speak.
>
> *Dṛḍhamati*: If they have no base, how can they speak?
>
> *The devaputra*: In the same way that I speak to you while not basing myself on anything.[13]

In his study on the "empty savior" concept in Buddhist thought, Malcolm David Eckel draws our attention to the *Tathāgataguhya Sūtra*, where this kind of action on the Buddha's part is more narratively described:

> O Śāntamati, between the night in which he attained perfect Buddhahood and the night in which he was to attain *parinirvāṇa* with no remainder, the Tathāgata did not utter a sound. He did not speak; he does not speak, and he is not going to speak. But all sentient beings, with their various dispositions and interests and in accordance with their aspirations, perceive as issuing forth the Tathāgata's diverse teaching. And each of them thinks: "The Lord is teaching the Dharma to us and we are hearing the Tathāgata's Dharma-teaching." On that point the Tathāgata has no conception and makes no distinction. O Śāntamati, this is because the Tathāgata is free from all the conceptual diversity that consists of the traces of the network of concepts and distinctions.

"In this image of Buddhahood," Eckel continues, "the disciples come face to face with the ultimate, and the confrontation is salvific. The Buddha says nothing and the disciples, in reality, hear nothing."[14] The disciples are able to "hear" the Buddha because of their own disposition toward the Dharma. Since they can only "understand" the Dharma by way of reference to their world-horizons, it seems to them as though they were hearing the Buddha "speak their language," as it were, while the Buddha in fact does nothing of the kind.[15]

13. Lamotte and Boin-Webb, *Śūraṃgamasamādhisūtra*, 166–67.

14. Eckel, "Gratitude to an Empty Savior," 60–61.

15. Those familiar with the Christian tradition will perhaps see a parallel here with the Pentecost account in Acts 2:5–13. From a Dharmic perspective, it is not that the apostles spontaneously became polyglots but that all within earshot heard their salvific message in accordance with each of their own various experiential, cultural, and

The compassion of the Bodhisattva, like that of the Buddha, is nothing if not *impersonal*, never forgoing the path to insight, never leaving off nonabiding nirvāṇa:

> Mañjuśrī, you should know that I exercise this supernormal power everywhere in innumerable (*aparamāṇa*) and infinite (*ananta*) koṭinayutaśatasahasrāṇis of *buddhakṣetras*, but the Śrāvakas and Pratyekabuddhas do not know this. Such is, O Mañjuśrī, the supremacy (*ārṣabha*) of the Śūraṃgamasamādhi: bodhisattvas, even while always manifesting in such wondrous feats (*vikurvaṇa*) in innumerable universes, never swerve from this *samādhi*.
>
> Mañjuśrī, just as the sun (*sūrya*) and moon (*candra*), without ever leaving their palaces (*vimāna*), illuminate villages (*grāma*), towns (*nagara*) and districts (*nigama*), so the bodhisattvas, without ever swerving from the Śūraṃgamasamādhi, manifest themselves everywhere in innumerable universes and expound the Dharma according to the aspirations (*adhimukti*) of beings.[16]

Advanced disciples perceive "the Buddha" in awakening to the Dharma. In the case of those as yet unawakened, however, they perceive—whom? The short answer is that you would have to ask them. The lists of various nirmāṇas offered in the sutras are hardly meant to be exhaustive; instead, they convey something of the limitless range of possible occasions by which sentient beings might come to insight. In all cases, though, that range is limited only by various beings' aspirations, not by a bodhisattva herself.

The "Parable of the Medicinal Herbs" delivered earlier in the *Lotus Sutra* helps shed some clarifying light on the impersonal nature of awakened activity in the world. There the Buddha likens his actions to that of "a great cloud":

> I appear in the world
> like a great cloud
> that showers moisture upon
> all the dry and withered living beings,
> so that all are able to escape suffering,
> gain the joy of peace and security,
> the joys of this world

---

linguistic horizons.

16. Lamotte and Boin-Webb, *Śūraṃgamasamādhisūtra*, 200.

and the joy of nirvana.
I look upon all things
as being universally equal,
I have no mind to favor this or that,
to love one or hate another.
I am without greed or attachment
and without limitation or hindrance.
At all times, for all thing
I preach the Law equally;
as I would for a single person,
that same way I do for numerous persons . . .
I bring fullness and satisfaction to the world,
like a rain that spreads its moisture everywhere.
Eminent and lowly, superior and inferior,
observers of precepts, violators of precepts,
those fully endowed with proper demeanor,
those not fully endowed,
those of correct views, of erroneous views,
of keen capacity, of dull capacity—
I cause the Dharma rain to rain on all equally,
never lax or neglectful.
When all the various living beings
hear my Law,
they receive according to their power,
dwelling in their different environments.
Some inhabit the realm of human and heavenly beings,
of wheel-turning sage kings,
Shakra, Brahma and the other kings.[17]

In most languages we just say some variation of "It rains," and the simile of the Buddha's actions being like a cloud of rain bears this out. There is no subject-verb-object structure involved, and even in the passage above it is clear that it is not the case that *someone* called "the Buddha" *sends* the rain *to* the various plants *in order to* water them; Buddha just *is* the rain. Moreover, we do not say that the rain watered the sycamore, and the begonia, and the grass, and the moss, and so on until each plant has been enumerated. It is understood that when it rains, any plant that happens to be out in the elements will receive moisture in its own measure, and will produce with it what it alone is capable of producing; the rain does not favor flowers over brambles, nor does it cherish prize roses over dandelions. Finally, we do not consider it a failure of the rain that one plant

17. Watson, *Lotus Sutra*, 103.

flowers beautifully, another produces thorns, or yet another produces toxins; all attest to the power of the rain in their myriad expressions.

In the same way one could say, "It Buddhas" or "It bodhisattvas,"[18] and those who inhabit the realms of Brahma, or of dragons, or of yakṣas, or of monks or nuns, or of violators of the precepts, receive the Dharma as if from Brahma, dragons, yakṣas, monks and nuns, and even violators of the precepts in their own way, without any differentiation in the "delivery" on the part of the Buddha or bodhisattva:

> The equality of the Buddha's preaching
> is like a rain of a single flavor,
> but depending upon the nature of the living being,
> the way in which it is received is not uniform,
> just as the various plants and trees
> each receives the moisture in a different manner . . .
> I rain down the Dharma rain,
> filling the whole world,
> and this single-flavored Dharma
> is practiced by each according to the individual's power.[19]

Some only respond to kindness; others only respond to aggression. Some need to hear "no," while others need to hear "yes." There is no contradiction in the seemingly contradictory nirmāṇas of the bodhisattva, because each is of "a single flavor" that is simply received in countless ways by those in their respective samsaric worlds. All of this is consistent with the understanding expressed in the *Diamond Sutra* that there is no being that can be called "a bodhisattva," for there is no one in particular "behind," as it were, each of the many nirmāṇas by which bodhisattvic activity is ascertained. In fact, there is "no such dharma as a bodhisattva"[20] at all.

Even the various iconographic representations of Avolekiteśvara bear this out. Oftentimes he is depicted as a multi-armed human, each hand holding a different implement useful for the benefit of sentient beings. A quick read of the figure might suggest that those many arms and hands and implements represent the many things the bodhisattva *does*, but the figure is perhaps better seen as a shorthand for (and a less costly version of) the kind of representation of Avolekiteśvara we see for example in Sanjūsangen-dō Hall in Kyoto, where presented is not a single

18. It is assuredly no coincidence that the tenth and highest *bhūmi* of the bodhisattva's attainment is called "the Dharma Cloud."

19. Watson, *Lotus Sutra*, 104.

20. Pine, *Diamond Sutra*, 19.

human form with one thousand arms, but one thousand full-bodied figures of the one and the same Bodhisattva, some of the many nirmāṇas by which he *is seen*. The misunderstanding that can arise from the multi-armed version is that one might be led to think that there is some entity—some being—at the center of all that business who carries out this or that particular task, when in truth there is no self and no being there at all, and, following the sutra on this point, no specific thing that is done.

Or again, we can think of the very diametrically opposed forms by which the Bodhisattva is sometimes portrayed. On the one hand, we have the form of Guanyin or Kannon, where Avolekiteśvara is cast as a kindly figure—motherly, in fact—with soft flowing robes and a tilted vessel in her hand pouring out a healing libation. As Hayagrīva-Avolekiteśvara, or Batō Kannon in Japanese, however, he is rendered fierce to the point of being grotesque—"hair standing on end, the eyes wide open and staring, and the mouth opened to reveal menacing fangs"[21]—all in a display by which the deluded—specifically those who are otherwise almost completely impervious to the Dharma when delivered with a kinder, gentler approach—might find themselves knocked off their high ego horse.[22] Sometimes compassion is experienced not as a gentle touch but as a dropped ton of bricks, and the Bodhisattva is then perceived not as grandmotherly but as something on the order of a drill sergeant.

In the end, perhaps the most to-the-point iconographic representation of Avolekiteśvara is the one in the "royal ease" posture—calm, serene, relaxed, not focused on this or that, doing nothing particular, utterly empty—and because of that ease compassionate beyond measure.

It is therefore not incidental that Avolekiteśvara at the beginning of the chapter is portrayed as a miracle worker, since his appearance on the scene takes place when he is called upon by someone in hardship or in a distressed state. That he is perceived as one who removes difficulties simply follows from the hard conditions in which the appellant finds herself and the relief that ensues once the Bodhisattva is brought into the picture by the entreatant who "single-mindedly calls" his name. To suggest, however, that the Bodhisattva somehow takes heed of the person's particular needs, modifies his actions accordingly, and seeks to produce a specific, conditions-altering outcome, would be to miss the point of the further exposition.

21. Mochizuki, "Compassionate and Wrathful," 344.

22. Makransky, "Confronting 'Sin' out of Love," 95.

We now arrive at the second and third of Bodhisattva Inexhaustible Intent's questions: Just how is the Dharma preached? How does a bodhisattva exercise *upāya*? In point of fact, the answers to these questions were already given by the answer to the first: a bodhisattva manifests emptiness in worlds of form.

Upāya is often rendered "skillful means," and while etymologically and historically that is accurate enough, we need to be cautious about where the emphasis is put. A bodhisattva is not in possession of some special *techné* or skill, nor are her actions to be evaluated according to some mean-ends standard. A bodhisattva, like the Buddha, is not plotting, scheming, or clever; she plans no strategy, develops no program of action, and calculates no gain or loss.[23] The only skillful means a bodhisattva really has at her disposal is ever-deepening insight into emptiness and the continual sloughing off of any lingering traces of attachment, aversion, and ignorance that get in the way of her being, simply, a manifestation of that emptiness in the worlds of others. Far from the model of putting the attainment of realization on hold until one has saved all beings, the bodhisattva understands that what one calls "saving beings" is but a correlative effect of further development on the path.

Upāya, like all of the other pāramitās, is developed as one's degree of ego-attachment abates. This is because in realizing ever more deeply her essential emptiness a bodhisattva is no longer blocked from an ever-wider range of expressions of her inherent wisdom. If I remain confined by tṛṣṇā, I will engage in activity that it is consistent with it and the samsaric worlds it creates. As that tṛṣṇā progressively ceases, I might find myself being and doing things I had never thought possible in places never before imagined. I might not even be aware that I am doing them. Others might see me as a "different kind of person" as a result, and they might even wonder about the consistency of my actions, since what I am doing today might not square with what I was doing yesterday. Of this, I (need) know nothing at all.

Śāntideva's litany of nirmāṇas in his paean to "Awakening Mind" in the *Bodhicaryāvatāra* likewise underscores the point that the upāya that issues from bodhicitta does not consist in being an agent that *does* things for others but simply in *becoming* what they need: "For embodied beings

23. As Daniel Taigen Leighton puts it, Avolekiteśvara is "responsive without deliberation." Leighton, *Bodhisattva Archetypes*, 177.

may I be the wish-fulfilling jewel, the pot of plenty, the spell that always works, the potent healing herb, the magical tree that grants every wish, and the milch-cow that supplies all wants."[24] This may mean being "medicine for the sick," or "food and drink" for the hungry, or "a servant for those in need of service," but these are just a very small sample of what it means to be anything at all that anyone might happen to want. As Charles Orzech put it, the personal transformation of which Śāntideva speaks "is identical with the bodhisattva's exercise of 'skillful means' (*upāya*), his extension of himself in *nirmāṇas*."[25]

Viewing upāya as an aspect of nirmāṇas helps avoid the snarls that come with focusing on determinate actions in their own right and assessing them for their skillfulness in demonstrating compassion. One would be hard-pressed to lump precept keeping and precept violating together as equivalent actions, for instance; either one keeps the precepts or one does not, and there is no overlooking the moral difference between the two. As actions arising within the world-creating framework of an observer, though, either may well be an occasion for precipitating insight on her part. Hence it would be more accurate to say, "a violator of the precepts appears salvifically to someone as a bodhisattva" rather than "a bodhisattva breaks the precepts in order to save someone." To take an oft-quoted case from *Lotus* itself as an example, one could say that the point is not that the father was *lying* to his children in order to get them out of the burning house but that the father was perceived *as a parent*, and the children, *being the children they were*, acted appropriately.[26]

Returning now to Bodhisattva Inexhaustible Intent's question, "How does the bodhisattva come and go in the saha world?" only one answer seems possible: "Not like everyday, tṛṣṇā-driven beings do."

In whatever the form the Bodhisattva of Compassion is perceived, the message received is consistent throughout: the liberating power of the

24. Śāntideva, *Bodhicaryāvatāra*, 21.

25. Orzech, *Politics and Transcendent Wisdom*, 43–44.

26. The parable recounts the story of a father who, in order to get his children to flee their burning house, promises them any number of fine toys that are just outside the gate. Of course, there are no toys, but the children, rushing out to find the toys, have been brought to safety all the same. Watson, *Lotus Sutra*, 56–58.

Dharma. As if to further emphasize this point, the Buddha in the *Lotus* goes on to say:

> Inexhaustible Intent, this Bodhisattva Perceiver of the World's Sounds has succeeded in acquiring benefits such as these and, taking on a variety of different forms, goes about among the lands saving living beings . . . The bodhisattva and mahasattva Perceiver of the World's Sounds can bestow fearlessness on those who are in fearful, pressing or difficult circumstances. That is why in this saha world everyone calls him Bestower of Fearlessness.[27]

There is only one way to become fearless in the sahā world, and that is to be free of the constraints of the sahā world through insight into emptiness whereby the tṛṣṇā that gives rise to that world falls away. Bodhisattvas are "fearless" (a common English translation of *bodhisattva-mahāsattva* is "fearless bodhisattva") because they are no longer swayed by phenomenal appearances the way sentient beings are.

From this perspective, it is possible to return to the Buddha's answer to Inexhaustible Intent's first question in order to see that the benefits there described might not have been what they first appeared to be. It would be a bizarre world indeed if there were someone who could make fire not burn flesh, cause bandits to stop in their tracks, rearrange storm fronts, cause women to bear male or female children on request, and the like. The Bodhisattva cannot be conceived of as a Santa Claus or some kind of miracle worker without denying the thoroughgoingly co-determining nature of all conditioned dharmas. But even as the Buddha was concluding the enumeration of all the great things Bodhisattva Perceiver of the World's Sounds could do, he added a small hint as to the real nature of the Bodhisattva's blessings: "Inexhaustible Intent, the bodhisattva Perceiver of the World's Sounds has the power to do all this. If there are living beings who pay respect and obeisance to Bodhisattva Perceiver of the World's Sounds, their good fortune *will not be fleeting or vain*."[28] Now sons get sick and daughters die, another storm might rise up tomorrow, and one's attackers might leave off for the moment only to return after redoubling their strength. Even if one were to be brought back from the dead, one would still have to die again. The fortunes dispensed by

27. Watson, *Lotus Sutra*, 302.

28. Watson, *Lotus Sutra*, 300; italics mine.

Avalokiteśvara as listed at the beginning of the chapter are all still subject to inconstancy, since they are all just further conditioned phenomena.

There is one good fortune, however, that is not fleeting or vain, and that is coming to the end of ego-delusion and its attendant dukkha. Fire is no longer able to burn *me*, when I understand that fire burns flesh but I am not my flesh. Thieves can no longer steal from *me*, when I see that there is no *me* to be stolen from or anything I can call "*my* possessions." Any child, girl or boy, is a gift when I no longer see *myself* defined by their gender. The Bodhisattva Perceiver of the World's Sounds in this way "delivers" beings from their suffering in the same way Tozan "delivered" his disciple from cold and heat in Case 43 of the *Hekiganroku*:

> A monk asked Tozan, "When cold and heat come, how can we avoid them?"
> Tozan said, "Why don't you go where there is no cold or heat?"
> The monk said, "Where is the place where there is no cold or heat?"
> Tozan said, "When cold, let the cold kill you; when hot, let the heat kill you."[29]

There is no place where the temperature is consistently a mild 75 degrees under partly cloudy skies with a light breeze out of the southwest. Yet there is a "place" where there is neither heat nor cold—the place where one with insight stands, which is no particular place at all, and, above all, not *not* this world of 110 degree days and -40 degree nights, either.

The *Śūraṅgama Sutra* states even more explicitly what is only somewhat obliquely stated in the *Lotus*, namely that the Avalokiteśvara's boons are not material mollifications of difficult circumstances but the realization of their thoroughgoing emptiness. There, listed among the ways the Bodhisattva bestow fearlessness, we find the following:

> First, because I did not listen to sounds and instead contemplated the listener within, I can now hear the cries of suffering beings throughout the ten directions, and I can bring about their liberation.
>
> Second, I was able to turn my awareness around and restore it [to its original nature], and therefore, should beings be caught in conflagration, I can make sure they are not burned.

29. Quotes from the kōan collections *Hekiganroku*, *Mumonkan*, and *Shōyōroku* are taken from the internal training materials of the Chicago Zen Center and are in manuscript form.

> Third, since I was able to turn my awareness around and restore it, I can make sure that beings who are adrift in a flood will not be drowned.
>
> Fourth, because I have put an end to deluded acts of mind, and so have no thoughts of harming or killing, I can make sure that any being who enters the realms of ghosts will not be harmed by them.
>
> Fifth, when I had succeeded in merging my faculty of hearing with the enlightened nature of hearing, my six faculties dissolved into each other to become one with my faculty of hearing. Therefore, if beings are about to be attacked, I can cause the others' blades to shatter so that these beings suffer no hurt, any more than water will be hurt by a knife that is plunged into it, or any more than light will be affected by a puff of wind.
>
> Sixth, my hearing was infused with an essential brilliance that illuminated the entire Dharma-Realm and dispelled the darkness of all hidden places. Therefore, I can ensure that beings will be invisible to any yakṣas, rākṣasas, kuṃbhāṇḍas, piśācas, pūtanas, or other such ghosts that might approach them.[30]

The Bodhisattva Perceiver of the World's Sounds has seen into the emptiness of the skandhas, here particularly hearing, thereby sundering the bonds that cause all suffering. In "calling upon" him, the supplicant is, in effect, opening herself up to what the Bodhisattva has realized, thereby coming to see into the emptiness of her own situation for herself. "Restoring awareness to its original nature" or "putting an end to deluded acts of mind" is far from extinguishing a fire, or tossing a drowning person a life preserver, or performing CPR, yet they are thoroughly salvific. Hence, the individual's "calling upon" the Bodhisattva is, at bottom, much more on the order of "I want to know what you know, Avalokiteśvara," rather than "Avalokiteśvara, fix my troubles for me."

This effective power of the Bodhisattva extends to all areas of life, social as well as personal or physical. Consider these more socio-political cases from the closing verses of the chapter:

> Suppose you encounter trouble with the king's law,
> face punishment, about to forfeit your life.
> Think on the power of that Perceiver of Sounds
> and the executioner's sword will be broken to bits!
> Suppose you are imprisoned in cangue and lock,
> hands and feet bound by fetters and chains.

30. Buddhist Text Translation Society, *Śūraṅgama Sutra*, 241.

> Think on the power of that Perceiver of Sounds
> and they will fall off, leaving you free! . . .
> If living beings encounter weariness or peril,
> immeasurable suffering pressing them down,
> the power of the Perceiver of Sounds' wonderful wisdom
> can save them from the sufferings of the world . . .
> When law suits bring you before the officials,
> when terrified in the midst of an army,
> think on the power of that Perceiver of Sounds
> and hatred in all its forms will be dispelled.[31]

There is no discussion here as to whether the king's law is legitimate, the sentence humane, the sufferings of the world fair, or the war just. There is no indication that the person in question either did or did not merit his sentence. All of that falls by the wayside, for none of that matters here. What matters is "the power of the Perceiver of Sounds," the power to see all dharmas as empty. From the standpoint of śūnyatā, there is no sword and no cangue, and hence they can no longer cut or bind. As soon as the convicted or the prisoner sees this, he is free.

We can pursue this a bit further from the other side as well. The executioner, the jailer, and the soldier all have their jobs to do, and one can only imagine the dressing down they will receive when they have to report to their superiors that they botched the execution, lost a prisoner, or failed to complete the mission. There is nothing in the accounts of Avolekiteśvara to suggest that the Bodhisattva's assistance to one person is such that it will require a material overhaul of currently existing states of affairs or lead to any sort of trouble for others, which is exactly what would be required if the executioner's sword were actually breaking into bits and the jailer's chains were really opening up through the Bodhisattva's power. The *Śūraṅgama* provides further clarity on this point. There, again among the list of the ways the Bodhisattva bestows fearlessness, we read:

> Eleventh, once perceived objects had disappeared from my mind as I turned the light of my understanding inward, my body and mind and entire Dharma-Realm were as bright and translucent as crystal. Therefore I can bring freedom from stupidity to beings whose natures have been so darkened by their dullness that they have had no intention of ever becoming enlightened.[32]

31. Watson, *Lotus Sutra*, 304–5.

32. Buddhist Text Translation Society, *Śūraṅgama Sutra*, 243–44.

From the clear standpoint of emptiness, the executioner remains the executioner, the jailer the jailer, and the soldier the soldier; though they persist in their dullness and have no intention of changing, the power of the Bodhisattva covers them all the same. From the clear standpoint of emptiness, no one's behavior needs to be altered in any way.

The implications of this understanding of the Bodhisattva's activity are profound and far-reaching. Once again, we can multiply examples, taking into consideration all of the difficult, troubling, and even harmful social situations someone might face: discriminatory practices, unevenly stacked economic opportunities, standing in want in the midst of a world of luxuries, suffering the many indignities and insults everyday people throw at one other, and the like. The "fearless power" the Bodhisattva offers to the afflicted is the realization that these, too, are devoid of an essential nature. If we were to paraphrase the interchange between Tozan and the monk along these lines, we might hear a conversation like this:

> A monk asked Tozan, "When homophobia or racism come, how can we avoid them?"
> Tozan said, "Why don't you go where there is no homophobia or racism?"
> The monk said, "Where is the place where there is no homophobia or racism?"
> Tozan said, "When there is homophobia, let the homophobia kill you; when there is racism, let the racism kill you."

This is not to be glib about deeply disturbing social situations any more than Tozan was being glib about the effects of frostbite and sunstroke on unprotected bodies. It is simply to put the emphasis where the Dharma suggests we look for liberation and to stop getting caught up in conditions as those bound by tṛṣṇā do. Without insight into śūnyatā, one could spend one's entire life trying to get people to be something other than they are and to get them to do something other than they do. This is an element of the "exhaustion" Vasubandhu referred to when discussing the near enemy of karuṇā; far from liberating beings through that process, one effectively sentences them (and oneself) to further rounds of samsaric world formation.

Although it is cast at times in what can only be considered hyperbolic language, the account of Avalokiteśvara in *The Lotus Sutra* offers much guidance for would-be compassionate bodhisattvas.

First, it is clear that bodhisattvic action is agenda-free, with "no mind to favor this or that, to love one or hate another."[33] Consistent with the infinite expanse of karuṇā, a bodhisattva has no point of view, no preferential option, no tug of solidarity with this group over that one, no partisanship of any kind. Having seen into the emptiness of all formations, there are simply no sides to take. Far from rendering the bodhisattva an impervious bystander to the ills of sentient beings, this actually makes her boundlessly efficacious; one of the great mercies of the Bodhisattva of Compassion is that *no one* need find a stumbling block in her.

Second, bodhisattvic action is not readily captured by any set of criteria. The wide-ranging lists of the bodhisattva's nirmāṇas in the various sutras, importing both the mythic elements of Brahmanic religion as well as characters from everyday life, cut off the possibility of saying that the bodhisattva appears only under such-and-such conditions or only as a thus-and-so. Yakṣas, petty kings, violators of precepts, and the like might well be replaced in a modern context with authoritarian leaders, invading armies, Wall Street financiers, and drug lords; and Brahma, bhikkhunīs, and keepers of precepts could be replaced with the Virgin Mary, imams, and Hasidic Jews—to the extent, that is, that these provide encounters that precipitate insight into emptiness on someone's part. This stands as a corrective to common considerations of upāya as consciously formulated exercises aimed at producing net gain. It would be as much of a mistake for someone to say of her own activity, "I am exercising upāya," as it would be for one to say, "I am being compassionate," for all of the reasons we saw in conjunction with karuṇā above. It would also be a mistake to make such an assessment from a third-party perspective ("Jason is exercising upāya toward that person over there"), for the same reasons. Whether some activity can be called skillful has to do with whether it happens to be precipitous in my coming to some measure of awakening, and, even then, it has to be understood that although the action was such for me, it may not be for others.

Finally, calls to "change the world" or "change society" do not issue from a bodhisattva's mouth, for a bodhisattva is not one who seeks to

33. Watson, *Lotus Sutra*, 103.

make conditions on the ground otherwise than they are. If a bodhisattva is no magician or demiurge, still less is she a world-changing activist in robes. Having seen into the emptiness of the sahā world, yet abiding among those still bound to it, she bears witness to the truth of the Dharma in the very conditions that obtain among men and women—just as they are—no matter how pleasant or unpleasant, no matter how easy or difficult. Whereas sentient beings seek to be free of their hardship through various strategies, much like Gotami seeking medicine to "cure" her dead son, the bodhisattva is able to model the endurance of hardship knowing it to be empty and, by so doing, guilelessly demonstrate the power of the Dharma. This is no easy task. It comes as no surprise, then, that the sahā world we hear so much about in the *Lotus Sutra* is also often referred to as *the world that is endured*, and it is to the patient endurance (*kṣānti*) of the bodhisattva as she comes and goes in the sahā world that we now turn.

6

The Ultimate Austerity: Patient Forbearance

After the Buddha had instructed Puṇṇa in the emptiness of self, the Buddha asked him,

> "Now that you have received this brief exhortation from me, Puṇṇa, in which country will you dwell?"
>
> "There is, venerable sir, a country called Sunāparanta. I will dwell there."
>
> "Puṇṇa, the people of Sunāparanta are wild and rough. If they abuse and revile you, what will you think about that?"
>
> "Venerable sir, if the people of Sunāparanta abuse and revile me, then I will think: 'These people of Sunāparanta are excellent, truly excellent, in that they do not give me a blow with the fist.' Then I will think thus, Blessed One; then I will think thus, Fortunate One."
>
> "But, Puṇṇa, if the people of Sunāparanta do give you a blow with the fist, what will you think about that?"
>
> ". . . I will think, "These people of Sunāparanta are excellent, truly excellent, in that they do not give me a blow with a clod."
> . . .
>
> "But, Puṇṇa, if the people of Sunāparanta do give you a blow with a clod, what will you think about that?"
>
> ". . . I will think, "These people of Sunāparanta are excellent, truly excellent, in that they do not give me a blow with a rod." . . .
>
> "But, Puṇṇa, if the people of Sunāparanta do give you a blow with a rod, what will you think about that?"
>
> ". . . I will think, "These people of Sunāparanta are excellent, truly excellent, in that they do not stab me with a knife." . . .

> "But, Puṇṇa, if the people of Sunāparanta do stab you with a knife, what will you think about that?"
>
> . . . I will think, "These people of Sunāparanta are civilized, very civilized, in that they don't take my life with a sharp knife" . . .
>
> "But, Puṇṇa, if the people of Sunāparanta do take your life with a sharp knife, what will you think about that?"
>
> "Venerable sir, if the people of Sunāparanta take my life with a sharp knife, then I will think: 'There have been disciples of the Blessed One who, being repelled, humiliated, and disgusted by the body and by life, sought for an assailant. But I have come upon this assailant even without a search.' Then I will think thus, Blessed One; then I will think thus, Fortunate One."
>
> "Good, good, Puṇṇa! Endowed with such self-control and peacefulness, you will be able to dwell in the Sunāparanta country. Now, Puṇṇa, you may go at your own convenience.[1]

Puṇṇa had learned the Buddha's instruction well. He understands emptiness thoroughly when he realizes the actions of others, even if harmful—or downright fatal—to himself, demand no concomitant response on his part. He will neither look to turn the Sunāparantans from their fierce ways, nor will he try to defend himself against their rough treatment. Instead, he will laud them for their civility and thank them for their generosity in helping him along his path. In this way he is fit to dwell not only among the Sunāparantans but among any group of people, no matter who they are or what they do. Out of insight into emptiness Puṇṇa manifests the pāramitā of patient forbearance (*khanti/kṣānti*).

The pāramitās describe the character or conduct of the awakening ones. They are *perfections*, as the terms are translated into English, not precepts. This means that they are understood not so much as tools for cultivating bodhicitta prior to awakening but rather as the flower and fruit of one who has come to some measure of awakening already. While one may certainly practice them in a limited degree with a limited degree of insight, thereby cultivating bodhicitta even further, they arise as the spontaneous activity of bodhicitta already operative. Thus they are said to be the "character or . . . conduct"[2] of the excellent ones. In the Theravādin tradition there are ten: giving (*dāna*), right conduct (*sīla*), renunciation (*nekkhamma*), wisdom (*paññā*), vigor (*virya*), patient forbearance (*khanti*), truthfulness (*sacca*), determination (*adhiṭṭhāna*),

1. Bodhi, *Connected Discourses*, 1168–69.
2. Dhammapāla, *Treatise on the Pārāmis*, 9.

loving-kindness (*mettā*) and equanimity (*upekkhā*). In the Mahāyāna the list is six: giving (*dāna*), right conduct (*śīla*), patient forbearance (*kṣānti*), vigor (*vīrya*), meditation (*dhyāna*), and wisdom (*prajña*). Sometimes four more are included: skillful means (*upāya*), aspiration (*praṇidhāna*), spiritual power (*bala*), and knowledge (*jñāna*). While all the pāramitās describe the conduct of a bodhisattva, patient forbearance is particularly instructive for understanding how a bodhisattva acts in the social world.

We have already seen how the bodhisattva's compassion unfolds: he simply manifests awakening mind in the sahā worlds of those around him who are still clouded by attachment, aversion, and delusion. As might be expected, some of the actions of those people are pleasing and beneficial to themselves and others; some of them are distasteful and harmful in the same measure. The bodhisattva, while himself not contributing (as much as before) to this incessant cycle of good and ill, is nevertheless subject to it, and weal and woe befall him no less than anyone else.

As one who has come to some measure of insight, however, the bodhisattva's response cannot be the same as those who are not as yet awakened. Nāgārjuna puts it this way:

> The bodhisattva reminds himself, "I should not be like everyone else who constantly follows along in the flowing current of cyclic births and deaths. I should move up against the current in order to seek out the very source and enter the path to nirvāṇa.
>
> "All common people, when met with attack, are hateful, when met with benefit, are delighted, and when in a frightening place, become fearful. In becoming a bodhisattva, I cannot act in the way that they do. Even though I have not yet succeeded in cutting off the fetters, I should nonetheless still exert self-restraint as I pursue the cultivation of patience.
>
> "When tormented and injured, I will not become hateful, and when encountering respect and offerings, I will not be moved to delight. I should not be fearful of the intense difficulties involved in the manifold forms of suffering. And, for the sake of beings, I should let flourish the mind of great compassion."[3]

"Moving against the current" is an appropriate metaphor for the exercise of patient forbearance, since it is so patently counterintuitive to our everyday understanding. Almost everything about our constitution speaks for self-defense—heightened reactions to certain visual and auditory stimuli, a fight-or-flee response, the release of adrenaline when

3. Nāgārjuna, *Six Perfections*, 389.

threatened, the various psychological forms of self-protection, and so on. Of course, almost everything about our constitution tends to fuel ego-delusion as well, so appealing to common human sensibilities is an unsound strategy, at least from a Dharmic perspective. Patient forbearance cuts to the deepest roots of ego-attachment, since it holds out the prospect of hurt, injury, and death. If there is one pāramitā that calls for the greatest fearlessness, it is patient forbearance. It is no accident that *The Dhammapada* calls it "the supreme austerity":

> Patient endurance is the supreme austerity.
> The Buddhas say that Nirvana is supreme.
> One who injures others is no renunciant;
> One who harms others is no contemplative.[4]

Indeed, Śāntideva openly acknowledges that the value of patient forbearance lies precisely in its "shock value" for our everyday unawakened understanding: "The virtue of suffering has no rival, since, from the shock it causes, intoxication falls away and there arises compassion for those in cyclic existence, fear of evil, and a longing for the Conqueror."[5]

The pāramitā of patient forbearance as described in the commentaries is exercised on two fronts, first toward sentient beings and secondly toward dharmas, or circumstances. They are distinguished because, absent insight, we are wont to think that there is something significantly different about the actions of a conscious actor as opposed to, say, atmospheric phenomena. I put up with a rained-out picnic because I understand that rain happens. It is not immediately obvious that I should put up with someone who is attacking me or otherwise treating me poorly. "They shouldn't do that!" or "No one should have to put up with this!" seem to make sense to say in response to the actions of such a person, whereas no one of right mind would exclaim, "It shouldn't rain!" or "No one should have to put up with getting drenched!" Further, while no one will seek to alter the weather, there is no shortage of those eager to change the actions of others, so we need to look particularly closely at the exercise of forbearance towards sentient beings, and that is the focus of this chapter. Patient forbearance toward dharmas, including the dharma called *society*, will be taken up in chapter 7. While all schools of the Dharma are of one voice on the matter, here we will be focusing primarily on the exposition of

4. Fronsdal, *Dhammapada*, 49.
5. Śāntideva, *Bodhicaryāvatāra*, 51.

patient forbearance in Nāgārjuna's *Mahāprajñāpāramitā Upadeśa*, from which we have just heard.

The pāramitās are expressions of the realization of emptiness. They are that mix of attitudes, comportments, and actions that obtain in the place where previously tṛṣṇā would have led to different attitudes, comportments, and actions. Just as dukkha arises in connection with both pleasant and unpleasant situations, patient forbearance is demonstrated toward the two corresponding kinds of beings, those who treat me well, who "are respectful and who contribute offerings," and those who treat me poorly, who "are hateful, who scold, and who may even bring injury through blows."[6] Our present concern is with the latter, but the former case is instructive as well and sets up the discussion to follow.

Nāgārjuna points out that whatever good I might receive from others comes in three different ways: as a result of past efforts, as a result of my present state, or as a consequence of deceiving others. We can leave the third to the side, since it hardly needs to be argued that one should not delight in ill-gotten gain; as Nāgārjuna puts it, "If I were to employ . . . falseness and then obtain offerings as a result, it would be no different from an evil thief committing a robbery to obtain his sustenance."[7]

As far as good received as a result of past efforts, Nāgārjuna states that it would be similar to the case of winning an award for one's work over the course of years. Suppose I study hard and get good grades, engage in any number of extracurricular activities ranging from glee club to varsity lacrosse, and consistently act as a "good citizen" of my school. Come senior year, I find that I have been named class valedictorian. I have no particular reason to think kindly toward those who put my name forward, nor do I have any reason to take particular pride in the award itself. Anyone who had an equally impressive record would have been chosen, and the selection committee simply applied the criteria anyone in their position would have used. Given the structure of high schools, selection committees, etc., no other outcome would have been likely. I simply got out of it what I put into it:

6. Nāgārjuna, *Six Perfections*, 359.
7. Nāgārjuna, *Six Perfections*, 369.

> If one now obtains offerings through previous-life causal circumstances involving diligent cultivation of merit, this is just something created through personal diligence and thus is obtained in the natural course of things. What would be the point in becoming haughty over something like this? This is just like planting in the spring and reaping in the fall."[8]

As a matter of fact, persons who are "successful" in this way oftentimes don't understand what all the brouhaha is about. Finding oneself bright, diligent, gifted, and acting accordingly, what other outcome is there likely to be? This is not arrogance; it is simply a straightforward account of the matter at hand.

It is just as indicative of a deluded understanding to develop attachment to those who are good to me because I have some quality they admire. Nāgārjuna, writing as a monk, addresses the point from the perspective of an adept:

> This [kindness] comes to me perhaps on account of my having some measure of wisdom, perhaps through awareness of the true nature of dharmas, or perhaps through being able to cut off the fetters. It is on account of these meritorious factors that this person makes such offerings. It does not actually have anything specifically to do with me . . . Truly this is just a case of people having a fondness for certain meritorious qualities. It is not that they have any specific fondness for me as such.[9]

We could just as well think of this kind of goodness as the kind one receives because one has blue eyes, or a pleasing voice, or a sunny disposition, or happens to be of the gender another person is interested in for a possible romantic relationship. Or perhaps someone has a thing for entertainers, athletes, public officials, or clergy. The good that is shown towards people in those professions has not to do with the person, but with the fact they happen to be entertainers, athletes, or the like. One would be equally taken with anyone else who happens to possess those attributes. This may help explain the confusion many sometimes experience when a celebrity is found to have a shadow side, for example in the case in which a professional athlete is found out also to be someone who commits domestic violence. It was just their athletic abilities that were admired, not the person himself, nor his other—here negative—qualities.

8. Nāgārjuna, *Six Perfections*, 367.

9. Nāgārjuna, *Six Perfections*, 367–68.

Skillfulness in some area does not imply overall goodness, nor does it cancel out unskillfulness in other areas of life.

Still, we do require good things for our lives. A gift of money that arrives just when I'm down to my last cent, a free meal offered when I am hungry, the return of health after a period of illness—all of these come with a sense of relief, and it seems only natural that they should prompt expressions of gratitude toward the source of the boon. Even when a particular giver is lacking, say in the case of the return of health after an illness, it is not uncommon to hear expressions like "Thank God," or, more impersonally perhaps, "Thank heavens" or "Thank goodness." Feelings of attachment to a giver, perceived or not, are however still an attachment and hence an impediment to proper insight. Nāgārjuna continues:

> Question: When a person has not yet achieved realization of the Path, clothing and food remain as urgent issues for him. How then does such a person adopt a skillful means to gain that patience which prevents the mind from developing attachment and affection for benefactors?
>
> Response: One resorts to the power of wisdom to contemplate the mark of impermanence, to contemplate the mark of suffering, and to contemplate the mark of the absence of an inherently-existent self so that the mind is influenced to abide in a state of constant renunciation and vigilant concern.[10]

Gratitude, in its deepest sense as gratitude that issues from insight, is not simply a matter of rendering thanks to a benefactor for a good received. Instead, it has to do with welcoming *all* circumstances with an open heart and an open mind, and above all without turning them into issues of self-and-other. Robert Aitken offers this anecdote to capture the point:

> When Seisetsu Shuryo Koskushi was roshi of Engaku Monastery in Kamakura, the dojo needed to be rebuilt to accommodate the large number of monks who had gathered to practice. A wealthy merchant brought five hundred pieces of gold, an immense sum of money, for this purpose.
>
> The story varies at this point, but according to the version I heard from Nakagawa Sōen Roshi, Seisetsu Zenji just said, "Okay, I'll take it."
>
> The merchant was miffed that he had not been thanked, and so he said, "In that sack are five hundred pieces of gold."

10. Nāgārjuna, *Six Perfections*, 371.

> Seisetsu was playing a game of go at the time and he looked up again from his board and said simply, "You said that before."[11]

Far from being rude, Seisetsu was demonstrating through his equanimity the emptiness of all giving, and, with it, the pāramitā of patient forbearance toward benefactors, in this case to the merchant and those around him.

It is this very same equanimity that is manifest in the second form of patient forbearance, forbearance towards those who do me harm. Here, the danger is not that I will become attached with kindly feelings, but quite the opposite, namely that I will fall prey to anger and aversion. While attachment and aversion are both kleśas, aversion is the more toxic of the two on the path to awakening:

> Upāli asked Buddha, "World-Honored One, suppose a Bodhisattva breaks a precept out of desire, another does so out of hatred, and still another does so out of ignorance. World-Honored One, which one of the three offenses is the most serious?"
>
> The World-Honored One answered Upāli, "If . . . a Bodhisattva continues to break precepts out of desire for kalpas as numerous as the sands of the Ganges, his offense is still minor. If a Bodhisattva breaks precepts out of hatred, even just once, his offense is very serious. Why? Because a Bodhisattva who breaks precepts out of desire [still] holds sentient beings in his embrace, whereas a Bodhisattva who breaks precepts out of hatred forsakes sentient beings altogether."
>
> "Upāli, as the Buddha has said, desire is hard to give up, but is a subtle fault; hatred is easy to give up, but is a serious fault."[12]

This is because attachment still affirms the lay of the land. It singles out a dharma here or there for particular affection, perhaps, but nothing is thereby rejected. In opting for butter pecan out of the range of offerings at the ice cream shop, I am not for all that saying that none of the other flavors should have a place in the freezer case; in giving my last five dollars to the woman begging at the intersection with a cup, I am not thereby putting the man at the next intersection out of the picture, even when I have no further money to give.

By comparison, singling out even one dharma out of aversion has the effect of clearing the whole playing field. This is because attachment and aversion act in two different ways. In attachment, I single out *another*

11. Aitken, *Mind of Clover*, 82.

12. Chang, *Treasury of Mahāyāna Sūtras*, 270.

for particular affection. In anger, I single out *myself* and seek to exempt myself from the perceived source of my hurt. Attachment *misunderstands* the connection between myself and others, revealing a *deficiency* of insight. Anger, however, *seeks to abolish* the connection between myself and others. Far from a mere weakness or deficiency of insight, Śāntideva suggests, it reveals instead its thoroughgoing *absence*:

> This worship of the Sugatas, generosity, and good conduct performed throughout thousands of aeons—hatred destroys it all. There is no evil equal to hatred, and [hence] no spiritual practice equal to forbearance.[13]

Insight is absent, because anger only arises in failing to see the essential emptiness of the actors, both the one who is causing me harm and the "me" who is harmed, by assuming there is something going on that demands to be averted—the threat to the self.

Nothing reinforces a sense of self more quickly than anger. The chapter on anger in the *Dhammapada* makes that connection explicit at the outset:

> Give up anger, give up conceit,
> Pass beyond every fetter.
> There is no suffering for one who possesses nothing,
> Who doesn't cling to body-and-mind."[14]

The conceit here, of course, is the root conceit of the self. Bodhidharma's version of the Ninth Grave Bodhisattva Precept makes the same point: "Self-nature is subtle and mysterious. In the realm of the selfless Dharma, not contriving reality for the self is called the Precept of Not Indulging in Anger."[15] Indeed, what is anger, at bottom, but an alternate reality, one in which I am at the center, contrived to distance me from the perceived source of my hurt?

Now the primary reason why anger arises in response the harmful actions of others is that they are assumed to have freely chosen that activity which now causes me harm. Rather than seeing them, like all conditioned beings, as a collection of states, as the teaching on the skandhas suggests, one ascribes to them a unique and autonomous source of agency. I feel anger at them because they presumably could have *chosen*

13. Śāntideva, *Bodhicaryāvatāra*, 50.
14. Fronsdal, *Dhammapada*, 59.
15. Aitken, *Mind of Clover*, 93.

to do otherwise. Almost all moral philosophy is united in claiming that moral culpability is only properly ascribed to more or less autonomous agents who elect their actions rather than find themselves in any way constrained or compelled to perform them. What separates responsible agents from children, the cognitively impaired, and animals is their ability to exercise conscious deliberation concerning their actions, a faculty the others are lacking.

It is precisely this ascription of autonomous free agency that the Dharma calls into question. Each of the pāramitās has a "proximate cause," an aspect of awakening life that prompts its manifestation, and the pāramitā of patient forbearance has its proximate cause in insight into emptiness, or as Dhammapāla described it, "seeing things as they really are."[16] Recall that in chapter 1 we saw that the teaching of the five skandhas was distinctive in that it provided an exhaustive account of persons without recourse to a governing faculty (soul, free will, etc.). "Seeing things as they really are" here means seeing that actions carried out toward me, whether for good or ill, do not arise *ex nihilo* from an otherwise unconditioned autonomous agent. Rather, they arise as a consequence of the afflictions to which the person carrying out the harm is subject. Following Nāgārjuna's line of thought, I can begin to practice patient forbearance, because I can see that there is no more reason for anger with respect to others because of their actions than there would be, say, toward a chair that happens to have been exactly where it was when I stubbed my toe on it. The comportment of the person and the characteristics of the chair are both equally, and non-autonomously, conditioned.

As long as beings are still unawakened, all of their actions can be seen as a form of acting out. Failing to understand the nature of their experiences, confusing them as "their own," they respond impulsively to situations impelled by attachment, aversion, and delusion. Nāgārjuna emphasizes the degree of their subjection to the defilements by likening them to puppets:

> Moreover, the bodhisattva knows that from long ago on up to the present, it has always been the case that causes and conditions come together and are falsely referred to as a "person" even though in actual fact there is no genuine dharma of a "person" involved at all. Who then is it that could be hated in such circumstances? There exist herein only bones and blood and skin and flesh. This is comparable to something laid up with bricks

16. Dhammapāla, *Treatise on the Pāramis*, 15.

> or to a wooden puppet displaying mechanical movements and manifesting comings and goings.[17]

The comparison to a puppet is particularly instructive: the arms swing, but there is no self-mover; the legs move, but they are not autonomously directed. When the puppet's arms or legs strike me, I do not blame the puppet but rather the one pulling the strings. However, the one who has seen into the truth of dukkha and its arising knows that even where sentient beings are concerned there is no puppeteer—not the "person" in question and still less some cosmic Director. There is just the continuous, mutually dependent, coarising of condition after condition, in other words, saṃsāra. That I now experience pain in conjunction with the actions of another is no more a cause of anger than experiencing pain in response to any other state of affairs.

Nāgārjuna is not alone on this score. As Śāntideva points out, "I feel no anger towards bile and the like, even though they cause intense suffering. Why am I angry with the sentient? They too have reasons for their anger."[18] "Reasons" here, of course, does not mean considered reasons but rather causes and conditions. Asaṅga in the *Bodhisattvabhūmi* makes the same point:

> Here a bodhisattva rightly learns the following: "This [person] is someone who is subject to causal conditions. He or she is a mere [collection of] formations. He or she is a mere [collection of] entities. There is no self here of any kind, no [real] sentient being, no [real] living beings, no [real] person that has taken birth who could scold [someone], who could anger [someone], who could beat [someone], who could speak abusively [to someone], and who could criticize [someone], or who could be scolded, who could be angered, who could be beaten, who could be spoken to abusively, and who could be criticized." For [a bodhisattva] who cultivates proper attention in this way, the notion of [someone] being a [real] sentient being will disappear and the notion of [him or her] being a mere [collection of] entities will remain. By relying on and establishing this conception of mere entities, [a bodhisattva] forbears and endures all the harms that are done [to him or her] by others.[19]

17. Nāgārjuna, *Six Perfections*, 404.
18. Śāntideva, *Bodhicaryāvatāra*, 52.
19. Asaṅga, *Bodhisattva Path*, 317.

Finally, Tsong-kha-pa in *The Great Treatise on the Stages of the Path to Enlightenment* puts it this way:

> When bodhisattvas are hurt by others, they think, "They do this because the demons of the afflictions have eliminated their ability to control themselves." Without even being the slightest bit angry with those persons they then must generate the spirit of enlightenment, thinking, "I will strive at the bodhisattva deeds in order to free them from these afflictions."[20]

Nāgārjuna cuts to the heart of the matter: "When one understands that the situation is of just this very sort, then one should reflect, 'If I become hateful, then this is just stupidity.'"[21]

I have marshaled a number of commentaries on this point of not ascribing autonomous agency to actors for two reasons. First, it is to show that this is not at all an ancillary aspect of the Dharma; it goes straight to the heart of what non-self entails. The realization of non-self requires a rethinking of all our everyday conceptions of guilt and innocence, blame and responsibility. The impetus to get angry at someone's actions and to seek to alter that person's behavior only makes sense against a backdrop of an assumption of conscious free agency. The teaching on the skandhas points to the fact that there is no control center, whether a rational soul or mind, in which to locate that free agency. Instead, our actions arise out of the interplay of the skandhas and the habit patterns one falls into by reinforcing certain of those configurations over others. The early lines of *The Dhammapada*, which show wherein the rising of anger lies, gets right to the point:

> "He abused me, attacked me,
>   Defeated me, robbed me!"
> For those carrying on like this,
>   Hatred does not end.
> "She abused me, attacked me,
>   Defeated me, robbed me!"
> For those not carrying on like this,
>   Hatred ends.[22]

When I clearly see that there is no autonomous "he" or "she" involved, and when I stop carrying on as if there were, anger simply vanishes.

20. Tsong-kha-pa, *Great Treatise*, 161.

21. Nāgārjuna, *Six Perfections*, 405.

22. Fronsdal, *Dhammapada*, 1–2.

But this viewpoint is not simply other-directed; the stupidity Nāgārjuna speaks of is compounded when I somehow imagine myself to be the hapless victim of others' hurtful actions as well. Avoiding this stupidity involves seeing clearly into my own contribution to the situation:

> How does one succeed in being patient even in the midst of people who are hateful and tormenting? One should reflect thus: "All beings are freighted with causes and conditions linked to transgressions and thus alternate in attaching and wreaking harm on one another. That I am now compelled to undergo such torment is also a consequence of such causes and conditions arising from my own past-life deeds.[23]

"Freighted with causes and conditions linked to transgressions" is compelling description of the human condition. The experience of harm requires both the one inflicting the harm as well as the one being harmed, and both of us find ourselves in the current situation as a result of the very many decisions and choices, propensities and habits, delusions and ignorance that have issued forth as this moment. We are co-complicit partners in the situation at hand. Śāntideva puts it surprisingly simply: "His the knife, and mine the body—the twofold cause of suffering. He has grasped the knife, I my body. At which is there anger?"[24] Attacker and attacked both showed up in the moment, brought to that point by everything that had gone on before. A knife attack is simply the present configuration of reality.

Nāgārjuna's referencing of "causes and conditions arising from my own past-life deeds" should not be read in the simplistic way karma is often thought about, as a kind of tit-for-tat proposition. There is no question of *desert* here. Rather, Nāgārjuna's observation is simply the obverse of the situation he described concerning receiving good from others. Just as in that case I had no ground for saying I deserved or earned the good, in the same way, when receiving ill treatment, I have no grounds for saying I should not have to deal with it. If I am honest, I recognize that I have done more than my share to bring the present infelicitous moment about, even if it is not immediately apparent in the current situation.

Perhaps a (non-lethal) example will serve to illustrate this point. Let's suppose I go for a swim at the local gym. After completing my laps, I return to my locker to find that I had left it unlocked, the padlock still where I had left it, right on top of the locker. I quickly check my shorts

23. Nāgārjuna, *Six Perfections*, 385.

24. Śāntideva, *Bodhicaryāvatāra*, 54.

pockets for the important items and find that my phone, keys, and wallet are all there. Relieved, I get cleaned up and head on my way. Before returning home, I stop at the grocery store and make my purchase with my debit card. Later that afternoon I go to pick up some dry cleaning, and, when I go to pay with cash, I find that the twenty-two dollars that had been in the wallet is gone.

Looking closely, I cannot not say that I was simply a victim, free of any contribution to the occasion of the theft. To begin with, I had placed my belongings in a locker in a locker room. Locker rooms are filled with all kinds of people, some of whom steal, even if most of them do not. I came ready with a padlock, fully cognizant of the fact that my possessions left unlocked were not at all safe from theft. I was under no illusions that I was opening myself to being stolen from just by virtue of showing up there bearing cash; if I really didn't want money taken from my wallet that day, I would have done well not to carry any. And, of course, I had forgotten even to use the lock.

I cannot be angry with the thief, either. It might seem be a simple matter to be angry with him, imputing culpability by saying, "He chose to steal from me," but things are not as simple as all that. To begin with, I have no idea what it would be like to be the kind of guy who rummages through unlocked lockers in a locker room. It never enters my mind to do such a thing. Further, I have no way to imagine what countless circumstances have led him to entertain such ideas, let alone commit them. Somewhere along the way, he got the bright idea to steal things. Perhaps it was on a dare from a friend as a kid, maybe it was out of some perceived necessity, maybe it was just a lark—it doesn't really matter. What matters is that over time he developed a disposition to stealing that even now prompts him to acts of theft.

Moreover, I don't know what possessed him to steal on this particular occasion. Was it compulsion? Was it because he had bills to pay? Was he getting cash to feed an addiction? A family? The thief may not even understand his motives at that point; he simply does not know what he is doing. I also do not know what kind of ongoing mental state he must be in as result of stealing. I would guess he is often fearful, suspicious, and guarded. I certainly do not envy him his lot in life.

But most importantly, the theft had nothing whatsoever to do with *me*. This person didn't know me. I wasn't targeted. I was just another guy in the locker room, and my belongings just happened to be accessible. Even if I had been targeted, it still would not have to do with *me*. As in the case of receiving good from others because of some quality I possess that they like, here I would be receiving ill because of some attribute or quality I possess that the person does not like, even if it is as simple as the attribute, "having money," seen from the perspective of one who does not (or who just wants more).

The conceit of the self comes into play when I begin to think that I am some kind of being who deserves not to have his things taken from him. I might even, in a moment of solidarity, extend that to others; "No one should have to put up with this!" I might say. But what does such an exclamation amount to? I live in a world in which people steal. Part of what it means for there to be thieves is that there are persons stolen from. I am no more immune from being on the losing end of theft than anyone else is. Of course no one wants to be stolen from; no one wants to be hurt in any way. But there is a world of difference between the kind of self-care that keeps oneself out of harm's way as much as possible and the sense of entitlement that one should not have to endure any hardship from others *at all*. In the first case, I will take common sense precautions, including the use of a padlock at the gym, to make stealing my things a little more difficult, even with the full knowledge that padlocks can be cut. In the second, I will take the theft as a personal assault, an attack on my personhood, and try to find a way to eliminate thieves.

Even taking common sense precautions in this case does not get to the very bottom of the exercise of patient forbearance; sentient beings do as much. The bodhisattva goes even further. As we saw, the compassion of the bodhisattva consists in manifesting whatever nirmāṇa is most congenial to those around him. This applies even when it might mean becoming for them the very object of their cruelty and disdain:

> Furthermore, the bodhisattva brings loving-kindness to his mindfulness of beings, looking upon them just as he would his own children, thinking, "The people of Jambudvīpa[25] have an abundance of every kind of distress and worry and they experience only a few days of happiness. If they find enjoyment in coming here and cursing and reviling or inflicting slander and injury, such happiness is only rarely enjoyed."
>
> He thinks, "Carry on then with the cursing as much as you please. Why? Because when I originally brought forth the resolve, it was done out of a desire to cause beings to be happy."[26]

25. Jambudvīpa is the "continent" in Buddhist cosmology where humans dwell. One could translate "the people of Jambudvīpa" simply as "the people of the world."

26. Nāgārjuna, *Six Perfections*, 393.

The bodhisattva is not daunted by any of this. In fact, it is for him the very occasion for the fruits of bodhicitta—self-sacrifice, readiness, contentment, and joy[27]—to have their free play. He does not go among the people of the world saying, "You think causing distress like this is a source of happiness; let me instruct you how to be truly happy," nor does he think, "These people . . . Let's see what we can do to change conditions so they don't give rise to thoughts of taking pleasure in others' distress." Instead, he offers himself as their plaything, letting them dispose of him as they see fit. He preaches the Dharma not in words but by being the very manifestation of emptiness.

One cannot but call to mind here the example set by the poet-monk Ryōkan. In "Curious Accounts of the Zen Master Ryōkan," Kera Yoshinge recounts one of Ryōkan's encounters with a thief:

> 45. There was a thief who broke into the Master's hut at Kugami. Finding nothing to steal, he pulled at the Master's sleeping mat, attempting to remove it without waking him. Pretending to be asleep, the Master rolled over, allowing the thief to pull the mat out from under him and carry it off.[28]

This was not Ryōkan's only run-in with thieves, and among his poems we find an account of a similar episode:

> Making off with the backrest and cushion
> A thief has struck my tumbledown hut
> How can I refuse him?
> All night, by the window
> I sit alone in the stillness
> The drip-drip of the rain
> filling the forest of bamboo.[29]

And, of course, there is Ryōkan's oft-cited classic,

> Left behind by the thief—
> The moon
> In the window[30]

apparently written after a thief had made off with all of his clothing. Ryōkan did not recoil from a would-be thief, protecting himself and his possessions. Rather, he met the thief on the thief's own terms, even going

27. See Brassard, *Concept of Bodhicitta*, 46–49.

28. Ryōkan, *Great Fool*, 104.

29. Ryōkan, *Great Fool*, 126.

30. Stevens, *One Robe, One Bowl*, 38.

so far as to make the thief's job easier. For one with deep insight like Ryōkan there is simply no ground upon which to set up a barrier between oneself and the thieves.

Intimacy with all beings means being intimate even with those we would rather see act otherwise than they do. Asaṅga captures this very intimate relationship when he offers the idea of "embracing" sentient beings as an antidote to anger and an encouragement to patient forbearance:

> Here a bodhisattva rightly learns the following. "Now in generating the mind [that aspires] to [attain] enlightenment, I have embraced all sentient beings in the manner that a spouse [is embraced] and I have pledged to accomplish what is beneficial for all sentient beings. Therefore, having declared, "I shall do what is beneficial for all sentient beings," it would be unseemly for me to do something injurious [to a particular sentient being because] I was unable to endure the harm [inflicted by him or her]. For [a bodhisattva] who cultivates proper attention in this way, the notion of being a foe that is held toward those sentient beings who harm him or her will be relinquished and the conception of embracing them will arise. By relying on this conception of embracing [sentient beings], [a bodhisattva] forbears and endures all the harms that are done [to him or her] by others.[31]

The first line of bodhisattvic "assistance" or "benefit" is the exercise of forbearance that leaves others just as they are. This is true compassion, as we saw exemplified by Avalokiteśvara above. Asaṅga glosses on this form of embracing:

> He or she embraces all sentient beings in the manner that a spouse [is embraced] and yet is untainted by the fault of embracing a spouse. Regarding this [topic], the fault of embracing a spouse is the following. It is the two qualities of developing afflicted forms of affection and hostility [respectively] in response to favorable or injurious actions [that are carried out] by one's spouse. Neither of these [faults] is found in a bodhisattva.[32]

With insight, notions of "friend" or "foe" do not even arise. These would be further instances of what Nāgārjuna calls my "stupidity." Therefore I neither attach myself to those who do me good nor separate myself from those who do me harm.

31. Asaṅga, *Bodhisattva Path*, 318.

32. Asaṅga, *Bodhisattva Path*, 30.

The vow to liberate all beings does not mean leveraging them from one state to another, say from bondage to liberation or from immorality to upright living. Striving for the ease of other beings, if we follow Nāgārjuna's and the others' line of thought, means primarily not standing in their way, of meeting them exactly where they are, no matter the attendant cost to oneself. This means that quite often there is simply nothing to do about others' actions, and Nāgārjuna goes on to relate the tale of the contentious monks of Kauśāmbī to illustrate the point. Seems these monks had let a small matter swell to such a degree that opposing camps had formed and were threatening to split the saṅgha into two factions, each going its own way. After a time, the Buddha came to them and gave the following instruction:

> You are seeking to gain nirvāṇa.
> You should cast aside and relinquish worldly benefits.
> When abiding in the dharmas of goodness,
> How could you be so hateful and full of disputation?
> When worldly men become angry and contentious,
> This is something one might yet forgive.
> But with men who have left the home life,
> How can it be that they dispute and struggle?

But the monks would hear none of it: "The Buddha is the Dharma King. He would prefer that we maintain a brief period of silence. However this group assailed us. We cannot but respond." The Buddha's response is noteworthy: "These men cannot be crossed over to liberation." As the sutra continues, "He then soared forth from the midst of that group of Sanghins and disappeared, going then into the forest where he remained in samādhi."[33]

The Buddha—the World-Honored One, Well-Gone, Teacher of Gods and Men—knew better than to try to budge these intransigent monks from their anger at the perceived slight from the other monks. They could not see that their response, driven as it was by the perception of self-and-other, had no standing in the Dharma. As long as they cast the situation at hand as one in which someone was doing something *to* them, ignoring their own contribution to the situation, failing to acknowledge their own wrongdoing in perpetuating the dispute at all, there was no toehold for the Buddha's teaching. Notice that the Buddha pays no attention to the merits of each side's case; no matter who was "in the right," it

33. Nāgārjuna, *Six Perfections*, 397.

does not override the root error to which both parties have fallen prey. Views, even purportedly "right ones," should not stand in the way of the unity and cohesion of the saṅgha that obtains when its members understand the conditioned nature of all views and hence their insufficiency as stand-ins in for the Dharma.

So the Buddha just leaves, heads to the woods, and sits in meditation. Sometimes patient forbearance means standing in the midst of rough situations or letting others have their way with me, but sometimes its exercise means letting the situation alone. The Buddha was not defensively fleeing the blows and insults of the monks; he simply acknowledged their imperviousness to the truth and walked away from it. The vow to liberate all beings may well involve letting them figure things out for themselves—or not.

The dispute of the Kauśāmbī monks is a cautionary tale in two respects. First, for those who would aspire to awakening it is a reminder that attachment to self-conceit acts as a repellant to the Dharma. Just like the monks, one whose heart has petrified in anger-driven ego-attachment is not at all amenable to the liberating truth of the Dharma. Hatred, following Śāntideva, destroys the very possibility of attaining insight, because it rejects at the outset what insight would entail, namely ego-attrition. If one finds oneself in the first stages of aspiration, the very best thing one could do would be to work to uproot the conceit of the self, to set clinging to views to the side, and to acknowledge one's shortcomings.

For those who would seek to change others and the worlds they create out of their own delusions, it is a cautionary tale in the other direction. Not everything is possible. As much as one might like to see people getting along, treating each other with dignity and respect, sometimes it is just not going to happen. As much as one might like to see those of means make it possible for those without to share in the wealth, sometimes it is just not going to happen. And as much as one might like to see people emerge from their self-constructed prisons, sometimes that is just not going to happen, either. The hortatory injunction, "May all beings be happy and secure; may they be inwardly happy,"[34] that one finds in the *Mettā Sutra* has its full strength and measure when uttered from the position of patient forbearance and enduring the effects of those beings' dis-ease. It is not a rallying cry to change those beings or to plot an escape route to a place where their shenanigans will no longer have an impact.

34. Bodhi, *Suttanipāta*, 179.

To return to one's own practice is, then, for a practitioner of the Dharma no less than the Buddha himself, one of the very best things one can do. Far from being a flight away from the business of the world, sitting in samādhi is the mark of ongoing openness to the truth of the world, even when—or *especially* when—that truth is unpleasant, harmful, or destructive.

7

The Social World Endured

Up to this point we have been following Nāgārjuna on the exercise of patient forbearance toward sentient beings, leaving until now a look at patient forbearance toward dharmas—circumstances, situations, phenomena. On the one hand, the distinction between the two is important. My treatment of others sets in motion further reactions on their part; if I treat them well, they will be at ease, but if I treat them poorly, there is no telling what actions they may be prompted to carry out in response. By contrast, my frustration with traffic, or the construction detour, or my personality quirks that get me in trouble with my neighbors, or the table I just stubbed my toe on, do not engender further actions in the same way. The table, traffic, and my temperament are not affected in the least by the vitriol I might hurl in their direction.

From the start, then, it is rather counter-intuitive that one should be patient with dharmas at all. Why should I be patient with cold and heat? Why shouldn't I seek to avoid hunger and thirst, difficulties, sickness and the like? Shouldn't I try to make myself a better person? Such aims certainly underlie the vast majority of the actions we undertake as we try to make things better or, at least, less worse, than they happen to be. And this is not just a matter of comfort. Whole systems of thought, spiritual practice, physical wellness, and social engineering have been developed in order to ameliorate just about every imaginable aspect of life, and in innumerable cases they have succeeded in alleviating some trouble or another to the benefit of many.

Nāgārjuna addresses this issue head-on:

> Question: If, in relation to other beings, one becomes hateful, engages in torment, and inflicts injury on their lives, one commits a karmic transgression, whereas, if one acts out of sympathy for them, one gains karmic blessings as a result. However, in reacting to cold, heat, wind, and rain, there is no production of any gain or any loss for anyone. Why is it then that one should remain patient with such phenomena?

The answer is that there is still plenty of damage done by failing to be patient even with these:

> Response: Although one does not thereby bring about any gain or loss for anyone, still, if one brings forth disruptive afflictions and distressful bitterness, one does inflict injury upon one's own practice of the Bodhisattva Path. It is for this reason that one should maintain patience.
>
> Additionally, it is not the case that one commits karmic transgressions solely through the killing and tormenting of beings. Wherever one courses in causes and conditions associated with evil thoughts, one generates karmic transgressions as a consequence.[1]

Failure to practice patient forbearance towards circumstances reveals the same "stupidity" Nāgārjuna mentioned in conjunction with lack of patience toward beings, namely a failure to understand the nature of conditioned phenomena, myself included, as inherently empty. If emptiness were not the nature of conditioned phenomena, then pursuing certain conditions and curtailing others would be appropriate as a way of consistently working to improve the lot of the self, further myself by making adjustments so as to render my condition more felicitous and pleasant, or at least less troublesome and painful. One who has come to a measure of insight knows that such tactics miss the point entirely. Thus, even when no sentient being is affected, the value of patient forbearance toward dharmas stems from its ability to deepen my own realization and to school myself even further in the emptiness of all things, whether conditions, others, or myself. The distinction between sentient beings and dharmas, at least from the perspective of practice, not as important as it may have first appeared.

In what might perhaps strike modern sensibilities as a surprising move, Nāgārjuna includes social structures under the heading of what he calls "non-mental" dharmas, thereby placing social phenomena on the

1. Nāgārjuna, *Six Perfections*, 410–11.

same level as atmospheric phenomena, at least as far as being a field for the exercise of patient forbearance goes. The implications for a possible Dharma-based understanding of social responsiveness are significant: talk of "changing society" from this perspective would be on par with talk of "changing the weather"—a fool's errand if ever there was one. Instead, Nāgārjuna will argue for the exercise of patient forbearance even when one finds oneself in a society rife with troubles and difficulties. To see how he gets to that point, we need to attend closely to the smaller steps he makes along the way. Proceeding from his reflections on embodiment, it will be but a short step to his considerations of patience with respect to the social environment.

Put simply, "non-mental" dharmas are those things that populate the causes and conditions that surround me. Nāgārjuna points out that these may be more "outwardly" oriented or more "inwardly" oriented. Outward non-mental dharmas include those things that affect me from outside my bodily form, such as wind and rain, cold and heat. Inward non-mental dharmas include those circumstances that arise from within my bodily form, such as hunger and thirst, sickness, aging and death. Whether "inward" or "outward," these dharmas in the end all point to the nature of embodiment itself:

> Then again, the bodhisattva considers, "I have taken on this body composed of the four great elements and the five aggregates. It ought therefore to be the case that it is freighted with all manner of aspects entailing suffering as a consequence. There is no one who takes on such a body and yet remains invulnerable to suffering."
>
> Whether one is rich and of noble birth or poor and of humble status, whether one is a monastic or a householder, whether one is foolish or wise, and whether one is intelligent or dull, no one is able to avoid it.[2]

In short, "there is no one who takes on a body who does not thereby become subject to suffering. Therefore the bodhisattva should course in the practice of patience."[3]

2. Nāgārjuna, *Six Perfections*, 413.
3. Nāgārjuna, *Six Perfections*, 414–15.

We know much more about bodies in the twenty-first century than Nāgārjuna could have possibly known in the second, but what we now know only underscores even more boldly his point that my very embodiment lays out a very rich field for the practice of patient forbearance. Already at conception genetic dispositions were dealt out that set up, say, my likelihood of needing corrective lenses, extensive dental work, insulin shots, hypertension medication, or an inhaler to treat my asthma. As an infant, my body was further modified and even more trajectories were set in motion: did I receive adequate nutrition for brain growth? Vaccines? Was I subject to secondhand smoke? As a child or adolescent, I might have been allowed (or left) to sit in front of a screen for most of the day, or I might have been thrown into too many sports and suffered a broken ankle in gymnastics or too many concussive hits to the head in football. Any of these and more can leave me in a situation in which now, as an adult, I have things to attend to, restrictions on my activity, and dispositions to even further conditions and illnesses. Even with welcome advances in medicine, I still have to take the time to go to the doctor, submit to testing, undergo surgery or radiation or chemotherapy, take my medications regularly and deal with their side effects—all because of my embodiment.

In addition to the more expressly pathological limitations on my body, I could be seven feet tall, or left-handed, or colorblind, or be beset with any number of conditions that make living in a world engineered for people of average height, or right-handedness, or color-sightedness, and the rest cumbersome. Or I might not be very attractive, and I find that making friends or getting romantic partners is unusually challenging. Gender comes into play here as well, for my embodied experience is in many respects extensively conditioned by whether I have XY or XX chromosomal pairs, or whether testosterone or estrogen has the upper hand in my system; even if I am transgender, I have to stick to a regimen of hormone shots long after successful reassignment surgery to keep the chromosomal pair I was conceived with from expressing.

I also find that I have certain psychological, affective, and emotional dispositions, and I no more chose these than I chose to have blue eyes, a receding hairline, or an allergy to tree pollen. Perhaps I prefer my eggs with ketchup, have a taste for Gregorian chant, or show an inordinate fondness for tulips. I might have a hard time refraining from making wisecracks or an easy time getting teary-eyed at a film in which the underdog finally triumphs. I could be sexually attracted to men or to women, or to both or neither. I may be the firstborn child in the family and display all the usual firstborn behavioral traits.

All individual differentiation aside, our bodies are all of them subject to environmental conditions. It is not an arbitrary coincidence that all non-aquatic life on this planet is sustained with an atmosphere of 78.09% N_2, 20.95% O_2, 0.93% Ar, and 0.04% CO_2, and every land-based organism is equipped to make use of that mix in varying measures. Nor is it coincidence that our cellular pressure is roughly equivalent to 1 atmosphere; too far above or below that and our cells either explode or implode. Nor again is it coincidence that we heterotrophs live only on the condition that there are ample autotrophs. (Even the creation account in Genesis wisely has the plants on the scene two days before the dryland animals and humans appear.) Far from being self-contained, self-sufficient entities, our bodies are at all times but possible effects of any number of causes and conditions that, as they change, change our bodies as well.

Finally, as our telomeres shorten over time and the effects of aging slowly make their appearance, we become increasingly aware of our finitude, our frailty, and the futility of fighting what is inevitable as long as we continue to draw breath—the steady, progressive breakdown of bodily systems that, sooner or later, ends with death. Even here, some deaths will be painless and swift, and others will be more laborious and protracted.

If I have gone on at some length multiplying cases here, it is to emphasize the point that there is no *generic* embodiment, only *this* configuration of skandhas, "freighted with causes and conditions," as Nāgārjuna pointed out above.[4] When I attend to the particulars of my constitution, I find nothing I can call "me" that is adjunct to the appearance and interplay of all these constituent moments by which I might measure positive and negative deviations from what I fancy I "should" be. I can certainly fantasize about what life might be like without the effects of aging, without the slight limp I have from a broken ankle suffered in my teens, or without the fact that I really like oatmeal raisin cookies. That fantasy, however, does nothing when it comes to navigating the onset of menopause, or walking any distance, or craving a cookie (or four) at the

4. Much of the "Theology of the Body," popular in certain Catholic circles and beyond, fundamentally misses the specificity and complexity and fluidity of embodiment, opting instead to focus on rather generic abstractions about embodiment generally.

strangest times. I have no idea why I am the way I am, but the way I am is all that I have to work with.

Dōgen referred to all of this as *the teisho of the body*: "The teisho of the actual body is the harbor and the weir. This is the most important thing in the world. Its virtue finds its home in the ocean of essential nature. It is beyond explanation. We just accept it with respect and gratitude."[5] Like all teishos, the body is a complete and forthright expression of the Dharma, if I but have the ears to hear it. Like all teishos, I can ignore it, pretend it isn't saying what it's saying, or substitute what I would like to hear in place of it. Unlike other teishos, I didn't ask for this one, nor does it end. There is no pause and reset function here, no remixing, and no fast-forward. I am left with a simple choice to make: keep fighting my embodiment, or succumb to its teaching and let tṛṣṇā abate.

The Zen adage, "When hungry, eat. When tired, sleep," finds its place here. Being patient with the dharma of hunger, I feed myself. Being patient with the dharma of drowsiness, I sleep. Taking my cues from these dharmas rather than, say, orthorexic projections of "how much (or what) I should eat" or success-driven conceptions of "how much work I need to get done," I neither reject the teaching of the body, nor do I attach to ideas of what I "should" or "would rather" do instead. In the same way, when the dharma of the urge to let loose a bit arises, it might mean that it is time to have a little fun:

> A monk asked Caoshan, "What's it like when you put aside your mourning clothes?"
> Caoshan said, "Today I have fulfilled my duty to my parents."
> The monk asked, "What about after you have fulfilled your duty?"
> Caoshan said, "I love to get drunk."[6]

Of course dharmas do not show up one by one, and there are hardly any controlled environments in which only one dharma, say tiredness, is the only thing I have to attend to. There are countless dharmas opening all of the time, and I sometimes have to work with a number of them at once. If I find myself a monk, and I am to be in the meditation hall for long

5. In Aitken, *Mind of Clover*, 103. *Teisho* in the Zen tradition is the verbal presentation of the Dharma by a teacher.

6. *Shōyōroku*, Case 73. In the Christian tradition there is a similar anecdote concerning Theresa of Ávila. Seems she was fond of partridge, and once, when the sisters of her convent were taken aback when they saw her tearing into a whole roasted bird with great relish, she said, "When I fast, I fast; when I eat partridge, I eat partridge."

stretches of time, patient forbearance with respect to the dharma of being tired may well just entail enduring sleepy meditation:

> A monk asked Kyorin, "What is the meaning of Bodhidharma's coming from the West?"
> Kyorin said, "Sitting long and getting tired."[7]

I will not berate myself for not being a "good" monk, nor will I bemoan the lack of clarity and focus in my meditation. If I am juggling work and family commitments with a sick child and a spouse that just had an appendectomy, it will mean just doing the best I can without turning it into a narrative of "how much better it would be if . . ." or "this is not what life is supposed to be like." Patient forbearance is the only sane choice I have.

Patient forbearance with respect to bodily dharmas, therefore, indicates yet a further aspect of The Middle Way. The Middle Way is often portrayed as "the Goldilocks way"—not too hot, not too cold, but just right. As we saw above, the Middle Way is the path that transcends clinging and aversion, not, for example, one that helps to find the sweet spot between hot and cold temperatures. With right view I can see that it is not an affront that my body should be clammy, uncomfortable, and dripping with sweat on a sunny ninety-five-degree day with 90 percent relative humidity. If there is a broad, leafy tree nearby, I may perhaps avail myself of its shade. But if there is no tree in the vicinity and I find myself in open country with no respite from the sun, then sunburn and heatstroke are quite likely. Similarly, it is not an affront that my body should be subject to frostbite and hypothermia in sub-zero conditions. If there is shelter and warmth nearby, I will no doubt avail myself of them. But if neither shelter nor warmth are to be found, then frostbite and hypothermia will be forthcoming. Patient forbearance does not mean that I should not take advantage of the tree or warm shelter if they are present. It simply means that, absent the tree or warm shelter, my body will be subject to the stated conditions, physical hardship will ensue, *and there is no flaw in the design.*[8] All relevant dharmas—the sun, the air, the cold, my body—are just as they are. There is no possible ground for gainsaying them.

7. *Hekiganroku*, Case 17.

8. Nāgārjuna, *Six Perfections*, 433: "One contemplates and knows [the true character of] dharmas as free of any flaw."

All of this is preparatory for understanding Nāgārjuna's point that the structure we have just seen for bodily dharmas holds true for the social conditions I find myself in as well. His argument is essentially this: just as I assume difficulties in taking on a flesh and blood human body in the natural world, I assume difficulties in being one human among others in a social world. Just as I will be subject to cold if I am in the Arctic or to heat in the Sahara, I will be subject to all the calamities of war if I am in a war zone, to the vicissitudes of local politics in my hometown, to the gross and subtle pressures to conform to the customs of the times, and to the gains and losses that come with the ups and downs of global, national, and local economies. These are just so many aspects of the social landscape that constitute my life as I know it; I have no everyday life apart from these many factors.

As with external dharmas generally, some social conditions are conducive to furthering my life, and some are not. But just as I have no reason to feel particularly lucky about finding myself on a pleasant summer afternoon or particularly unfortunate in being caught in a blizzard, so, too, I have no reason to take particular delight in finding myself in a station of privilege or economic affluence, nor do I have reason to take umbrage in finding myself enduring, say, discrimination, political disenfranchisement, or economic hardship. While we somewhat readily understand this when it comes to the body and to weather conditions, it feels like a stretch to extend patient forbearance to social, political, and economic conditions. The standard objection is that the social environment, unlike the natural environment or the particulars of my embodied makeup, is the product of human deliberation and choice. No one commands the weather, but societies are seemingly capable of structuring themselves, whether through laws or policies or any of the other mechanisms of social and political cohesion.

Recall that for Nāgārjuna, sentient beings are, from the point of view of their conditioned nature, just "puppets" responding to the ceaseless interplay of conditions. If that is the case, it follows that he should consider the whole social arena to be just one big puppet show, the production of so many conditioned and conditioning non-autonomous agents. Acting out their attachment, aversion, and delusion, they cast about this way and that. What emerges by way of social structures and policies is therefore not the product of a rational design but a hodgepodge of whatever happens to be possible as these tṛṣṇā-driven actors play off each other—in other words, saṃsāra. The social dynamic, so considered, resembles Brownian motion far more than the unfolding of a rational or divine plan, a forward movement toward freedom and justice, or a collective learning exercise. Economies and polities rise and fall in response to myriad conditions that no one agent, whether a singular or a plural one, is in charge of. There is not even something like Adam Smith's "invisible hand" at work here, for Smith used that term as way to describe the social benefits that accrue from otherwise discrete individual aims. If we follow Nāgārjuna, there is not even the least warrant for assuming the puppet show will turn out at all well. There is change, of course, but there is no discernible trajectory.[9]

In the canon the broad contours of these changes are identified as "the eight worldly conditions":

> Bhikkhus, these eight worldly conditions revolve around the world, and the world revolves around these eight worldly conditions. What eight? Gain and loss, disrepute and fame, blame and praise, and pleasure and pain. These worldly conditions revolve around the world, and the world revolves around these eight worldly conditions.[10]

In calling them "worldly conditions," the Buddha recognized that these are on par with all other dharmas in that they are generated by the interplay of other causes and conditions without specific rhyme or reason. In fact, they are sometimes referred to as the "eight winds" because of their ability to buffet beings in this direction or that. Like atmospheric winds, they have no particular singular source, nor are they purposefully aimed in a particular direction. They just blow. Natural gas prices fall, and coal falls out of favor, prompting further job loss in Appalachia. A new emperor takes the throne, and Buddhist monasteries are disbanded and the monks laicized. Major highways are built, and mom and pop restaurants along the old route go out of business. Email becomes widespread, and the postal service loses revenue. Irish Catholic immigrants, previously the subject of discrimination and suspicion, become mainstreamed, and some of them now treat Pakistani Muslims with the kind of discrimination and suspicion visited upon their grandparents and great-grandparents. Vaccines are developed and rates of childhood disease and death

9. This point will be taken up in more detail in chapter 9.

10. Bodhi, *Numerical Discourses*, 1116.

fall. Pony Express riders stable their horses when the telegraph line is finally stretched across the plains. There is money in my pocket because at some point someone pulled some out of theirs. Each of these shifts prompts further shifts, further rounds of gain and loss, further affirmation and rejection, and so on and on and continuously on.

There is nothing in the teaching of the Buddha to suggest that there is anything out of the ordinary in any of this, anything at which to take offense, and certainly nothing that needs to (or even could) be fixed. To lean on one side of any of the oppositional pairs of worldly dharmas is to prompt a concomitant inverse effect on the other side. This is simply what unfolds when sentient beings governed by tṛṣṇā act. When people pursue their own constructed view of what an ideal situation for them looks like, there are going to be winners and losers. Anyone who would take a sober look at the vicissitudes of human interaction will simply not be surprised at the twists and turns social forces make.

What the Buddha did teach, however, is how one might stop being afflicted by dukkha in response to all of this ebb and flow. The sutra continues that these worldly dharmas affect the instructed noble ones no less than uninstructed everyday persons; no one is exempt from them. The noble one, however, does not respond to them the way the everyday person does. As far as the everyday person goes, failing to see that these winds are marked by anattā, anicca, and dukkha,

> gain obsesses his mind, and loss obsesses his mind. Fame obsesses his mind, and disrepute obsesses his mind. Pleasure obsesses his mind, and pain obsesses his mind. He is attracted to gain and repelled by loss, [etc.]. Thus involved with attraction and repulsion, he is not freed from birth, from old age and death, from sorrow, lamentation, pain, dejection, and anguish; he is not freed from [dukkha] I say.[11]

The noble one responds differently. Knowing the four winds are but conditioned dharmas, "gain does not obsess his mind, and loss does not obsess his mind, [etc.] Having thus discarded attraction and repulsion, he is freed from birth, from old age and death, from sorrow, lamentation, pain, dejection, and anguish; he is freed from [dukkha] I say."[12] Nāgārjuna expressly links this teaching of the Buddha to the practice of patient forbearance:

11. Bodhi, *Numerical Discourses*, 1117.

12. Bodhi, *Numerical Discourses*, 1117.

> Furthermore, the bodhisattva reflects, "Not even the Worthies and Āryās are able to avoid encountering circumstances precipitating the eight worldly dharmas. How much less could this be the case for me?" On account of this, one should be able to maintain patience.[13]

The stakes are even higher for one who has set forth on the path of the bodhisattva. If I cannot be patient with the comings and goings of the everyday world, Nāgārjuna muses, it is not clear I can even hope to fulfill my bodhisattvic aspirations, either:

> The bodhisattva makes vows with the great mind, "I will patiently undergo even the sufferings of the *avīci niraya* (hells). How much less might it be that I would fail to maintain patience with minor sufferings? If I fail to maintain patience with minor sufferings, how could I be able to maintain patience with major sufferings?[14]

Having vowed to liberate all beings, how could I now shield myself from the structural effects of their countless deluded choices and actions?

Any social structure or force one presently encounters, then, is best seen to be as empty and as conditioned as a summer rain shower or winter snowstorm and calls for the same kind of patient forbearance. Both prompt one to do things that one in all likelihood would rather not do, or else they put one in a position of not doing what one rather would do. If twelve inches of snow fall during the night, it is clear that, whatever else I would like to do, I'm going to have to shovel before much else happens with my day. If I am militantly anti-gay, and the state compels me to offer services at my establishment to gay couples, whatever else I would rather be doing, I would do well to comply. By the same token, if I am out and proud, and I find myself in the middle of a militant (and possibly violent) anti-gay crowd, it is probably best if I do not make a big point about being gay at that place and time. Of course, in each of these cases—shoveling, baking a cake, or keeping a low profile—if one does what one would rather do instead of what the circumstances call for, one should not be surprised at the untoward consequences that follow. Whether one concedes or holds fast to one's principles, no one is exempt from the consequences of doing so; holding fast will bring praise from

13. Nāgārjuna, *Six Perfections*, 411–12.

14. Nāgārjuna, *Six Perfections*, 415.

some while drawing disdain from others, and making concessions will play out similarly.

But it is not fair, one might object, that some persons seem to be able to exercise their preferences unhindered while I do not. Why should I have to endure pushback from others concerning my beliefs, my autonomy, or my personal expression? Why should I (or anyone) have to endure social structures that demonstrably give preferential treatment to some group or another but not to me? We will look more closely at the question of justice in the next chapter, but for the moment, following Nāgārjuna, this much can be said. Yes, it is not fair that social structures favor some more than others. By the same token, though, it is not fair that drought conditions obtain but a couple hundred miles from an area with ample rainfall, or that the tornado razed my house to the ground while it left yours intact some scant hundred yards away. It is not fair that the boy with muscular dystrophy is not able to play soccer with his schoolmates, and it is not fair that some children are born to drug addicts while others are born to clean and sober parents. What Dōgen said concerning the teisho of the lived body could just as well be said of the teisho of the body in society: "It is beyond explanation. We just accept it with respect and gratitude."[15] We do not know why it is the way it is, but it is all we have to work with.

The one distinction Nāgārjuna does make between patience with respect to natural phenomena and patience with respect to social phenomena is that, because social structures and institutions are human constructs, and I am a human, I recognize that I have contributed to their makeup and character. While I do not participate in the arrival of a snow squall, I have participated in the movement of social forces. Hence difficulties I might be experiencing in social life are, like the difficulties I encounter when another is causing me harm, traceable in part to my own activities up to that point. The circumstances of my birth and my responses to them; the conditions of my family and my responses to them; the neighborhood I grew up in and my responses to it; the schooling I was offered (if any) and my responses to it; the kind of classmates, teachers, coaches, guides, clergy I encountered (again, if any) and my responses to them; the job I was able to secure (if any) and my responses to it; the nature of my work and my responses to it; the mores, customs, attitudes, social pressures, cultural expectations around me and my responses to

15. In Aitken, *Mind of Clover*, 103.

them; the things I just so happened to find interesting because of those around me (team sports, maybe, or the cello, street drugs or hesychasm, crocheting or volunteering, saving endangered species or gratuitously killing insects) and the ways in which I responded to and acted upon them; the country I was born in and its current geopolitical standing and level of internal development and my responses to them—all of this and more precipitates the present moment, with all of its fret and trouble, thrown into the mix of the myriad circumstances and responses of those I share the planet with now as well as those of all who have come before.

This is the condition Nāgārjuna has in mind when he writes,

> The bodhisattva naturally realizes, "It is on account of the causes and conditions associated with karmic offenses in previous lives that one is reborn in a place so fraught with suffering. This is something I created myself. Hence I ought to be bound to personally endure it."[16]

The mention of "previous lives" here need not raise the specter of reincarnation; "previous lives" here primarily refers to the many forms of life one takes on in the span of this human birth—the rising and falling of one's samsaric worlds. One lives a child's life, a student's life, the life of a young adult, a sick person, a teenager, taxpayer, spouse, parent, neighbor, coworker, or stamp collector. As one lives through each of these and more without awakening, one sets in motion subsequent causes and conditions to which others then respond. They, also without awakening, respond to them likewise prompted by their own attachment, aversion, and ignorance, and further causes and conditions are set in motion. Standing now in the midst of this large-scale mess is not an accident, nor could it be otherwise: it is the very life I have helped contribute to with my own delusion and ego-attachment. Even if I now have attained some measure of awakening, I am not for all that absolved of living through the consequences of my previous actions.

Michel Foucault, paraphrasing a line from Charles Baudelaire, once wrote, "You have no right to despise the present."[17] Although Foucault and Baudelaire were addressing somewhat different concerns, the maxim is well taken here, and it is one with which Nāgārjuna I think would agree. This place and time so fraught with suffering for me is also the place and time that has given rise to those things I happen to enjoy and

16. Nāgārjuna, *Six Perfections*, 411.

17. Foucault, "What Is Enlightenment?," 40.

that benefit me in some way or another; the wheat is not to be winnowed from the chaff, and in any case, what is wheat today may be chaff tomorrow and vice versa. If I am honest, I know that I helped bring all of this about, so by seeking to eliminate, rather than act in light of, unpleasant social conditions I am, in effect, carrying out a cherry-picking exercise in reality. Rather than seeing all dharmas with the mind of equanimity, I seek to advance those most conducive to my perceived well-being and to eliminate those that run counter to that perception. In this respect, aversion to dharmas and anger toward sentient beings are cut from the same cloth; both are attempts to "contrive reality for oneself" out of the conditions that currently obtain.

Of course, the Buddhist tradition is not free of lamentations concerning the state of the world. Perhaps the most classic example of this is the discourse surrounding "The Declining Age of the Dharma," or *mappō* in Japanese. Originally developed in China out of a few Pāli and Sanskrit sources, the doctrine gained ground in the wake of Chinese imperial opposition to Buddhism in the fifth and sixth centuries, and it was developed even further in Japan by Saichō, the founder of Japanese Tendai, in the eighth century, and Shinran, the founder of Jōdo Shinshū, in the thirteenth. In brief, the theory was that after an initial True Dharma Age following the life of the Buddha and lasting for some five hundred years, the teaching had deteriorated to a point that the Imitation Dharma Age began. After five hundred years of further decline the Last Dharma Age would begin, initiating a period of defilement, the corruption of the Dharma, and the advent of any number of unfortunate developments like earthquakes, famine, war, and pestilence.[18] Monks would violate the precepts, the faithful would be misled, and the light of the Dharma would grow dimmer. (Interestingly enough, the story of the disputatious monks of Kauśāmbī we heard about in chapter 6 was advanced in various retellings as the precipitating moment for initiating the decline of the Dharma.[19])

But champions of *mappō* theory did not, on the whole, advance it in order to prompt the faithful to change the social and political and religious institutions around them for the better. Instead, they used it to urge their followers to repent of their own wrongdoings and to encourage

18. Marra, "Development of *Mappō* Thought (I)," 27.

19. Nattier, *Once Upon a Future Time*, 130–32.

them to ever more diligent practice. Shinran was particularly keen to stress that one could not separate oneself from the goings-on of the day:

> As a man of *mappō* living with other beings with whom he was sharing the same nature, Shinran, for the first time in this history of Japanese thought, realized that *mappō* was not something outside human beings, so he was able to say that "I cannot consider my existence apart from the existence of *mappō*." . . . To escape *mappō*, therefore, meant in Shinran's judgment to escape oneself, a thing impossible to do from the perspective of this world.[20]

One could counter that this is not at all surprising coming from one who championed Amidism, who saw human efforts as futile and therefore counseled complete faith in the salvific power of Amitābha Buddha. Still, we find much the same sentiment expressed in the interchange between Mañjuśrī and Mujaku in Case 35 of the *Hekiganroku*:

> Mañjuśrī asked Mujaku, "Where have you just come from?"
> Mujaku replied, "The south."
> Mañjuśrī said, "How is southern Buddhism faring?"
> Mujaku answered, "The monks of the latter days of the Law have little regard for the precepts."
> Mañjuśrī said, "Are there many or few?"
> Mujaku said, "Here about 300, there around 500."
> Mujaku then asked Mañjuśrī, "How does Buddhism fare in this part of the world?
> Mañjuśrī said, "The worldly and the holy dwell together; dragons and snakes intermingle."
> Mujaku asked, "Are there few or many?"
> Mañjuśrī said, "In front, three by three; in back, three by three."

Mujaku speaks for the party of "good Buddhists," those who are doing their part to do well by the Dharma in the Last Age. He is fastidiously doing his best to uphold the precepts, and he is keenly aware of who is and who is not equally dedicated—even to the point of counting each and every head. Mañjuśrī is not at all impressed with this display of zeal. When asked how Buddhism is doing in his neck of the woods, the Bodhisattva of Wisdom shows Mujaku wherein the Dharma lies: in the realization of emptiness. In emptiness, "dragons and snakes intermingle," and they are *everywhere*—six of one, half dozen of the other. Insight frees one from the bonds of discriminations such as good and bad, high and

20. Marra, "Development of *Mappō* Thought (II)," 292.

low, precept-following and precept-violating. This does not mean that one denies the distinction between dragons and snakes, saints and sinners; Mañjuśrī does not say to Mujaku that everyone is the *same*.[21] Removing the bonds of discrimination means that one can acknowledge the dragons *as* dragons and the snakes *as* snakes without being compelled to take the subsequent step of promoting the one and seeking to eliminate the other. One's own practice is not contingent upon the quality of the practice of others. One's existence is not separate from a snake-infested *and* dragon-bearing world.

What does a bodhisattva do, then, in unwelcoming and unwholesome social environments? Nāgārjuna's answer is, what a bodhisattva always does; he diligently practices in the direction of Buddhahood:

> Additionally the bodhisattva considers and realizes that there are two kinds of countries: There are those which are pure and there are those which are impure. If the bodhisattva is born into an impure country and experiences these bitter sufferings, hunger, cold, and manifold torments, he makes a purifying vow to himself: "When I achieve buddhahood, the country will have none of these manifold sufferings. Although this place is impure, it will ultimately work to my benefit."[22]

The country will have none of those sufferings once buddhahood is attained, Nāgārjuna points out, because as a Buddha he will generate no karmic outflows with which to sully the social landscape and cause others or himself further hardship. More to the point, however, the difficult social situations he currently perceives himself to be in reveal much more about his own lingering attachments and aversions than anything else about conditions. Coming to the end of attachment and aversion, he will have come to the end of his views on pure versus impure countries, not unlike Mañjuśrī. Until then, the difficulties this seemingly "impure" country throws in his path are best treated as occasions for honing his insight and practicing the pāramitās.

All language of future Buddhahood aside, the key insight here is that at no point does it cross the bodhisattva's mind that it lies within his or anyone else's purview to turn an impure country into a pure one. Just as it can never be a matter of creating a climate in which I will at all times be

21. That would, of course, be an instance of wrong view. Mañjuśrī is indicating the second form of right view, a reflection of the Noble Truths.

22. Nāgārjuna, *Six Perfections*, 411.

comfortable, it can never be a matter of creating a social milieu in which I will not have troubles. The demand for a difficulty-free social life is on par with an expectation of sunny June days all year round.[23] It is simply unreasonable to expect that things will always go well, no matter what one's social station in life. The injunction to "change the world" is bought in the coin of denying one of the fundamental aspects of reality arrived at with insight into emptiness, the identity of saṃsāra and nirvāṇa:

> There is nothing that distinguishes *saṃsāra* from *nirvāṇa*; there is nothing that distinguishes *nirvāṇa* from *saṃsāra*, and the furthest limit of *nirvāṇa* is also the furthest limit of *saṃsāra*; not even the slightest difference between the two is found.[24]

It is for this reason that Hakuin's observation that "this earth where we stand is the pure lotus land, and this very body, the body of Buddha"[25] means *this* body and *this* land, populated with *these* people, under *these* conditions, just as they are.

Recall the quote from Aldo Leopold with which this book began:

> One of the penalties of an ecological education is that one lives alone in a world of wounds. Much of the damage inflicted on land is quite invisible to laymen. An ecologist must either harden his shell and make believe that the consequences of his science are none of his business, or he must become the doctor who sees the marks of death in a community that believes itself well and does not want to be told otherwise.[26]

We can now rework this in light of the Dharma:

> One of the penalties of awakening is that one lives alone in a world of wounds. A bodhisattva cannot harden her shell and make believe that her insight exempts her from the consequences of living among those without. Instead, she functions as the awakening one who has seen the cause of dukkha in herself

23. It is telling, for example, that in his *News from Nowhere* (1890) William Morris's depictions of life after the socialist revolution are always set on a sunny day in June.

24. Nāgārjuna, *Mūlamadhyamakakārikā* XXV, 19–20; in Gethin, *Foundations of Buddhism*, 239.

25. Rochester Zen Center, *Chants & Recitations*, 35.

26. Leopold, *Round River*, 165.

> and sees it now in others who are as yet incapable from freeing themselves from it.

The bodhisattva goes against the current in patiently enduring all circumstances, even when common sensibilities would have her do otherwise. Neither hardening her shell nor carrying out interventions, her compassion consists in manifesting, through her forbearance, the power of insight over conditions.

The lesson Puṇṇa learned at the feet of the Buddha is not to be lost these many years hence without a concomitant loss of the Dharma. The social and economic, technological and political changes that have occurred over the last two and a half millennia have not altered the fundamental lay of the land, namely that all contingent circumstances, all conditioned beings, and even myself, are marked by anattā, anicca, and dukkha. Whether at Sarnath or in Silicon Valley, each person in every generation has to navigate the prevailing landscape for him- or herself. And just as the basic lay of the land and the nature of beings has not changed, neither has the path to the end of dukkha, either. There is a price to pay in following that path, both then and now: patiently enduring the small- and large-scale effects of countless beings—myself included—having acted out of attachment, aversion, and delusion.

III

Upāya Born of Emptiness

8

Justice Is a Word not Uttered by the Wise

It is widely acknowledged that *justice* is not a word in the lexicon of the Dharma as it is in the religious and philosophical systems of the Mediterranean basin—Abrahamic religion and Greek and Roman philosophy. These systems for the most part presuppose an understanding of actors and the world that is, from top to bottom, precisely what the Dharma calls into question. Rather than viewing the world as a God-ordained or rational system in which everything has its proper place and relation to the rest, the marks of conditioned existence point to the fact that there is in experience no evidence of an intended or rational order, and hence no ground for postulating an Orderer or ordering principle. Rather than affirming an autonomous center of agency within every actor, made in the image and likeness of the Orderer or in accordance with the order of the world, the teaching on the skandhas leads one to see that there is no such governor to be found. And rather than assuming a clear means-ends relationship that the postulate of the well-ordered world and the self-possessed governor makes possible, it is understood that actions and their expected effects do not immediately line up with one another, making the swift imposition of retribution and the restructuring of the social order accordingly questionable as a matter of both principle and pragmatics. It comes as no surprise, then, many Buddhist theorists who nevertheless want to take up the issue of justice have spoken in terms of *appending* a conception of justice to the Dharma and modifying the core teaching as needed to accommodate it.[1]

1. See Blumenthal, "Buddhist Theory of Justice," 321–27, 328, 339–49.

But if significant swaths of the Buddhist tradition have been consistently silent on[2]—or seemingly intractable with respect to—the issue of justice, it is not without reason. For one who would attain to the liberation of the Dharma, the pursuit of justice shows itself to be an unskillful enterprise on two, closely related, fronts. First, it is always ever marked with the kleśa of anger or aversion, and as long as anger or aversion are present, one has not yet uprooted the defilements, making steady progress on the path impossible; as indicated in the *Nissaraniya Sutra*, there is "no such possibility" that where loving-kindness, compassion, altruistic joy, equanimity, etc. have taken root, that ill will, harming, resentment, lust, and pursuit of marks can at all arise.[3] Even if one has not yet eliminated them completely (and so few have) electing to pursue a path that runs counter to them cannot but thwart one's steadfast aspiration; either one is heading in the direction of the path outlined by the Noble Truths or one is not, and there is no splitting the difference between the two or finding a *tertium quid* that could.

Second, the active pursuit of justice reveals a misunderstanding of the relationship between actions and consequences. The everyday demand for justice requires that compensation for harm be both manifest and swift; as Martin Luther King Jr. in "Letter from Birmingham Jail" put it, "Justice too long delayed is justice denied." While it is central to the Dharma that "there are evil actions, there is the result of misconduct"[4] and "there are good actions, there is the result of good conduct,"[5] this in no way implies that the results of misconduct or good conduct will be either openly visible or timely—in other words, that they will obtain in a way that would be materially satisfactory to the aggrieved. The Buddha challenged the naïve realism that would claim to be able to assess actions on their face, to see plainly the causal structure involved, and to know just what, exactly, will prove compensatory or corrective in balancing out pain and pleasure within a time frame that would satisfy the demand for justice. It was with due consideration for the Dharma that Walpola Rahula, one of the first expositors of the Dharma for the West, felt compelled to note, "The term 'justice' is ambiguous and dangerous, and in its name more harm than good is done to humanity."[6]

2. See, for example, Lele, "Disengaged Buddhism," 239–89.
3. Bodhi, *Numerical Discourses*, 867–68.
4. Ñāṇamoli and Bodhi, *Middle Length Discourses*, 1062.
5. Ñāṇamoli and Bodhi, *Middle Length Discourses*, 1063.
6. Rahula, *What the Buddha Taught*, 32.

For the sake of framing this discussion with some degree of precision, let us recall briefly John Stuart Mill's account of justice in *Utilitarianism*.[7] Mill was of the view that "the two essential ingredients in the sentiment of justice are the desire to punish a person who has done harm and the knowledge or belief that there is some definite individual or individuals to whom harm has been done."[8] The second of these serves to separate situations of perceived injustice from unsatisfactory states of the world generally. One may well find it distressing that people suffer and die from contagious diseases and cancer, or from famine and drought, but these are not instances of injustice. Part of what it means to be human is that we are all of us susceptible to disease and the vicissitudes of conditions around us—no one is singled out, and there is no discernible causal agent at work.[9] By contrast, situations are called unjust that involve a harm perpetrated on a particular individual by a particular agent. If John takes a baseball, aims it at me, and hits me on the head with his throw, then John, it is said, has acted unjustly. But if John happens to hit a foul ball that lands on my head while I am seated in the stands behind the plate, then John has not acted unjustly, and the harm he caused with the ball on that occasion is purely fortuitous.

The first component of the sentiment of justice, the desire to punish, arises out of a straightforward calculus of pleasure and pain. Our affective life is, on Mill's account, exclusively conditioned by circumstances and their effects on us; we naturally greet pain with measures to counter the pain, and we naturally greet pleasure with the urge to sustain it. Moreover, our perception of pain and pleasure is marked out against the standard of the self; we like those who like us, and we feel antipathy toward those who threaten our person in any way: "Now it appears to me that the desire to punish a person who has done harm to some individual

7. Mill's reflections are helpful here because they, like the teaching of the Buddha, do not rely on universalizing claims concerning the intended order of the world nor do they predicate human action on a transcendental conception of the self. Moreover, to the extent to which utilitarian thought shares in the progressive tradition's aim of social amelioration, it rests on a rather straightforward calculus of pleasure and pain, gain and loss, punishment and reward that is similar to that which the analysis of action provided by the Buddha seeks to correct. It is fair to say that, for the most part, proposals for an engaged Buddhist conception of justice remain at the level of progressive thought, leaving what is distinctive and liberating about the Dharma behind.

8. Mill, *Utilitarianism*, 51.

9. With this, of course, Mill leaves the issue of theodicy to the side. The justice with which he is concerned is very much a this-worldly, everyday affair among human actors.

is a spontaneous outgrowth from two sentiments, both in the highest degree natural and which either are or resemble instincts: the impulse of self-defense and the feeling of sympathy."[10] The sentiment of self-defense prompts me to respond to instances of harm or benefit to my person; the sentiment of sympathy prompts me to respond to instances of harm or benefit to others I happen to be concerned about, that is, those I perceived as extensions of myself.

This impulse to self-defense, Mill maintained, is one we share with animals:

> It is natural to resent and to repel or retaliate any harm done or attempted against ourselves or against those with whom we sympathize. Whether it be an instinct or a result of intelligence, it is, we know, common to all animal nature; for every animal tries to hurt those who have hurt, or thinks are about to hurt, itself or its young.[11]

The only difference Mill saw between animals and us on this score is that we are capable of sympathizing with more than just our immediate relations—indeed with all of humanity—if we are properly cultivated. Mill considered it to be one of the signs of continuing social improvement that we expand our root feelings of self-preservation to include sympathy with all others who suffer, even if their suffering is not immediately connected to kith and kin. The benchmark of the self remains, but it is now an expanded, social self. An injury to humans generally is now seen as an injury to myself, and the instinct for self-defense is applied on an ever-widening scale.

Mill thought it only natural that we should harbor resentment toward those who cause us, or those we identify with, harm. The naturalness of that response was rooted in the idea, inherited by Mill from Jeremy Bentham, that there is no action that is not undertaken save with respect to pain and pleasure. As Bentham starkly put it:

> Nature has placed mankind under the governance of two sovereign masters, *pain* and *pleasure*. It is for them alone to point out what we ought to do, as well as to determine what we shall do. On the one hand the standard of right and wrong, on the other the chain of causes and effects, are fastened to their throne. They govern us in all we do, in all we say, in all we think: every effort

10. Mill, *Utilitarianism*, 51.

11. Mill, *Utilitarianism*, 51.

> we can make to throw off our subjection, will serve but to demonstrate and confirm it.[12]

The Buddha was familiar enough with the workings of pleasure and pain, and he was not unmindful of this very natural tendency to resentment. In the *Nikāyas* we find a catalogue of its many manifestations:

> Bhikkhus, there are these ten grounds for resentment. What ten? (1) Thinking: "They acted for my harm," one harbors resentment. (2) Thinking: "They are acting for my harm," one harbors resentment. (3) Thinking: They will act for my harm," one harbors resentment. (4) Thinking: "They acted for the harm of one who is pleasing and agreeable to me," one harbors resentment. (5) Thinking: "They are acting for the harm of one who is pleasing and agreeable to me," one harbors resentment. (6) Thinking: "They will act for the harm of one who is pleasing and agreeable to me," one harbors resentment. (7) Thinking: "They acted for the benefit of one who is displeasing and disagreeable to me," one harbors resentment. (8) Thinking: "They are acting for the benefit of one who is displeasing and disagreeable to me," one harbors resentment. (9) Thinking: "They will act for the benefit of one who is displeasing and disagreeable to me," one harbors resentment. (10) And one becomes angry without a reason. These, bhikkhus, are the ten grounds for resentment.[13]

Unlike the Utilitarians, however, who saw no reason to call this very natural impulse into question but simply sought to raise it from its base animal origins to a broader, more socially serviceable and humane form, the Buddha identified this impulse as but a further instance of the exercise of the kleśas, which meant that its cessation was, indeed, possible. The chains forged by the dual sovereignty of pleasure and pain *could* be broken.

The path to the end of resentment offered by the Buddha consists not in acquiescing to resentment by countering the pain that gave rise to it with retributive pain but in coming to see clearly that there is—rather baldly stated—*nothing* to be done in the face of it. The Buddha continues:

> Bhikkhus, there are these ten ways of removing resentment. What ten? (1) Thinking: "They acted for my harm, but what can be done about it?" one removes resentment. (2) Thinking: "They are acting for my harm, but what can be done about it?" one

12. Bentham, *Principles of Morals and Legislation*, 11.

13. Bodhi, *Numerical Discourses*, 1439.

> removes resentment. (3) Thinking: "They will act for my harm but what can be done about it?" one removes resentment. (4) Thinking: "They acted for the harm of one who is pleasing and agreeable to me, but what can be done about it?" one removes resentment. (5) Thinking: "They are acting for the harm of one who is pleasing and agreeable to me, but what can be done about it?" one removes resentment. (6) Thinking: "They will act for the harm of one who is pleasing and agreeable to me, but what can be done about it?" one removes resentment. (7) Thinking: "They acted for the benefit of one who is displeasing and disagreeable to me, but what can be done about it?" one removes resentment. (8) Thinking: "They are acting for the benefit of one who is displeasing and disagreeable to me, but what can be done about it?" one removes resentment. (9) Thinking: "They will act for the benefit of one who is displeasing and disagreeable to me, but what can be done about it?" one removes resentment. (10) And one does not become angry without a reason. These, bhikkhus, are the ten ways of removing resentment."[14]

This "What can be done about it?" is not apathetic resignation or cold indifference, though it will no doubt seem so to the everyday person for whom self-defense and its extension toward others out of sympathy are so perfectly natural and appropriate that no other options present themselves. Despite appearances, the Buddha's "what can be done about it?" actually reflects a clear—even wise and compassionate—response to the situation at hand.

To begin to see how this is so, we need only recall the structure of right view. The first kind of right view involved a recognition of, among other things, that there are good and bad actions and that each of them has markedly different consequences. This stood counter to the wrong view that there are no distinctions between good and bad, and therefore no particular results that follow in their wake one way or the other. In light of the first kind of right view, "What can be done about it?" would, indeed, indicate callous indifference. But this first kind of right view is, however, still "affected by taints, partaking of merit, ripening in the acquisitions."[15] Driven by attachment and aversion, and deployed with a view to outcomes, it strives to maximize good actions and their consequences and to minimize bad actions along with theirs as well. It is still tied to the self in that it seeks to better that self's lot.

14. Bodhi, *Numerical Discourses*, 1440.

15. Ñāṇamoli and Bodhi, *Middle Length Discourses*, 934.

If the teaching of the Buddha were nothing more than an Iron Age version of utilitarianism from the Indian subcontinent, this would be the end of the matter. The second kind of right view—the one that arises with the clarity of insight into the Noble Truths of dukkha, its cause, its cessation, and the path to its cessation—sees that the truth of things is not exhausted with considerations of good and bad, pain and pleasure, better and worse because the self that had served as their benchmark is nowhere to be found. Things happen, but they are not about *me*; I am neither advanced nor hindered by any of them. When there is no self-concept to be challenged by the activity of those around me, there is no drive for self-defense, evasive or corrective action is abandoned, and resentment abates. The compulsive drive to do this or that in response to the harm inflicted by another simply dissipates as a matter of course, and the straightforward, "What can be done about it?" begins to issue forth as a spontaneous assessment of the situation at hand.

Because the abatement of resentment is come to only within the context of one's own aspiration for awakening, it has to be admitted that it does not provide much of a basis for a social program the way, say, Mill's does, or as advocates of a socially engaged Buddhism hope it might be. It is one thing to say, "I harbor no resentment and have no need to retaliate," and it is another to say, "You should not be resentful, or you should not retaliate," and still yet another to claim, "No one should be resentful, and no one should retaliate." Since the Buddha's counsel here is always only ever meant as a skillful means for an individual aspirant, it remains open to the charge that it is essentially asocial, that it does not do its part toward advancing the well-being of society, and that it sequesters individual purity from the messy world of human interaction. But this is a charge that fails to appreciate the place of the Dharma in the world.

The *Aggañña Sutra* helps situate the place of the non-resenting, and hence non-justice-seeking, practitioner within the broader social environment. The sutra begins with an interchange between the Buddha and two of his disciples who had belonged to Brahmin families. The Buddha asks whether the Brahmins revile and abuse them now that they have gone forth into the homeless life, and the two answer affirmatively; the Brahmins now chastise them for associating with persons of every social strata, throwing the order required for the upholding of society to fall into disarray. The Buddha then goes on to illustrate the baselessness of such a system of social stratification, and while it is generally well-known that the Buddha criticized the Vedic concept of *varṇa*, or social class, it is often overlooked that his critique is, in part, rooted in the idea that such a class-based system grew out of a particular view about how best to maintain the social order in accordance with the demands of justice. Pursuing the Dharma will require setting that view of maintaining the social order to the side.

The Buddha begins by tracing human society back to its primitive origins in the development of agriculture.[16] At that time, humans without distinction began to move from gathering food for the day's meal to setting up plots of land to cultivate crops for many days' worth of meals. Once the land had been divided up into plots, trouble began to emerge:

> Then, Vāseṭṭha, one greedy-natured being, while watching over his own plot, took another plot that was not given to him, and enjoyed the fruits of it. So they seized hold of him and said: "You've done a wicked thing, taking another's plot like that! Don't ever do such a thing again!" "I won't," he said, but he did the same thing a second and a third time. Again he was seized and rebuked, and some hit him with their fists, some with stones, and some with sticks. And in this way, Vāseṭṭha, taking what was not given, and censuring, and lying, and punishment, took their origin.[17]

So far there is nothing surprising in this account. Humans, when threatened in their possessions or livelihoods, will try to make their attacker stop. Here all is fair game, and neither party is restrained in any way in the pursuit of his or her ends; from the side of the aggrieved, if rebukes are not sufficient, fists and stones and more will do quite nicely. The first, quite natural and straightforward, answer to the question, "What can be done about it?" is "Make the person stop by any means at one's disposal."

It is telling that in this account the censuring and punishing are not viewed as praiseworthy in their own right, nor are they even tolerated simply as morally neutral expedients. Taking what is not given *and* censuring both are here identified as unskillful actions; so too are lying *and* punishing the liar. When I respond to another's greed on the basis of my

16. The sutra takes human development back even further to its mythic beginnings, but those aspects are not relevant for the discussion at hand.

17. Walshe, *Long Discourses*, 412.

resentment toward that greed, neither one of us stands on particularly high ground. We are each simply playing out our ego-attachments—the one seeking to augment his lot, the other seeking to defend his, both of us gripped by the defilements all the same. This point was not lost on those proto-landholders: "Then those beings came together and lamented the arising of these evil things among them: taking what was not given, censuring, lying and punishment."

It was precisely these considerations, the sutra continues, that led to the establishment of a policing force. Rather than relying on their own resentment and acting as was necessary in light of it, these persons, beginning to sense that their own administration of justice was as defilement-driven as the perpetrator's actions themselves had been, collectively agreed to free themselves of such taints by placing the burden of social maintenance on the shoulders of an appointed agent:

> And they thought: "Suppose we were to appoint a certain being who would show anger where anger was due, censure those who deserved it, and banish those who deserve banishment! And in return, we would grant him a share of the rice." So they went to the one among them who was the handsomest, the best-looking, the most pleasant and capable, and asked him to do this for them in return for a share of the rice, and he agreed . . . This, then, Vāseṭṭha, is the origin of the class of the Khattiyas.[18]

Some have read this as a Buddhist version of social contract theory,[19] and in a way it is. But rather than setting up an efficient and all-powerful authority to hold everyone in awe, as in Hobbes, or erecting an impartial arbiter to transcend the limits of our own idiosyncratic perspectives, as in Locke, here we find the contract arising as a way for the general population to take the evil of exercising chastisement and meting out punishment off their shoulders and to place that burden on those of another out of ethical considerations. The warrior class (*khattiyas/kṣatriyas*) is established, they are paid for their willingness to take on the onerous duty of

18. Walshe, *Long Discourses*, 413.

19. Matthew J. Walton has cautioned against reading the *Aggañña Sutta* as straight-up equivalent modern European social contract theory, and I agree with him. Particularly interesting for the issue here is that neither Walton nor the authors he takes up follow the sutra through to the point where the appointed guardians of the social order set their mandate aside in favor of becoming renunciants and pursuing the Dharma. In other words, the *Aggañña* is still being read here exclusively for its social-political import, not for its critique of the business of social management in favor of the holy life. See Walton, "*Aggañña Sutta*," 374–93.

"showing anger where anger is due," and everyday people are now free to go about their business secure in their persons and possessions but without having to sacrifice their uprightness to do so. At this point the answer to the question, "What can be done about it?" is "Create a class of persons other than ourselves to engage in the morally compromising duty of social policing and the administration of justice."

Many have rightly pointed out that the Buddha did not withhold advice to persons in a position of civil authority, but it is important to remember that such discussions belong at this level of social life. One can certainly exercise civil authority more or less humanely, more or less fairly, more or less equitably, and it should come as no surprise that, when asked, the Buddha was happy enough to speak to such matters. All of this is well and good, but it still does not touch upon the point of the Buddha's teaching (or even the point of this sutra), which is not the establishment of a humane civil authority, which many have addressed, but the unshakable deliverance of mind, the unique contribution of the Dharma.

The sutra continues that it is precisely because of the moral compromise inherent in the exercise of civil authority that a further step is taken by some of those who, until this point, had been responsible for the administration of justice:

> And then, Vāseṭṭha, it came about that some Khattiya, dissatisfied with his own Dhamma, went forth from the household life into homelessness, thinking: "I will become an ascetic." And a Brahmin did likewise, a Vessa did likewise, and so did a Sudda.[20]

That Khattiya with little dust in his eyes could sense that the discharge of his duties—even though he was thoroughly authorized in carrying out his task, had the support of the population, and might have taken some solace in knowing that through his actions justice was served—meant that he was still not free of dukkha and still not rid of the defilements that give it rise. So he simply walks away from it all. So, too, does the Vessa, who had been responsible for the material sustenance of the community. So, too, does the Sudda, charged with providing necessary labor and craftsmanship. So, too, does the Brahmin, whose knowledge and spiritual insight were considered necessary for the proper determination of the affairs of life in accordance with the order of the cosmos. The point is clear: the definitive end to one's dukkha begins with the surrender of, among other things, one's socially-imposed responsibility for the maintenance

20. Walshe, *Long Discourses*, 414.

of the social order, and the highest praise is reserved, not for those who keep the peace or secure the common weal, but for those who have set all that aside and set out on the path of realization:

> And, Vāseṭṭha, whoever of these four castes, as a monk, becomes an Arahant who has destroyed the corruptions, done what had to be done, laid down the burden, attained to the highest goal, completely destroyed the fetter of becoming, and become liberated by the highest insight, he is declared to be chief among them in accordance with the Dhamma, and not otherwise.[21]

For one who has begun to be aware of the path to liberation and sets out upon it, the answer to the question, "What can be done about it?" is "Nothing, for 'this is not mine, this I am not, this is not my self.'"[22]

We may no longer subscribe to a social theory that would assign determinate places for the maintenance of the body politic already at birth, and we see value in allowing individuals to find their own place in society in accordance with their talents and aspirations.[23] In rendering everyone in the polity a plain and equal citizen, however, the responsibility of enforcing with appropriate measure the basic rules of social life is borne by all of the members of the population themselves. Although some individuals may be deputized for the day-to-day aspects of the task, they exercise whatever authority they have in the name of the people as a whole. If we add to this the tendency to blur—or erase—the distinction between ordained and lay, aspirant and everyday person, then there would seem to be no exemption from this burden for anyone. The duty to "show anger where anger is due" now belongs to everyone, and everyone, no matter his or her spiritual aspiration, is implicated in its execution.

One way that has been attempted to mitigate the necessarily untoward effects of that general exercise of anger on those who have taken up the Dharma has been to rework the everyday resentment that follows upon harm into a form that is less tied to raw emotion and blatant ego projections but retains some social efficacy all the same.[24] Following the

21. Walshe, *Long Discourses*, 415.

22. Bodhi, *Connected Discourses*, 902.

23. Even if current conditions do not allow for the freest possible movement of individuals between classes and occupations, it nevertheless remains the ideal by which to measure how near or far a society is from the mark of a free and open society.

24. This is precisely the compromise come to when, once Christianity became the religion of the empire, the need was felt to reconcile the loving and self-effacing demands of the Gospel with the job of exercising civil authority. By the time of Augustine,

long tradition of the West in the assumption that the pursuit of justice has its origin in appropriate anger, some have raised the question whether there might not be a form of anger that, despite all that the Dharma teaches, is not toxic, which, in proper measure, can actually promote rather than hinder progress on the path—a kind of anger that, far from being "stupid," as Nāgārjuna had called it, actually reflects wisdom and compassion. So it is that we now find anger being cast as a necessary complement to other key elements of practice, as reflected, for instance, in the neologism, *right anger* (and cloaked in Pāli no less!): "[W]e might have a newly compounded term, *samma kodha*, which means something like proper or appropriate anger. That is, anger at violence, oppression, and injustice by which suffering beings impose on other beings."[25] In other instances, anger is cast as something of a virtue, and references to "loving-anger"—clearly intended to parallel the brahmavihāra of loving-kindness—have been advanced as well.[26] While no one appears to be advocating for "right greed" or "loving-ignorance" as necessary complements to the Dharma, "right anger" or "loving-anger" seem to be compelling notions precisely because of the connection of anger to justice.

Part of what is confusing here is terminology. The Sŏn Buddhist teacher, Seung Sahn, speaks of four kinds of anger: "attached anger," "reflected anger," "perceived anger," and "loving anger." In a letter to a practitioner he writes:

> Before yong maeng jong jin,[27] your anger was only reflected anger. If you do more hard training, the reflected anger will change to perceived anger. After more practicing the perceived anger will disappear. Then you will have only loving anger—inside you will not be angry, only angry on the outside.

The progression is from pure gut emotion to merely the show of anger without any attendant emotion or ego-investment:

> Attached anger sometimes lasts for three hours, sometimes three days, and does not quickly return to love-mind. When

---

it was incumbent upon the now imperial church to transform the Gospel injunctions against anger generally into a theory of righteous anger and set forth a theory about the just use of forceful coercion. The theory of the just war was born.

25. Senauke, "Right Anger and the Path," para. 15.

26. Loori, *Invoking Reality*, 55.

27. This is the Korean name for the extended meditation retreat known in the Zen world as sesshin.

> you were crying, you had reflected anger; it did not last long . . . After more hard training, your reflected anger will change to perceived anger. You will feel anger but not show it; you will be able to control your mind. Finally, you will have only loving anger, anger only on the outside to help other people—"You must do this!"—but no anger on the inside. This is true love-mind.[28]

Loving anger, then, would be the dispassionate expression of a moral authority exercised in order to rectify an improper or unjust situation for the well-being of all.

It is certainly better to act dispassionately rather than from raw emotion, but even if it is cleared of its emotive underpinnings, justice is still tainted with aversion in that through it one seeks to put distance between conditions at hand in favor of other, better, ones. The kleśas are not simply or even primarily *emotional states* but more particularly *defilements of the mind* arising from the conceit of the self. Aversion is a defilement that puts distance between self and other, and is every bit as operative with a cool head as with a hot one. No matter how one happens to *feel*, there is implicit in all talk of justice a rather clear invocation of a *gap* between obtaining conditions and some preferred state. As Amartya Sen put it (in a thoroughly non-Dharma-related context), "the contrast between what is happening and what could have happened . . . is central to the advancement of justice."[29]

We find this point echoed without qualification among contemporary Buddhist sources as well. Kristen Johnston Largen was of the view that "compassion . . . requires the spur of justice to bring about the social change that is necessary for the thriving of sentient beings";[30] and while John Makransky rightly steers away from anger language on this point, his take on appropriate response to harm still carries with it the separation inherent in the playing out of aversion:

> Fierce compassion is the power to confront—forcefully if necessary—someone who thinks and acts harmfully both on behalf of those he harms and on behalf of his own positive potential, his fuller personhood. Such a fierce, confronting compassion is possible only if it is the expression of a de-reifying wisdom rather than any kind of reifying anger.[31]

28. Sahn, *Only Don't Know*, 69.
29. Sen, *Idea of Justice*, 389.
30. Largen, "Liberation Theology and Engaged Buddhism," 52.
31. Makransky, "Buddhist Critique of Liberation Theology," 648.

The issue is not whether one is being forceful out of "de-reifying wisdom" rather than emotion. As we saw above, bodhisattvas may well *come across* as fierce, and their severity might indeed be the spur that prompts another further on the path to awakening, but the bodhisattva does not *choose to act* fiercely with the intent of changing others, their behavior, or social conditions in any way. The relevant point is not *how* one happens to come across but *why* one is entering the fray in the first place. If it is at all connected with the intent to change the actions of others then one is already caught up in aversion, and it is not clear that doing so on my own behalf or that of others makes much difference here. In either case, one would be at pains to show that the structure of tṛṣṇā ("May I/you/they/we be thus because of this") is not operative, leaving one with the choice to participate in that endeavor or to surrender that attachment if one would keep to the path.

Now it is an oft-repeated charge against those who would set down the burden of social policing that they, through their non-participation, are far from the blameless, morally neutral players they imagine themselves to be but actually contribute to the further spread of injustice and other social ills through their non-action. This was precisely the charge made by the Brahmins against the Buddha's two disciples who had formerly been members of their ranks. In abandoning their station, they were precipitating the descent of social life into chaos, for it was the duty, according to Brahmanic thought, of all members of society each to do their part in the maintenance of the social order. We find this same critique clearly articulated in Mill's writings as well:

> Let not any one pacify his conscience by the delusion that he can do no harm if he takes no part, and forms no opinion. Bad men need nothing more to compass their ends, than that good men should look on and do nothing. He is not a good man who, without a protest, allows wrong to be committed in his name, and with the means which he helps to supply, because he will not trouble himself to use his mind on the subject. It depends on the habit of attending to and looking into public transactions, and on the degree of information and solid judgment respecting them that exists in the community, whether the conduct of the nation as a nation, both within itself and towards others, shall be selfish, corrupt, and tyrannical, or rational and enlightened, just and noble.[32]

32. Mill, *Inaugural Address*, 36.

From this perspective, religious renunciants of every tradition, from the noble ones of the Buddha's family to the saddhus of India and hermits of China, from the Desert Elders of the Christian tradition to their anchoritic, coenobitic, and mendicant heirs—not to mention the Church of the Brethren, the Quakers, and the Mennonites—would all of them be co-complicit in the advancement of evil. This squares quite well with the widespread suspicion of the renunciant life we find currently in society generally and even within many religious bodies as well. One cannot but imagine that some of the widespread contemporary impulse to render the Dharma serviceable for the pursuit of justice can be traced to the fear of being, whether in one's own estimation or others' perceptions, co-responsible for evil by taking no concerted action against it.

But the Buddha had pointed out that the highest praise was to be reserved precisely for those who, like the Khattiya having become aware of the dukkha inherent in administering justice, simply put down that burden in favor of pursuing the path to release. If one reads the Buddha's defense of those who would abandon responsibility for the social order in order to live the holy life simply as a self-serving justification for swelling the ranks of the bhikkhus and bhikkhunīs, then one might well be inclined to say that that is all well and good for monks and nuns, but the noble lay practitioner cannot be held to such a standard. The *Aggañña Sutra*, because it ends with individuals becoming monastics, might still remain open to such a criticism. Turning to the *Mahākammavibhanga Sutta*, or "The Greater Exposition of Action," we find a useful explanation of why Mill's indictment—no less than the Brahmins' indictment of the social defectors above or contemporary attempts at articulating "right anger"—misses the mark, and why even a noble householder will not be inclined to try to find a way around the moral compromise inherent in the demand for and exercise of justice.

The Buddha begins by identifying four cases of persons based on the particular alignment of their actions and the observed consequences that follow from them. First is the case of the person who commits moral wrong in life and, upon death, reappears in "an unhappy destination, in perdition, even in hell."[33] Second is the case of one who abstains from moral wrong and who, upon death, reappears in "a happy destination, even in the heavenly world."[34] Third is the one who abstains from wrong

33. Ñāṇamoli and Bodhi, *Middle Length Discourses*, 1060.

34. Ñāṇamoli and Bodhi, *Middle Length Discourses*, 1060.

yet ends up in an unhappy destination; fourth is the one who commits wrong yet reappears in a happy destination. So far, there is nothing particularly remarkable here, and we are all familiar with cases where scoundrels enjoy bliss and the upright endure hardship, just as we are familiar with cases where scoundrels meet with hardship and the upright find their lives proportionally pleasant. The social landscape is a mix of all of these cases, each of them obtaining as conditions warrant.

But while the Buddha grants the general principles, "there are evil actions, there is result of misconduct" and "there are good actions, there is result of good conduct,"[35] he does not agree with those who would claim, based on their experience of some particular case or another, that *everyone* who commits wrong or who refrains from wrongdoing will find that the expected results discernibly follow. Suppose, he offers, that a someone has seen a person commit evil and ended in a hell realm, or that he has seen a person do good and end in a heavenly realm, or that he has seen a person commit evil and end in a heavenly realm, or, finally, that he had seen a person do good and end up in a hell realm. What that person sees with his own eyes is not for the Buddha to gainsay, but he points out that the observer is unwarranted in moving from his experiential information to the general principle that *everyone* who commits evil *of course* ends (or *should* end) in a hell realm, or that *everyone* who does good *of course* ends (or *should* end) in a heavenly realm, or that *everyone* who does good *does not* enjoy happy recompense or that *everyone* who commits wrongdoing *does not* meet with ill.

The reason for this is that at any given moment the observed connection between action and consequence is at best a snapshot of an ongoing process whose origins and final consummation are impossible to know. Since I do not perceive all of the causes that led to this action, I cannot possibly know the full extent of how this action will now play out. To take two of the Buddha's examples:

> Therein, Ānanda, as to the person who here kills living beings . . . and holds wrong view, and on the dissolution of the body, after death, reappears in a happy destination, even in the heavenly world: either earlier he did a good action to be felt as pleasant, or later he did a good action to be felt as pleasant, or at the time of death he acquired and undertook right view. Because of that, on the dissolution of the body, after death, he has reappeared in a happy destination, even in the heavenly world. But since he

35. Ñāṇamoli and Bodhi, *Middle Length Discourses*, 1062–63.

> has here killed living beings . . . and held wrong view, he will experience the result of that either here and now, or in his next rebirth, or in some subsequent existence.[36]
>
> Therein, Ānanda, as to the person here who abstains from killing living beings . . . and holds right view, and on the dissolution of the body, after death, reappears in a state of deprivation . . . even in hell: either earlier he did an evil action to be felt as painful, or later he did an evil action to be felt as painful, or at the time of death he acquired and undertook wrong view. Because of that, on the dissolution of the body, after death, he has reappeared in a state of deprivation . . . even in hell. But since he has here abstained from killing living beings . . . and held right view, he will experience the result of that either here and now, or in his next rebirth, or in some subsequent existence.[37]

Some may wish to read these cases primarily as illustrations of the idea of rebirth, but what is most instructive here for present purposes is that they are reminders of the finitude of our awareness, first with respect to agents and second with respect to consequences. We are limited with respect to agents, since, as the teaching on the skandhas indicates, I am not *one* but a *conglomeration* of various processes that are constantly at work, coloring my thought and action now this way, now that. What I know for myself I can as well assume for others—that even as some aspect of them has led to this action at this time, other aspects of them are also always at work, and in any case no one's self is *exhaustively* captured in any one given action. That I now see that person at this moment committing evil or performing good tells me nothing of the full causal background that led to the situation I am now seeing with my own eyes.

Second, we are limited with respect to consequences, because the chain of consequences any intended action sets in motion trails off far beyond the reach of graspable space and time, and certainly beyond the immediate observational present. Hence, the charge that failing to meet evil with justice will *of course* lead evil to triumph has no basis, any more than meeting evil with justice will *of course* lead good to triumph. There is simply too much going on over too great a length of time based on such a variety of factors for such a conclusion to be drawn. Everyday actors may well be *impatient* with such a state of affairs, but that does not mean they *must* be altered. For one who would clearly see the nature of actions

36. Ñāṇamoli and Bodhi, *Middle Length Discourses*, 1064.

37. Ñāṇamoli and Bodhi, *Middle Length Discourses*, 1065.

and their causes in accordance with the Noble Truths, acquiescing to and acting out such impatience reveals a sure lack of understanding.

This is particularly manifest in actions aimed at righting wrongs or setting the scales of justice to balance. Since the drive for justice is an attempt to see to it that happy consequences line up with meritorious action and that unhappy consequences line up with misconduct in relatively short order, it is all too easy to move from the view, "every evil deed is eventually requited," to the programmatic, "let us now give the evildoer his due." If it is going to happen sooner or later, one might think, best to get on with it now, lest one give the impression that one is somehow tacitly approving the perpetrator's actions. This is precisely the conclusion that Immanuel Kant, for one, was led to:

> Even if a civil society were to be dissolved by the consent of all its members (e.g., if a people inhabiting an island decided to separate and disperse throughout the world), the last murderer remaining in prison would first have to be executed, so that each has done to him what his deeds deserve and blood guilt does not cling to the people for not having insisted upon this punishment; for otherwise the people can be regarded as collaborators in this public violation of justice.[38]

Mill, too, for all of his disagreements with Kant, thought that capital offenses required capital punishment for rather similar reasons:

> When there has been brought home to any one, by conclusive evidence, the greatest crime known to the law; and when the attendant circumstances suggest no palliation of the guilt, no hope that the culprit may even yet not be unworthy to live among mankind, nothing to make it probable that the crime was an exception to his general character rather than a consequence of it, then I confess it appears to me that to deprive the criminal of the life of which he has proved himself to be unworthy—solemnly to blot him out from the fellowship of mankind and from the catalogue of the living—is the most appropriate as it is certainly the most impressive, mode in which society can attach to so great a crime the penal consequences which for the security of life it is indispensable to annex to it.[39]

Since the "security of life" requires such consequences, failure to deliver those consequences would be to abandon the commitment to that

38. Kant, *Metaphysics of Morals*, 116.

39. Mill, "Speech on Capital Punishment," 65.

security. In other words, those who would not punish the offender with death would effectively be condoning his actions.

It seems to be pushing the limits of credulity to say that unless the murderer is executed his compatriots are necessarily *collaborating* in the act. The perpetrator's act does not require either my approbation or my censure, any more than any dharma requires my evaluation and judgment, so it is not at all clear that anyone is ever complicit in the action of another based simply on whether one responds to it or not. The only way to make such a claim stick is on the basis of the assumption that someone's crime, if left unchecked, will necessarily entail further crimes, either on the part of the perpetrator himself or on the part of those who, seeing no swift repercussions to his actions, will be prompted to commit similar crimes. The account of action and its consequences offered by the Buddha calls that very assumption in to question.

Now it is true that the one who renounces participation in social policing should not expect society to come to her aid when she is beset by others' harmful actions; it would be inappropriate to demand for oneself what one has not granted to others. For the pursuer of the Dharma this is simply one of the many opportunity costs of living the holy life. From its inception, the Dharma has understood itself to stand at the periphery of society. As we saw in chapter 3, the bhikkhu was presented with any number of ways in which he was going to face a lack of social support for his efforts, and we would not have heard of Puṇṇa in chapter 6 had he called the authorities rather than submit to the harsh treatment of the Sunāparantans. The question, of course, arises concerning what one does when seeing harm inflicted on another. It is all well and good, one might argue, to adopt such a perspective for oneself and forgo the impulse to self-defense, but does all of this go so far as to say that one should stand idly by while the perpetrator has his way with someone else? Here we find a consistent response in the likes of Śāntideva and Nāgārjuna. Suppose the practitioner happens upon someone being attacked. One with awakening insight has the avenue closed to her that remains open to others: confronting the attacker out of solidarity with the victim. Śāntideva points the reader in the other direction: "When people harm one's teachers, relatives, and others dear to us, one should, as above, regard it as arising on the basis of conditioning factors and refrain from anger towards them."[40] The perpetrator is simply playing out his delusions, attachments, and aversions, which is why Nāgārjuna thought it a kind of stupidity to become angry with the perpetrator in any way.

This stance is not particular to the Madhyamaka or even the Mahāyāna generally; we find it already in the *Nikāyas* as well. In the *Kakacūpama Sutra* the Buddha chides the bhikkhu Moliya Phagguna for associating so much with bhikkhunīs to the point that, if anyone spoke ill of bhikkhunīs, Phagguna would become angry and "make a case of it." The Buddha reminded him that such attachments stand in the way of the cultivation of dispassion and equanimity:

> If anyone gives those bhikkhunīs a blow with his hand, with a clod, with a stick, or with a knife in your presence, you should abandon any desires and any thoughts based on the household life. And herein you should train thus: "My mind will be unaffected and I shall utter no evil words; I shall abide compassionate for his welfare, with a mind of loving-kindness, without inner hate." This is how you should train, Phagguna.[41]

As we saw in chapter 1, "thoughts based on the household life" are the thoughts related to the view that everything is to be evaluated in terms of gain and loss, pleasure and pain, right and wrong—the first kind of right view that the practice of the holy life took one beyond. Phagguna is showing a kind of compassion toward the bhikkhunīs in being solicitous of their welfare, but as long as he harbors resentment toward their attackers, it is more properly seen as the near enemy of compassion, as karuṇā would extend compassion toward the attackers as well.

If there is any kind of intervention to be carried out when others are set upon, it is simply that of offering oneself in the place of the perpetrator's victim. This, at least, was Nāgārjuna's recommendation:

> Also, the beings of the world are constantly tormented by the many sorts of diseases. Additionally, they are constantly pursued and spied upon by the insurgents of death which stalk them like an enemy always waiting for an opportunity to seize advantage . . . One should prefer that, before suffering falls on someone else, one would first take the injury on himself.[42]

40. Śāntideva, *Bodhicaryāvatāra*, 56.
41. Ñāṇamoli and Bodhi, *Middle Length Discourses*, 218.
42. Nāgārjuna, *Six Perfections*, 395.

Again, this is not a recommendation particular to the Mahāyāna, and the Jātaka tales are replete with stories of the Buddha's previous lives as an aspiring bodhisattva recounting how he willingly gave his life to spare others ill fortune and misery. It would run contrary to good sense to expect that kind of response out of everyday individuals, inured as they are to their defilements, but for the son or daughter of the Buddha, such a response would be a straightforward consequence of having adopted the path: "Bhikkhus, even if bandits were to sever you savagely limb by limb with a two-handled saw, he who gave rise to a mind of hate towards them would not be carrying out my teachings."[43] As the noble disciple can see what the average run of persons does not, it is only fitting that the noble disciple stand in their stead. The drive for self-defense, which Mill pointed out lies at the heart of the sentiment of justice, and which, of course, lies at the heart of the kleśa of aversion, is precisely what the practice of the pāramitā of patient forbearance undercuts and what the pāramitā of giving would here also set to the side for the welfare of all, whether perpetrator or victim.

Renouncing the job of policing the vicissitudes of social life and satisfying the everyday demands of justice that lies at the start of one's path in the Dharma and only deepens over time is not a censurable offense against the wellbeing of the social order, as Mill and others would claim. It is, rather, a standing reminder of the reality of our essential emptiness and the thoroughly conditioned nature of actions. Everyday persons, taking their cues as they do from pleasure and pain, attachment and aversion, may not understand the import of that reminder and so perceive it as a "do-nothing" response, but their lack of perspicacity about the matter is just that—a deficiency of understanding, not a sound objection. From the very first promulgation of the Dharma it has been acknowledged that the path that leads to liberation goes against the stream of everyday ways of looking at things, and it cannot have much presence in the world at all if, despite everything it teaches, it succumbs to those everyday perceptions and tries to accommodate them. There is no point trying to concoct something to do or find ways the Dharma might support something to do in cases where, as we have seen, there is ultimately nothing to be done.

43. Ñāṇamoli and Bodhi, *Middle Length Discourses*, 223.

Many other theological and philosophical system have already assumed the role of trying to render unproblematic the connection between spiritual aspiration and the imposition of justice. The promise of the Dharma lies elsewhere.

There is perhaps no better way to conclude these considerations than by offering a case from the tradition where we find the Buddha's "What can be done about it?" exemplified. For this we turn to an account of the great Zen teacher, Hakuin:

> The Zen master Hakuin was praised by his neighbors as one living a pure life.
>
> A beautiful Japanese girl whose parents owned a food store lived near him. Suddenly, without any warning, her parents discovered she was with child. This made her parents angry. She would not confess who the man was, but after much harassment at last named Hakuin.
>
> In great anger the parents went to the master. "Is that so?" was all he would say.
>
> After the child was born it was brought to Hakuin. By this time he had lost his reputation, which did not trouble him, but he took very good care of the child. He obtained milk from his neighbors and everything else the little one needed.
>
> A year later the girl-mother could stand it no longer. She told her parents the truth—that the real father of the child was a young man who worked in the fishmarket.
>
> The mother and father of the girl at once went to Hakuin to ask his forgiveness, to apologize at length, and to get the child back again.
>
> Hakuin was willing. In yielding the child, all he said was: "Is that so?"[44]

Hakuin's "Is that so?" is a skillful expression of the Buddha's "What can be done?" For one who has insight into the marks of conditioned existence, reputation, treasure, and livelihood are not things that one can be unjustly deprived of; they have already been surrendered in the uprooting of ego-attachment with insight into the truth of the Dharma. There is no perceived wrong to make right, and hence no justice that needs to be served.

According to the account it took the young mother a year to tire of her ruse, name the real father, and take back her child. It might have taken less time, sparing Hakuin further expense and ridicule. It might

44. Reps and Senzaki, *Zen Flesh, Zen Bones*, 26–27.

have taken more time, or she may never have come forward with the truth at all, and Hakuin's troubles would have simply continued. We can assume that none of those possible scenarios would have changed his response to the situation at hand in any way, for whether recompense of harm is short or long or seemingly forever in coming, *this moment* is the open field for the exercise of the Dharma and the manifestation of awakening, and it will not be made more or less so in light of the long lapse of ages, no matter how the consequences fall out.

9

All the Time in the World

In the Museum Schloss Hohentübingen in Tübingen, Germany, there is a carving of a horse that dates back some thirty thousand years or more. The "Wild Horse from Vogelherd" was carved by humans living in that area during the Middle Aurignacian Period, which ran roughly between 38,000 and 29,000 BCE. It is a beautiful piece, even though the legs have since broken off. There is an elegance to the work, a grace and flow in the neck and head. It is also quite small (4.8cm x 2.5cm x 0.7cm), bespeaking a keen facility with tools and an impressive dexterity of hand. Whatever significant differences there are between those of us who live in the twenty-first century CE and those who lived in the three-hundred-eightieth century BCE, it cannot be doubted that we are of the same stock; near as we can tell, no other species makes gratuitous art objects. When we begin to think that far back, we tend to lump millennia together as if they were days or months. "Some twenty to twenty-two thousand years ago" trips off the tongue without pausing to consider that the difference between them is roughly equivalent to the entire span of the Common Era. It is, quite frankly, incredibly hard to wrap one's mind around the kind of time in question here. Perhaps that is a good thing.

Talk of justice, social change, and social revolution is inextricably caught up with an understanding of time. Specifically, it is caught up with an understanding of time that carries with it a profound sense of urgency. "How long will it take until . . . ?" or "How much longer do we have to put up with . . . ?" are some of the questions that fuel the impetus for change and prompt the demand for swift justice. Conversely, there is a feeling that certain elements of the past should have been put to rest by now, often reflected in exclamations such as "I can't believe this is still happening in the twenty-first century!" or "I'm surprised people still think that way in this day and age!" The future cannot come soon enough; the past cannot disappear quickly enough. There is a clock ticking somewhere, so it would seem, and it is already well past the eleventh hour. Buddhadāsa Bhikkhu, in advocating for what he called *Dhammic socialism*, did not mince words on this point: "Time is running out."[1]

There is perhaps no more famous example of the tie between temporal orientation and the drive for social change than the French Republican Calendar. As part of their efforts to purge the nation of any lingering ties to the *ancien régime* and to mark the advent of the new social order, the Convention nationale instituted a new calendar, begun on the date of the establishment of the Republic and stripped of any references to mythology and religion. In one fell instant, September 22, 1792 became 1 Vendémiaire, Year I. The calendar was in use for about twelve years until it was abolished under Napoléon, only to be used again briefly by the Commune de Paris, another short-lived revolution of sorts, for a few weeks in 1871.[2] A new calendar was in order because the world had just been created anew. (For the sake of comparison, the reckoning of the Common Era was devised by Dionysius Exiguus in 525 CE as part of his calculations for determining the date of Easter each year. Dionysus set the year following Diocletian 247 as *anno domini* 525. This means that roughly a quarter of Western Christian history was recorded using the Roman imperial calendrical system. Even still, the Dionysian calendar did not gain widespread use until some time after 800 CE with the establishment of the Holy Roman Empire, by which time the Christianization of Europe was already a *fait accompli.*)

The *Républicains* who imposed their calendar wore their hubris on their sleeves. Yes, Louis Bourbon was dead, but the *Terreur* was yet to come, and the guillotine would fall many more times before it was all over. For all the revolutionaries' tirades against Roman Catholicism, the faithful continued to be faithful, the sacraments were still administered (at least secretly), and by 1801 Napoléon would be signing a concordat with Pius VII restoring the status (if not the lands) of the Catholic Church. Royalists were still present in large enough numbers to support the return of the monarchy several times off and on until 1870, and a monarchist group, *Nouvelle Action Royaliste*, maintains offices in Paris even today. Some things changed, some things did not, but the days and

1. Buddhadāsa, *Dhammic Socialism*, 115.

2. From May 6–23, 1871, or 16 Floréal–3 Prairial Year LXXIX.

months and years—however they were numbered—kept passing all the same.

Change is a fact of conditioned existence. The kind of change envisioned by social transformers is of a different order. It is the kind of change that anticipates rather quickly putting to rest certain forms of action and thought and setting new, improved, versions of the same—or completely different ones—in their stead. It is the kind of change that dreams of starting over fresh. In addition, it assumes a telos, a movement from point A to point B, with points A and B lying squarely within a conceptually graspable timeframe. Looked at more closely, it is clear that it is not simply change that social transformers have in mind, but progress; and *progress*, unlike *change*, is not a word in the lexicon of the Dharma.

It is important to recall that talk of progress requires the presumption of an historical trajectory with defined reference points as well as a neutral vantage point from which to assess the proceedings. This view as it comes to us today is in large measure a secularized version of a certain understanding of Christian salvation history in which the *felix culpa*, the "happy fault, the necessary sin of Adam" brought about the advent of the Redeemer, whose perduring Spirit continues to work to reconcile all things unto the Father. The A and Ω are clearly indicated, even if only eschatologically intuited. Hence the Christian can perhaps anticipate an end time in which every tear will be wiped away, and Rev. Dr. Martin Luther King Jr., following Theodore Parker, the Unitarian Universalist, could speak of "the long moral arc of the universe" bending towards justice.

It is not at all clear, however, that such a perspective is compatible with the Dharma. This is not a judgment that the moral arc of the universe does or does not bend towards justice; it is an observation that the essential emptiness of all dharmas precludes the invocation of *any* arc, moral or otherwise, in the first place. As all dharmas are marked by anicca, anattā, and dukkha, there is simply no fixed point of reference by which to ascertain forward progress (or backward regress) over time; any mooring that would serve to tether such a perspective has been taken away. Moreover, as saṃsāra is without discoverable beginning and nirvāṇa is without any kind of end, where could one find the terminal points by which to inscribe an arc of any kind?

The lack of an historical sensibility is not a failure on the part of the Buddha's teaching. The liberating promise of the Dharma requires no conception of historical progress, because its aim—that unshakable deliverance of mind—is not the end product of a series of causal connections that will coalesce "just-so" on a widespread scale at some future time; there is no functional equivalent of an advent of the Messiah, the establishment of a kingdom of God on earth, or even a successful social revolution to anticipate. The cessation of tṛṣṇā is possible *now*, and no configuration of past, present, or future conditions is, of itself, particularly favorable or particularly unfavorable to its realization. As Asaṅga put it:

> Sentient beings in the human realm
> Realize awakening at each and every moment
> In places beyond reckoning.[3]

Since it is ignorance of the nature of dharmas—not dharmas themselves—that gives rise to the worlds of saṃsāra, overcoming ignorance—not rearranging dharmas, producing new ones, or making others go away—brings saṃsāra's grip to an end. So we need to take a look at what the tradition and our own straightforward experience say about time, about past, present, and future points of view, and about the drive to wrap all that up in a tidy narrative that would account for the whole from start to finish. In particular, we need to explore that temporal urgency that would prompt the sheer reaction to fix the ills of the world *right away*, particularly if that reaction has some purported sense of compassion and pretense of awakening attached to it.

In the *Bhaddekaratta Sutta* the Buddha addresses the issue of temporal orientation head on:

> Let not a person revive the past
> Or on the future build his hopes;
> For the past has been left behind
> And the future has not been reached.
> Instead with insight let him see
> Each presently arisen state;
> Let him know that and be sure of it,
> Invincibly, unshakeably.[4]

3. Asaṅga, *Summary of the Great Vehicle*, 63.
4. Ñāṇamoli and Bodhi, *Middle Length Discourses*, 1039.

He then goes on to explain what reviving the past and building hopes on the future entails:

> How, bhikkhus, does one revive the past? One nurtures delight there thinking, "I had such material form in the past." One nurtures delight there thinking, "I had such feeling in the past," . . . "I had such perception in the past," . . . "I had such formations in the past," . . . "I had such consciousness in the past." That is how one revives the past.[5]

As Bhikkhu Bodhi points out, "nurtures delight" here is not simply a memory that this or that happened but rather a "relishing of past experiences with thoughts of craving."[6] To the simple recollection of a past event, tṛṣṇā is been added. Wistful hankering for the days of youth, nostalgia for past circumstances, the effort to recapture past feelings, thoughts, or sensations—all of these pull one out of direct engagement in the present moment and in so doing reinforce the conceit of a self that transcends the present moment. "I was class valedictorian" can be a simple description of a matter of fact in response to being asked, "Who was your class valedictorian?" "I was class valedictorian . . ." can, however, also reflect a longing for the good old days when one was something of a success and enjoyed the admiration of one's peers and mentors, recalled to mind as one is attending, say, a niece's high school graduation some thirty years after one's own.

Although "nurturing delight" would appear to be most closely associated with attachment to past pleasant experiences, we have seen that the currents of tṛṣṇā run in the other direction as well, namely along the lines of aversion. Keeping old grudges alive, fueling anger at past insults and hurts, and defining one's present life with reference to unpleasant circumstances long since passed are also included here. These, too, seem to have their "delight" about them, given the tenacity with which we tend to keep them in play. In fact, one might go so far as to say that we tend to define ourselves more by our past painful experiences than by past pleasant ones. I am more likely to let fade the memory of a nice enough day at the park with my family as a child, for instance, than I am to let go of rehearsing certain slights or harmful acts received from those very same people. Most days I got to work without incident, but I have no difficulty

5. Ñāṇamoli and Bodhi, *Middle Length Discourses*, 1039–40.

6. Ñāṇamoli and Bodhi, *Middle Length Discourses*, 1344n1215.

recalling (and find I am all too eager to recount) the day I totaled the car on the commute.

Hope in future states exhibits the same structure that obtains with respect to reviving past states:

> And how, bhikkhus, does one build up hope upon the future? One nurtures delight there thinking, "May I have such material form in the future!" One nurtures delight there thinking, "May I have such feeling in the future!" . . . "May I have such perception in the future!" . . . "May I have such formations in the future!" . . . "May I have such consciousness in the future!" That is how one builds up hope upon the future.[7]

One makes the present moment tolerable by making it part of a narrative that will lead to a future outcome based on present desires. I can put up with a grueling training regimen by telling myself it will lead to a speedier promotion, perhaps, or a larger paycheck down the road. The flipside to this from the perspective of aversion is a kind of catastrophic thinking—"I may have such a painful form in the future if this keeps up," or "I will die soon if nothing changes!"—and rather than simply enduring out the present as it is, I employ corrective measures to avert the supposedly impending disaster.

Many religions systems hold out the prospect of hope, and some might suggest it is precisely the bailiwick of religion to do so. The Dharma stands well outside this understanding of religion in that it is ultimately a *hopeless* teaching. Norman Fischer, in a recent essay on anger, echoes the Buddha's suggestion to abandon hope. "To hope," he writes, "usually means to reject the experience of this moment, and therefore hope can be a kind of cowardice. Rather than face what's going on right now, we focus our attention on later, when things will hopefully be much more pleasant than they are at the present moment."[8] In this respect, hope is actually another form of aversion, and Fischer is right in seeing the surrender of hope as an antidote to anger. As long as I hold out hope that the object of my dislike will change, I run the very real risk of remaining angry for quite a long time. It is only when I surrender that hope, when I settle into the matter at hand, just as it is, that anger can dissipate and the presumed "need" to nurture the hope that things will change can abate. The same would hold true for the everyday frustrations that arise in conjunction

7. Ñāṇamoli and Bodhi, *Middle Length Discourses*, 1040.

8. Fischer, "Acupressure Point of the Heart," 74.

with sentient beings and dharmas, as Nāgārjuna described above. The pāramitā of patient forbearance is nothing if not a resolute setting aside of hope in favor of opening up oneself fearlessly to present circumstances.

For those used to thinking about the present in terms of the past and future, and who might derive some comfort from thinking that the present moment is securely "tethered," so to speak, between these two poles, surrendering the past and setting aside hope is no doubt a disconcerting proposition. "How will I know where to head if I do not know where I came from?" one might ask, or "How can I orient my efforts if I don't know where to direct them?" "Will they ever pay off?" Such questions reveal that the drive to nurture delight in the past and the future stems from the fact that what is most interesting is not the past or the future purely and simply; I honestly do not care about *everything* that has, in point of fact, happened or will happen, as connected as it might be—ultimately and in principle—to the present. What I am most concerned about are things related to *me*, to *my* past and *my* future, and how all of that hangs together into a coherent whole. This, at least, is where the Buddha put the crux of the matter:

> The uninstructed worldling, who is not a seer of the noble ones and is unskilled and undisciplined in their Dhamma, who is not a seer of superior persons and is unskilled and undisciplined in their Dhamma, regards form as self or self as possessing form, or form as in self, or self as in form. That form of his changes and alters. With the change and alteration of form, his consciousness becomes preoccupied with the change of form. Agitation and a constellation of mental states born of preoccupation with the change of form remain obsessing his mind. Because his mind is obsessed, he is frightened, distressed, and anxious, and through clinging he becomes agitated.[9]

I am concerned about the past because what I had heretofore taken to be me is now different—If this is me now, what was I then? How did the I that was there get *here*? I am concerned about the future because what I take to be me now is subject to change, and I want to hold on to what I happen to value about my present state or perhaps leverage it towards a better tomorrow, a happier future, or a fulfillment of what I perceive to be my duty or my vocation. Any way I look at it, I will remain forever fretful if I try to keep my past in line with my present self-conception, or I will be forever busy—and no less fretful—should I strive to line up the

9. Bodhi, *Connected Discourses*, 865.

future in response to what I happen to either like or dislike about present conditions trying to get it all just right.

We understand well enough the trouble such questions can cause on the everyday level. I can walk just fine without thinking about how and where my feet will land even five paces hence. I start my week on Monday not knowing how Friday will turn out, let alone Tuesday. I bring a child into the world not knowing how long she will live, what talents she might develop, or how she will fare in her adult relationships or her retirement years—if she even gets that far. There is just that next step, the setting of the alarm, and the changing of the diaper. If I dwell too long (or even at all) on any of these future states, I run a good risk that I will end up botching the job that is right in front of me right now. The same holds true with respect to dwelling on past states. While everything I have ever done has contributed to bringing this present moment about in the most general of senses, I do not rely what I had for lunch on Tuesday, October 9, 2012 or what color shirt I wore on Friday, September 26, 1997 (assuming I can even remember) to pick today's meal or get dressed this morning. If I hold on too tightly to the past in these regards, I might never stop ordering from the children's menu, or I might find myself dressing like a teenager well into my sixties.

One might interject that those are trivial enough matters, and that where my foot lands on the sidewalk or whether I have a peanut butter and jelly or a portobello and aioli sandwich for lunch matters little in the big scheme of things—and that would be a fair enough observation. But as we saw with respect to samsaric formations generally, *anything* can be taken up and turned into a storyline about oneself. The issue is not whether the matter at hand is comparatively weighty or consequential; the issue is whether it gets rolled into a narrative of *me now* as opposed to *me then*, or of *me now* as opposed *to me in the future*. In both cases, the large and the small, there persists a fundamental ignorance of the truth that that I cannot be in two places at the same time. If anything, focusing on the "big picture" aspects of self—career, family, sense of calling or vocation—just makes matters worse. Just as I might trip if I am focused on the 113th footfall after the present one, I might not pass organic chemistry if I keep fantasizing about what being a physician is like, or I might not go out on a date with someone I happen to meet if I keep holding on to projections of what my future spouse and life with them will of course have to be like.

The Buddha's injunction to see each presently arisen state as it is and to become unshakeable and invincible with respect to it involves relinquishing the view that any circumstances past or future reflect or portend anything at all beyond what is currently the case:

> And how, bhikkhus, is one invincible in regard to presently arisen states? Here, bhikkhus, a well-taught noble disciple, who has regard for noble ones and is skilled and disciplined in their Dhamma, who has regard for true men and is skilled and disciplined in their Dhamma, does not regard material form as self, or self as possessed of material form, or material form as in self, or self as in material form. He does not regard feeling as self . . . perception as self . . . formations as self . . . consciousness as self, or self as possessed of consciousness, or consciousness as in self, or self as in consciousness. This is how one is invincible in regard to presently arisen states.[10]

There is invincibility, because at any time the skandhas are just as they are. Any presently arisen configuration of them does not *get* old, *turn* gray, *get* promoted, *lose* abilities, and the like. This set of skandhas simply shows signs of senescence, has this job now, or has a prosthesis from the knee down. It does not matter that prior to this there was an ensemble that manifested differently or a subsequent one that might present yet differently again in the future. At this moment, nothing in this is out of place, none of these conditions are untimely, and all of them together constitute all I happen to be right now.

Dōgen's reflections on time in the *Shōbōgenzō* fascicle, *Uji*,[11] pick up on the understanding of temporal relations in the *Nikāyas* and offer a helpful way of seeing what such invincibility with regard to present states entails. He begins with the rather common view that temporal change is a matter of focusing on "states before" and "states after":

> An ordinary man . . . thinks: "At one moment someone was an asura, at another moment he was a Buddha. This is just like crossing a river, passing a mountain. Even if the mountain and the river continue to exist, I have passed them; my place is now in this jewel palace and vermillion tower. I and the mountains-rivers are like heaven and earth to each other."[12]

10. Ñāṇamoli and Bodhi, *Middle Length Discourses*, 1040–41.

11. Translations of the title vary. "The Time-Being" or "Being-Time" are frequently found.

12. Raud, "Existential Moment," 162.

It is easy to see the birth of the personal narrative in this everyday observation. "At one moment I was a toddler; now I am an adult and being a toddler lies in the distant past," one might say, or "Five years ago I was a junior sales representative; now I am in charge of the whole team." While these statements are true enough, speaking this way has the effect of reinforcing the idea that there is an "I" that is somehow independent of all of those various conditions, one that now stands at enough remove from them that it can describe them with the benefit of distance.

The problem is that one cannot reconcile that view of the self with an understanding of action in the world. Such an "I" cannot cross a river, and such an "I" does not direct the sales team. That "I" that may well exist as an idea in thought but nowhere else. It is the commentator, not the doer. The "I" that acts in the world does not enjoy the leisure of making such commentary for it is wholly caught up in what is going on. Dōgen continues:

> Yet there is more to this principle than just such thoughts. At the mentioned moments of climbing the mountain or crossing the river, there was also an I, and there had to be the moment of the I. Whenever there is an I, the momentariness is unavoidable. If a moment is not just a sign of the transition, then the immediate present of the existential moment is there for me. *This* is the existential moment. The moment of climbing the mountain and crossing the river, the moment of palace-tower, does it not swallow them up and spit them out [simultaneously]?[13]

This "I" is not of the same stripe as the disengaged "I" that surveys the past, present, and future from a position of some remove. Rather, this is the experiential I that co-arises with the nexus of what-and-when in action. "I am drinking my coffee," "I am in rehab," "I am climbing a mountain"—these broad descriptions cover many moments that, as they occur, have an aspect of self to them that is momentary and fleeting. Each sip comes and goes, and, as it does, every thought I have or word I utter or movement I make during the course of those sips comes and goes as well. Each is "swallowed up and spit out," as Dōgen puts it, rising and falling, appearing and disappearing the whole time, never to return again. The "I" that comes and goes with each of those risings and fallings is also swallowed up and spit out, never to return again, either. If upon reflection there seems to be a certain obviousness to what happened while I was

13. Raud, "Existential Moment," 162.

drinking the coffee, I do well to remember that nothing about it was at all obvious at the time.

Still, things *do* change over time, and none of this goes so far as to deny the workings of causality. But rather than casting that change as movement of a discrete entity along a temporal line, and hence measurable in terms of progress or regress, Dōgen describes the process of change as a kind of "shifting":

> The existential moment has the quality of shifting. It shifts from what we call "today" into "tomorrow," it shifts from "today" into "yesterday," and from "yesterday" into today in turn. It shifts from "today" into "today," it shifts from "tomorrow" into "tomorrow." This is because shifting is the quality of the momentary. The moments of the past and the present do not pile on each other nor do they line up side by side.[14]

Elsewhere he illustrates this with respect to the seasons: "They are like winter and spring. You do not call winter the beginning of spring, nor summer the end of spring."[15] Although what we call winter includes things like snow and sub-freezing temperatures, winter is not made up of bits and pieces; simply getting rid of snow or forcing animals out of hibernation will not make it any less winter. When winter comes it *is* winter, and all things connected with "winter" are present. The same is true with respect to "spring." Although what we call spring includes birdsong and flower blossoms, spring is not a sum total of "things that make up spring." It just *is* spring; renting some birds and setting out some flowers in the yard in the middle of January will not make the day any more spring. Still, the day does come when we can look around and say, "It is winter," just as the day comes when we can look around and say, "It is spring."

I do not like the snow, and I do like the daffodils, but the shifting of winter into spring is not an *improvement* on winter. And while I do like the warm evenings of summer and do not much care for a whole mess of leaf litter, fall is not a *degeneration* of summer. The shifting of one temporal moment into another is not a matter of success or failure, progress or regress, but simply the rising of a *yet another* constellation of mutually conditioning dharmas. That those dharmas themselves do not admit of improvement or degeneration, gain or loss in themselves is sufficiently

14. Raud, "Existential Moment," 165.

15. Dōgen, *Moon in a Dewdrop*, 71.

enough attested to by the fact that what I see as a positive aspect in them might well be perceived otherwise. I might not like the winter's snow, but there are any number of ski enthusiasts who do, and, for them, an early spring is hardly a cause for joy. It is not that one of us is right and the other wrong as much as we are showing differences in our respective attachments and aversions; the matter at hand is still just the matter at hand. As we saw in the discussion of samsaric worlds, there is no grounds for any expectation that individuals' samsaric worlds will overlap all that much and every good ground for assuming they won't. But none of that matters much as far as shifting conditions over time goes, for, however we might value matters at hand, we find ourselves breathing the same air, getting drenched in the same rain, or trudging through the same twelve inches of snow at the very same time. There is no escaping this, and there is not much to say about it one way or the other, positive or negative, either, when all is said and done.

Both the Buddha and Dōgen took up the issue of time with reference to an individual person in relation to his or her past or future states, but the structure of their observations holds equally well *mutatis mutandis* when applied to social groups and their self-understanding. Just as the delusion of the *nos* is, at bottom, no different from the delusion of the *ego*, the vexation that arises in the individual by nurturing delight in the past and cultivating hope in the future is no different from the vexation that the same give rise to in social groups as well.

The ordinary understanding of time might prompt observations such as "Once we were in the Middle Ages; now we are Post-Moderns," or "That was before Civil Rights legislation; this is now." Whatever the past may have been, so the thought goes, we are no longer there. We have passed them. The self-congratulatory nature of such comparisons more often than not stands in inverse proportion to the degree of actual engagement in the present. It is true that property is no longer owned by nobles and administered as fiefs, and one would be hard-pressed to find a "Whites Only" drinking fountain, but that would be to focus on bits and pieces of the past and to imagine that one is beyond them simply because those particular bits and pieces are no longer to be seen. Whatever satisfaction might be found in that comparison is quickly lost when one understands that the same kleśas that gave rise to those previous formations are still every bit as operative, albeit in different form. The defilements of greed and aversion did not go away with the rise of private property for everyday persons or the elimination of Jim Crow laws.

There is nothing connected with the rising and falling of samsaric worlds that ever goes away as long as they are in play, so even though there is shifting, any given moment of social life is a condition whole and complete in itself with all the messiness all of those samsaric worlds currently operative together entail. This is why Shinran, as we saw above, understood that he could not consider himself apart from the troubled age he was living in; *mappō* was a constituent of him, and he was a constituent of *mappō*. What was true for Shinran is true for any of us as well. We are twenty-first-century kinds of persons in every respect, and every one of our actions is part of the mix that makes up the world today, as we saw with Nāgārjuna. Nothing is lacking and nothing is extraneous in this very moment—whether for good or ill—and none of us are ever out of place with respect to it, no matter what we might happen to call it or however it might stack up in comparison to other moments.

Dōgen's reflections on time are best understood in the context of a discussion of the nature of awakening. He was keen to offset what he saw as an overemphasis on awakening as a radical split between "states before" and "states after," a split that the language of "sudden enlightenment" seemed to support much too comfortably. That said, the *drive* to identify signs of the advent of awakening or to find markers by which to ascertain its presence that besets the over-eager practitioner is one that is shared by those keen for social change who look to identify signs of its proximate coming or to indicate in some small way its dawning in the present. One need only think about the eagerness with which seemingly transformative social events are often greeted—an eagerness indicated by the speed with which they sometimes get labeled "spring," as if a long winter of discontent was finally over and done with. Such eagerness tends to fade just as quickly as it arose. Prague Spring, as it turned out, did not give way to Prague Summer. It ended rather abruptly when Warsaw Pact tanks invaded Czechoslovakia some seven months after it had begun. Arab Spring had a somewhat longer duration, approximately three years by most accounts. While there are some who might say that it continues to this day, a sober accounting of the events of the early 2010s reveals mixed results in terms of liberties gained, oppression ended, and economic hardship alleviated throughout the region. A few protests, some governmental shake-ups or a change in administration, or some new legislation or policy directive do not a transformed society make, any more than a moment of clarity or some seemingly selfless act constitute awakening. Aung San Suu Kyi was considered something of a shining light by much of the progressive Buddhist community in the West—until she wasn't.

Of course, this is not just a mindset that afflicts those disposed to progressive thought, and we find no shortage of similar behavior on the part of those all too eager to find signs that things are going south. If one is convinced that society's best days are behind us, anything that does not correspond to past ways of doing things will be taken as a sure sign of calamity and doom. Gay marriage will be seen as a sign of the complete collapse of the institution of marriage, just as the emancipation of slaves or the abolition of feudalism seemed to speak to some of the decline of all that was good and holy in earlier centuries. If one takes certain Biblical accounts of the end times at face value, any earthquake or armed conflict will be viewed as a sign that the last days are indeed close at hand. Harold Camping was convinced the world would end on May 21, 2011—until it didn't.

We inevitably stand on rather uncertain ground when staking hope in any specific circumstances that seem to portend, or individuals who seem to herald, the dawn of the future, whether that future be thought of in positive or negative terms. Just as one warm day in February does not mean that spring has come any more than a crisp evening in mid-August means fall is just around the corner, some event that seems to correspond with a projection of "what things will be like" once a better or worse future has arrived does not mean that the present has in any way been done away with or that said future is on the horizon. Talk of spring and fall here can only take us so far in appreciating the unskillfulness of anticipating a future, since as long as the earth revolves around the sun there will be the next season. By contrast, when it comes to human affairs we simply do not know what will follow this present moment and what subsequent moments will bring with them. That history does not repeat itself as the seasons do does not automatically mean it is heading anywhere particular, and that fact alone may help explain the ongoing attraction of millenarianism in all its forms, both religious and secular. Faced with an utterly unknowable and uncertain future, thoughts of wrapping it all up soon—and *soon* here could mean a *week* or two or ten or a *century* or two or ten—can provide a semblance of security. Even if it means Armageddon, at least it will be an Armageddon whose certain coming I can count on.

The social optimist *and* the social pessimist, the progressive *and* the conservative, the iconoclast *and* the preservationist all suffer from the same root conceit of reading a perduring social self into ever shifting dharmas. If there seems to be a rift in social relations between "reactionary" and "revolutionary" or "liberal" and "conservative" camps, it may well be because both of them are vying over control of the one and the same temporal delusion. As we have seen many times now, the solution, according to the Dharma, is not to pick one delusion over another but to see these and *all* delusions as the delusions they are, to become dispassionate towards them, to be liberated from them. Here, curiously enough, time is on the side of the practitioner, so to speak, since, as the *Diamond Sutra* reminds us, delusions, like any other dharma, are never of terribly long duration anyway:

> As a lamp, a cataract, a star in space
> an illusion, a dewdrop, a bubble
> a dream, a cloud, a flash of lightning
> view all created things like this.[16]

Whichever delusion one is operating under, it, too, will not last long—unless it is kept going through the attachment and aversion anyone happens to take delight in maintaining towards it.

Historical moments are marked by emptiness no less than any other dharma. There is discernible shifting, of course; what was is not like what is. But it would be claiming too much to say that the past somehow abides, alongside the present, as a stable reference point from which to judge whether the shifting is positive, negative, or neutral. That point of reference is not given in dharmas themselves but only in the projections of tṛṣṇā ("We are because of what was," "We shall be thus because of what happened") on the part of a present-day agent or group of agents presuming to hold both moments in view at once. The same would hold true for future projections as well. But as long as there are mutually conditioning dharmas, there is time, and time is nothing but the ongoing mutual conditioning of dharmas. Attempts to end those dharmas, separate from them, or add to them are also dharmas, and they are also time. And although one may fancy oneself in some way separate from the nexus of what-and-when, the very exercise of fancying oneself separate is itself an

16. Pine, *Diamond Sutra*, 27.

element of what-and-when. Try as one might, one is never removed from the conditioned and conditioning stream.

All the same, *this* moment constituted by *these* dharmas together with *this* momentary configuration of the skandhas is the invincible field of practice. And while this moment may be confusing and messy—and, as ever, most assuredly unsatisfactory as long as I unequivocally bind my self-conception up with it—it is all that is going on, and anything anyone might be inclined to say about its connection to past states or projected future ones offers, ultimately, no surety with respect to it. Indeed, even invoking those states and nurturing delight in how they all might connect with one another only further muddies the waters of the present with elements that are, at bottom, rather extraneous to it.

To school us further in the emptiness of time, the Dharma would suggest that we have, as it were, all the time in the world. In Buddhist cosmology, and in the Mahāyāna in particular, expanses of time, when they are addressed at all, are cast in terms of *kalpas*. These are truly vast stretches of time:

> To provide an idea of the length of a kalpa, the *Maha Prajnaparamita Shastra* gives these examples: take a city (preferably a deserted one) several hundred square kilometers in area and fill it with mustard seeds. Then take out one seed every hundred years. When the city is empty of mustard seeds, a kalpa will still not be over. Or take a rock several hundred square kilometers in area and brush it with a silk scarf once every hundred years. When the rock is worn to dust, a kalpa will still not have ended.[17]

For those more numerically inclined, a single kalpa is reckoned in various sources as either 10^{51}, 10^{59}, or 10^{63} years.[18] To drive home the point even more forcefully, *The Diamond Sutra* speaks of "many hundreds and thousands of millions and trillions of kalpas,"[19] and according to one calculation, "a *bodhisattva's* career . . . covers about four times 3 x 1051 x 320 x 106 years or four times nine hundred sixty thousand million billion

17. Pine, *Diamond Sutra*, 255. These similes were first put down in the *Anamataggasaṃyutta Sutra*; see Bodhi, *Connected Discourses*, 654.

18. Keown, *Dictionary of Buddhism*, 135.

19. Pine, *Diamond Sutra*, 15.

billion billion billions of years."[20] This is most assuredly not a matter of physical science, but neither is it merely a matter of a hyperactive mythic imagination. Instead, it provides as fitting a temporal orientation for the practice of the Dharma as one is likely to get.

Tossing around such vast numbers is a skillful way of dislodging the mind from its attachment to past and future states of any kind. Immanuel Kant addressed the effect of such vast magnitudes on the mind in *Critique of Judgment*. He pointed out that in contemplating such immeasurables the cognitive mind finds itself beyond the limits of conceptualization, beyond the ability to assign values such as "larger" and "smaller." This is the domain of the *sublime*, to use the terminology of his day, the domain of that "*in comparison with which everything else is small*."[21] There is no phenomenon that can be described in this way, since every phenomenon is limited in cognition to what the finite understanding can grasp. Yet, he claimed, it is precisely in its incomprehensibility that the sublime attests to a power within us that is not limited to phenomena or to ourselves as discrete beings in the phenomenal world. Finding the power to be attuned to the sublime within ourselves is what, for Kant, provides the basis for elevating ourselves from perceived limitations and for "expand[ing] the soul"[22] beyond the conditioned world of sense.

When kalpas are invoked, the effect is intended to be quite the same. As recounted in the *Cūḷamālunkya Sutta*, the Buddha was once confronted by an inquisitive monk, Mālunkyāputta who demanded an answer to questions concerning, among other things, the eternality or non-eternality of the cosmos. The Buddha would not answer these questions one way or another—not because there isn't perhaps an answer one way or another, but because the answers to these questions simply do not matter for the practice of the Dharma:

> If anyone should say thus: "I will not lead the holy life under the Blessed One until the Blessed One declares to me: 'the world is eternal' . . . or 'after death a Tathāgata neither exists nor does not exist,'" that would still remain undeclared by the Tathāgata and meanwhile that person would die.
>
> Mālunkyāputta, if there is the view "the world is eternal," the holy life cannot be lived; and if there is the view "the world

20. Dayal, *Bodhisattva Doctrine*, 79; yes, the word *billion* is used four times in a row.

21. Kant, *Critique of Judgment*, 105.

22. Kant, *Critique of Judgment*, 135.

> is not eternal," the holy life cannot be lived. Whether there is the view "the world is eternal" or the view "the world is not eternal," there is birth, there is ageing, there is death, there is sorrow, lamentation, pain, grief, and despair, the destruction of which I prescribe here and now.[23]

Eternal or not eternal are not discussion points, because nothing about the practice has to do with getting somewhere or not according to an historic—or even cosmic—clock. From the point of view of practice, the universe is neither eternal nor not eternal but *immeasurable*. Just as living the holy life is not dependent upon the state of the world at any given point in time, it is also not dependent upon a particular duration of time. The Buddha is said to have practiced for countless kalpas as a bodhisattva before taking birth in this age, and the career of any other bodhisattva, as we have already seen, has traditionally been thought of in terms of such vast expanses of time. The many successive levels (*bhūmis*) of bodhisattvic attainment are the business of eons, as Asaṅga, for one, indicated concerning the marks and signs of attainment: "[s]ince [the marks and secondary signs] are attained by practicing [virtuous activities] for three [periods of] countless kalpas, there is an immeasurability of time."[24]

Here, too, time is on the side of the practitioner, so to speak, for the immeasurability of time is of a piece with the sheer vastness of karuṇā. While the spatial vastness of karuṇā takes me out of my attachments to particular beings, the immeasurability of time frees me from attachment to projected past conditions or anticipated future outcomes with regard to those beings as well. As long as I understand karuṇā as being exercised with reference to past and future states, the most I can practice is compassion's near enemy, because I am still bound up with everyday views about self and other. When I entertain the thought, "May you be like this," and compound it further by turning it into "May you be like this in the future" or "May you not be like you have been up until now," I now not only run up against the persistent chain of causality (despite my best efforts things never turn out exactly as I intend) but the shifting sands of temporality (despite my best efforts things never quite adhere to the timeframe I have set for them) as well. This is why the "I" of the Four Bodhisattvic Vows,

> All beings without number, I vow to liberate
> Endless blind passions, I vow to uproot

23. Ñāṇamoli and Bodhi, *Middle Length Discourses*, 535.

24. Asaṅga, *Bodhisattvabhūmi*, 618.

> Dharma gates beyond measure, I vow to penetrate
> The Great Way of Buddha, I vow to attain[25]

cannot be understood as referencing my everyday, conventional self. If they are taken to be such, then of course I will be keen to see their fulfillment within the context of my samsaric horizon, apply some measure to see how well that is going, and then use that to assess my progress on the path. I will tally the number of beings I've liberated, how many passions I have uprooted, and how many dharmas I have penetrated. I might fret that I have not yet liberated more, or I might congratulate myself for having liberated as many as I have. I might even look around me and see how my tally compares with that of others. Sensing that I only have so much time to work with I will soon enough become "frightened, distressed, and anxious, and through clinging . . . agitated,"[26] since the task (as I conceive it) well exceeds the resources at hand—the duration of my own present life first among them.

It is true enough that the configuration I now call *me* will dissipate, but that does not diminish the sincerity or the power of the vow, since the aim of aspiration is not the Buddhahood of my conventional self (whatever that could possibly mean) or even the liberation of such conventional others through the activity of that conventional self, but simply the unobstructed manifestation of enlightened mind among the samsaric worlds of others. As Jay Garfield points out:

> To confuse an altruistic impersonal aspiration for enlightenment for the sake of sentient beings with an aspiration for one's own enlightenment—to confuse a conviction that there is a future for the sake of which one should work with the view that it is one's own future—is a serious, though subtle form of *ātmanvāda* or even *ātmangrāha*."[27]

Just as this business I call *me* never attains nirvāṇa, this business I call *me* never liberates a being any more than it uproots a passion, or penetrates a dharma. Yet in the moment when I surrender the self, there is no being that is not liberated, no passion that is not uprooted, and no dharma that is not penetrated. This is why even Garfield's contrast of "a future for the sake of which one should work" with "one's own future" does not

25. Rochester Zen Center, *Chants & Recitations*, 36.

26. Bodhi, *Connected Discourses*, 865.

27. Garfield, "Nāgārjuna's Theory of Causality," 518. *Ātmanvāda* is the belief in a perduring soul or self; *ātmangrāha* is the grasping after that soul or self.

quite get to the heart of the matter. When it comes to the practice of the bodhisattva, there is no particular future orientation at all, for here where one with insight stands "there is no yesterday, no tomorrow, no today,"[28] in the words of the Third Chinese Ancestor of Zen, Xìnxīn Míng. The temporal field of bodhisattvic activity, like its spatial field, is thoroughly measureless because it is utterly selfless.

Surrendering the self is all that has ever been required for realization, but when that does not happen, it can seem as though time itself is the culprit, and one might find oneself looking for reasons why things have not turned out more favorably as of yet, despite one's best efforts. In Case 9 of the *Mumonkan*, for example, we read:

> Once a monk asked Master Seijo of Koyo, "Daitsu Chisho Buddha did zazen for ten kalpas in a meditation hall, and could neither manifest the Dharma nor attain Buddhahood. Why was this? Seijo said, "Your question is quite reasonable." The monk persisted, "Why did he not attain Buddhahood by doing zazen in the meditation hall?" Seijo replied, "Because he didn't attain Buddhahood."

The monk's question is reasonable from the ordinary person's perspective: why would one invest ten years—let alone ten kalpas—in a practice that showed no signs of paying off? Is there not something wrong with a practice that does not produce appreciable gains? Seijo could have tossed him a bone, saying something about gradual versus sudden enlightenment, perhaps, or that Daitsu Chisho Buddha had at least rooted out a bit of defilement or achieved a certain level of supramundane awareness, but Seijo is more astute than that. He knows that the monk's appetite for a narrative of progress will not be satisfied with a bit of historical detail or a small token of success. The tṛṣṇā that wants to see something where there is nothing to be seen can only be quelled by its own abandonment. When there is neither "Daitsu Chisho Buddha" nor "Buddhahood" as abiding formations to latch on to, what matter ten kalpas—or ten minutes? Since attainment has never been a question of getting somewhere within a certain amount of time, impatience with respect to attainment proves itself to be its own kind of insidious hindrance,[29] one that obscures

28. Rochester Zen Center, *Chants & Recitations*, 31.

29. Restlessness and remorse (*uddhacca-kukkucca*) is the name given to this particular nīvaraṇa. It grows from the fret and worry over one's conditioned states in their relationship to awakening and generates the vain search for a kind of spiritual "perfection," one that wants to get things "just right." In the *Nikāyas* it is said to reveal

the plain truth that awakened mind is always laid bare and ever present. Since the holy life is not contingent upon historical circumstances, there is no need to take stock of measurable successes and failures, as tempting as that might be.

The fearlessness of a bodhisattva consists in continuing to practice the pāramitās even in the face of seeming to get absolutely nowhere any time soon. Nicholas Bommarito has pointed out that the patient forbearance the pāramitās call for is not of the same sort one thinks of when one contrasts patience with impatience. In that case, patience means biding one's time until conditions change, like waiting for the teakettle to come to a full boil, or waiting out the game delay until the rain passes. As he notes, the patience of the pāramitā is more closely akin to the patience a parent has with a special needs child: "a person who is patient with the child is not waiting for improvement; they don't expect any improvement to come. They are patient because of how they deal with frustrations *in the moment*."[30] It involves a complete settling into the situation at hand without reservation, without the comforting dream of how things might yet turn out or when that might yet come to pass. As one settles yet further into the situation at hand, one often finds a deepening ability to respond more selflessly to that same situation and to others as well. For the bodhisattva, a future—and more to the point for our concerns here, *better*—state of affairs never needs to enter the picture. And yet practice continues.

The practice of the Dharma knows no calendars, no timetables, no history, and certainly no notion of progress to speak of, because it is rooted in the unshakable realization of the dependent coarising of empty phenomena. Dependent coarising implies many things. It means that things are inextricably bound up with one another. It means that nothing is fixed, static, or done. But it also means that everything is implicated—the good and the bad, the beautiful and the ugly—just as they are, right now. Manichaeism saw good and evil as locked in a perpetual conflict, with no absolute primacy of the good or the expectation that it will win out. The Dharma does not divide the world into a good/evil dualism. Instead,

a mind that is "too tense." Bodhi, *Connected Discourses*, 1739.

30. Bommarito, "Bile & Bodhisattvas," 271.

it simply calls for a sober recognition of the myriad ways in which the three poisons keep us asleep to our true nature as long as we live in a pre-awakened state. The sahā world is, after all is said and done, *endured*, and, as we saw, not even bodhisattvas are exempt from the present tangled mess. And since the sahā world is, for all we can possibly know, all that we have to work with, when it comes to social conditions one may well be inclined to ask the monk's "quite reasonable" question as to why things haven't gotten better yet, but in the light of the Dharma, Seijo's answer will be the one forthcoming: "Because they haven't." If one goes rushing off to create a "solution" to that "problem" in order somehow to move things along, then one will have missed the point indeed.

10

Nowhere Abiding

Dōgen observed, "To follow buddha completely means you do not have your old views. To hit the mark completely means you have no new nest in which to settle."[1] In this he was simply being a faithful student of the Dharma. In the *Suddhaṭṭhaka Sutra*, for instance, we read that

> A brahmin does not speak of purity by another,
> by the seen and the heard,
> by good behavior and observances, by the sensed.
> Untainted by merit and by evil he has discarded
> what was taken up without creating anything here.[2]

The path indicated by the Dharma is not complicated; it just means holding to nothing whatever, engaging in the work of surrendering what has been held, and having the fearlessness and presence of mind not to put anything in its place.

Over the course of the preceding chapters, I have brought the words of the Buddha and Dharma Ancestors to bear on the task of discarding what was taken up concerning some claims about the nature of social change and about the position of one pursuing the Dharma with respect to it. As this study nears its end, it would, of course, be out of keeping with that task to put something else in their place, so in this last chapter I would simply like to tease out some broader implications of the core argument as it concerns the life of practice and its relation to civic life. Setting aside all thought of using the Dharma as an instrument for social

1. Dōgen, *Moon in a Dewdrop*, 43.

2. Bodhi, *Suttanipāta*, 294.

transformation still leaves open the question as to how best to think about the exercise of the holy life in relation to public life more generally.

As mentioned at the start, it has come to be expected that religious groups and those who speak on their behalf weigh in on current events and the social concerns of the day. Watchdogs now monitor the media for statements from churches, temples, mosques, and synagogues to determine their relative degree of "tone deafness" on some social issue and to clock their comparative speed in condemning (or not) some tragic development that has just taken place. Even before some tragedy occurs, religiously affiliated think tanks, national conferences of bishops, synod presidents, and the like regularly offer their considered perspectives on broad social issues, the direction of policy and voter sentiment, and the distinctiveness of their brand of religious belonging in addressing them all. Being a "public theologian" is now a thing, but for every issue of *First Things* there is an issue of *Sojourners*, and the editorial staffs of the *National Catholic Reporter* and the *Catholic World Report* both consider themselves to be in line with Rome (or with versions of what they think Rome should be). Of course, Catholics are not alone in this, and the Anglican Communion, the United Methodist Church, and others have found themselves near the breaking point on questions of social policy. If one has ever sensed that the *public* tends to take precedence over the *theology* in such cases, one would probably not be misreading the situation; spokespersons take their places less along the lines that would separate orthodoxy from heterodoxy and more in lock step with the various social and political winds of the day across all points on the spectrum.

Although the expectation to produce social commentary is now felt by many religious bodies, its roots, it seems, are distinctively Christian. Specifically, it can be traced to the self-understanding of Christianity as a *kerygmatic* religion, one that is expressly charged with proclaiming its message to the world. While at its inception the kerygmatic content centered without gloss on the Christ and the salvation to be had through the redemption of the cross, over time that content inched into more detailed areas of human life, both personal and social. This permeation took off dramatically in the fourth century when, in the scant three score and seven years between the Edict of Milan (313 CE) and the Edict of Thessalonica (380 CE), Christianity went from being an outlaw sect whose followers were subject to torture and death to become, as formulated in the Nicene Creed, the state religion of the Roman Empire. The foundations of Christendom, the express alignment of political and religious authority, were laid, and the salvific message of the gospel was now seen as finding at least some of its fulfillment in the well-ordered Christian state.

Although a lasting and unproblematic union of civil and religious authority would remain more promise than reality, the dual and oftentimes contradictory expectation that that religion conform to social demands (in terms of it being relevant and helpful for the challenges faced by the polity) and that social life conform to the tenets of religion (in terms of being right and just and good for human flourishing or, at the very least, that it not get in the way of religious expressions of the right and the just) had taken root. Its branches are alive and well today, and this dual expectation was expressed not so very long ago by John Paul II on the occasion of his visit to Poland in 1979. He cast such an expectation as a characteristic of

> the fundamental mission of the Church, which everywhere and always strives to make people better, more conscious of their dignity, and more devoted in their lives to their family, social, professional and patriotic commitments. It is her mission to make people more confident, more courageous, conscious of their rights and duties, socially responsible, creative and useful.
>
> For this activity the Church does not desire privileges, but only and exclusively *what is essential for the accomplishment of her mission.*[3]

Although the pope was speaking as a Roman Catholic, the sentiment is not at all limited to Catholicism or even to Christianity. There are certainly echoes of it among socially-engaged Buddhists as well. As I mentioned at the start, some of the first teachers of the Dharma in the West were also engaged in capitalizing on the freedoms accorded to religion by civil law to make their own contributions to discussions of individual dignity, social justice, and overall human betterment during the heady days of the 1960s.

Modern constitutions may now codify the legal separation of church and state, but they do so, in principle at least, to safeguard public policy from being unduly skewed by sectarian leanings. But modern constitutions also guarantee the toleration of religious plurality, which means that the court of public opinion remains a wide-open forum for religious groups to use in an effort to influence society as a whole. And because

3. John Paul II, "Apostolic Journey to Poland," 4.

of the exceptionally broad freedoms accorded to religion,[4] there are few limits to the tools religious groups will make use of in pursuit of that task—from door-to-door proselytizing to dedicated radio and television stations, from renting billboards to booking concert venues and sports arenas—and few limits on what they might feel obliged to address—from scientific theories to foreign policy, from technological developments to race relations, and from vaccinations to immigration policy. While one may certainly be *at liberty* to engage in these ways, the question is whether entering the court of public opinion under the banner of freedom of expression or free exercise can be considered a *skillful* one for those who have set themselves to realizing the Dharma.

Recall that when the Buddha sent forth his disciples, he did so with the exhortation to "teach the Dhamma that is lovely in its beginning, lovely in its middle, and lovely in its ending, both in the letter and in the spirit, and display the holy life fully complete and perfect."[5] Though they were to teach, they were only to do so when asked and when conditions were appropriate. Primarily this had to do with the mind states of those whom they were about to instruct. The disciples were certainly not to hold forth in public to indifferent passersby, as we saw above in the case of the "dolt" bhikkhu, Kassapagotta, and even when someone did ask for the teaching, that person was to display a comportment and frame of mind that was respectful by prevailing social standards. At any other time, maintaining a noble silence was the order of the day.

But even when the disciples did teach the Dharma to parties asking in good faith, there was a limit to the range of topics to be addressed.[6] Disciples were not to speak on matters of practice beyond their respective levels of attainment, nor were they simply to repeat verbatim what they had heard. This shielded a bhikkhu from any form of vainglory or pride, and it served to strengthen the hearer's confidence that what was being said was not mere bluster or the stuff of deception. Moreover, the disciples were not to prognosticate on things to come, nor were they to insinuate themselves in the domestic affairs of everyday people lest they cause scandal. Above all, whether speaking to others or even among

4. There is such concern to avoid even the slightest appearance of establishmentarianism that just about any group that simply identifies itself as religious is automatically shielded from social scrutiny in ways that groups that do not style themselves that way are not.

5. Walshe, *Long Discourses*, 217.

6. Ariyesako, *Bhikkhus' Rules*, 106–17.

themselves, no one was well-served by the disciples engaging in what the Buddha called "pointless talk":

> On one occasion the Blessed One was dwelling at Sāvatthī in Jeta's Grove, Anāthapiṇḍika's Park. Now on that occasion, after their meal, on returning from their alms round, a number of bhikkhus had assembled in the assembly hall and were sitting together engaging in various kinds of pointless talk, that is: talk about kings, thieves, and ministers of state; talk about armies, perils, and wars; talk about food, drink, garments, and beds; talk about garlands and scents, talk about relatives, vehicles, villages, towns, cities, and countries; talk about women and talk about heroes, street talk and talk by the well; talk about the departed; miscellaneous talk, speculation about the world and the sea; talk about becoming this or that.

If the list seems rather exhaustive, it is because it is meant to be. From politics to potatoes, from munitions to mothers-in-law, and from the latest theories about the universe to the newest goods at the market, almost every possible subject is implicated here—and *none* of it, the Buddha told those assembled bhikkhus, was at all fitting for their station: "Bhikkhus, it is not suitable for you, clansmen who have gone forth from the household life into homelessness out of faith, to engage in various kinds of pointless talk, that is: talk about kings, thieves, and ministers of state . . . talk about becoming this or that."[7]

It is not difficult to see why any and all of these topics should merit the designation, *pointless*. Everything on the list is both utterly changeable in its particulars (as conditioned dharmas) while being utterly timeless in its form (as yet more manifestations of saṃsāric world formations). At any given moment, the subject matter of such pointless talk is just a snapshot of conditions created by the large-scale interplay of attachment, aversion, and ignorance, a snapshot that will be undone just as surely as it has come to pass. Taking such ephemera seriously enough even to weigh in on them endows them with a gravity and significance far beyond their measure. Still, none of that stops most folks from ardently consuming and producing such talk all the same. From one generation to another, there is always gossip about the neighbor's teenager. Whether it is hot or cold, sunny or snowy, there is always some commentary about the weather. No matter who is in public office or a position of authority, there is always a take on the decisions of the day or the quality of the

7. Bodhi, *Numerical Discourses*, 1424.

decision-maker, swiftly countered by someone else offering an opposing viewpoint. Modern technology, from the printing press to the internet, may have facilitated and exacerbated this phenomenon, but it certainly did not create it. The drive to engage in pointless talk is as old as the hills, and it is that *drive*, much more so than the particular evanescent *content* itself, that indicates why it is particularly unfitting for a son or daughter of the Buddha to engage in any of it.

In the cosmological folklore that came to be associated with the Dharma there are said to be beings in the realms of samsaric existence that suffer from an insatiable hunger or greed. Known as *pretas*, or hungry ghosts, they are often depicted with distended, but empty, bellies and necks so thin they are incapable of passing food. Their biggest problem, however, is not their anatomy but their menu choices:

> The main features of *preta*-s [*sic*] are linked to the food they consume or inhale, that is to say one of the fundamental features distinguishing their condition. In fact, the meaning of their names is often directly related to the specific "food" that allows them to subsist. Some of these creatures wander the human world or deserted areas with the specific aim of finding that food, usually to no avail. In most cases the kind of "food" these beings covet is particularly revolting. The "Vomit-eaters" (*shitu* 食吐), Panduopocha 槃多婆叉, and the "Excrement-eaters" (*shifen* 食糞), Pishituo 毘師哋, as their names suggest, search for these repulsive substances. Likewise, the "Spittle-eaters" (*shituo* 食唾), Qizha 哈吒, desperately roam the world seeking this kind of human secretion on the ground or on walls.[8]

This graphic—and rather pointedly scatological—portrayal of the pretas only underscores the direness of their plight: they are hell-bent on consuming the waste products of sentient beings. Not believing that they could be satisfied with anything else, yet oblivious to the fact that what their tastebuds crave their bodies have no use for, their ignorance and greed keep them from finding any satisfaction or tranquility. On and on they go, endlessly consuming the detritus that comes their way, persisting in their suffering.

From this perspective, the drive to engage in pointless talk can be viewed as the distinguishing characteristic of yet another kind of hungry ghost, one that feels the need to feed on and produce—in language wholly appropriate to the matter at hand—*bullshit*. In *On Bullshit*, the

8. Moretti, "Thirty-Six Categories of 'Hungry Ghosts,'" 49–50.

philosopher Harry G. Frankfurt hits upon a feature of such speech that is pertinent for our concerns here:

> Bullshit is unavoidable whenever circumstances require someone to talk without knowing what he is talking about. Thus the production of bullshit is stimulated whenever a person's obligations or opportunities to speak about some topic exceed his knowledge of the facts that are relevant to the topic. This discrepancy is common in public life, where people are frequently impelled—whether by their own propensities or by the demands of others—to speak extensively about matters of which they are to some degree ignorant. Closely related instances arise from the widespread conviction that it is the responsibility of a citizen in a democracy to have opinions about everything, or at least everything that pertains to the conduct of his country's affairs.[9]

The odd thing about bullshit, following Frankfurt's observation, is not that the bullshitter is necessarily lying, being disingenuous, or even unwittingly making a mistake as much as he or she is speaking with a *presumed responsibility* for coming up with something to say. That presumption may be based on the demands of others or have its source in one's own sense of self-importance, but, no matter the source, it remains that bullshitting is always a matter of wanton *editorializing* much more so than *reporting*. It is not engaged in to add materially to anyone's knowledge of the situation as much as to put one's stamp and spin on it. Even if the speaker's grasp of the facts remains somewhat fuzzy and incomplete, there will certainly be no doubt where he or she stands on the matter, for the three words that never seem to escape the bullshitter's mouth are *I don't know*.

One might excuse such behavior in everyday persons, even religious ones, as just so much stuff and nonsense, but for one who would take up the Dharma, the drive to engage in such talk is not simply pointless but downright inimical to the pursuit of the path. In the commentarial literature pointless talk is identified as one of the conditions that gives rise to the nīvaraṇa of doubt. The doubt it engenders is not of the skeptical kind, where one despairs of the truth of anything at all, but of the wavering kind, where one stands stock-still at a crossroads, wanting to go in both directions at once but not having confidence enough to commit to the one road and abandon the other. Engaging in pointless talk is one way for an aspirant to try to keep one foot in the stickiness of saṃsāra while at the

9. Frankfurt, *On Bullshit*, 63–64.

same time claiming to be progressing on the path that brings samsaric worlds to an end. It reveals a kind of hesitation with respect to the idea that the way of renunciation and seclusion is, indeed, the way to the end of dukkha—hedging one's bets, as it were, that should the Dharma fail, one will at least have one's everyday way of doing things to fall back on. When that fails to satisfy, as fail to satisfy it will, at least one will have the consolation of experiencing a very familiar kind of hunger.

The nīvaraṇas are all of them marked by a kind of fear, and the doubt that engaging in pointless talk manifests would be, to borrow a contemporary turn of phrase, the fear of missing out. Once one has constructed an identity on the basis of one's opinions regarding changing conditions, one will be driven to grab hold of each one that comes along, since the ability to maintain such an identity is only as good as one's familiarity, however tenuous, with the changing particulars of the domain in question. Of course, the fact is that one is *always* missing out. There are simply not enough hours in a day to keep up with everything going on in one's family or neighborhood, let alone regionally, nationally, or globally. If I read *The New York Times* in its entirety every day, check back the next day for errata or retractions, read that day's news, and then repeat, even for the span of one week, I will be filled with more details than I can possibly make use of, and I would *still* not have learned, perhaps, of recent legislative maneuverings in Costa Rica, the third quarter prospects for the Tunisian economy, or the new parking restrictions in downtown Pocatello, Idaho. And that is just the news. There are not enough hours in a day to listen to all the new music in every genre and style, to read the latest novels or collections of short stories and poetry, to keep track of every athletic competition and know the stats of all the best players in every sport, or keep pace with the breaking designs on the fashion runways of the world.

The Buddha's exhortation to abandon pointless talk, then, stems from recognizing the drive to engage in it for what it is: so many attempts to fashion the contours of a presumptive selfhood, a way of maintaining a public face bought in the coin of remaining inured to one's fundamental ignorance. It is not fitting for one who set out on the path because it fails to appreciate what the setting out was about to begin with—the end of following such fruitless paths in favor of the one that leads to succor and release.

If being a hindrance to one's own spiritual development were not trouble enough, the things listed as pointless talk are so many ongoing occasions for fomenting dissension as well. As each is weighed in on, individual likes, dislikes, and preferences of one kind or another, inevitably come to the fore. Whether it be a preferred political candidate or Mexican restaurant, a favorite movie or brand of toothpaste, a more attractive wallpaper or a more absorbent paper towel matters little; each is as good an option as any not only for staking out the parameters of an identity but also, in the process, for creating at the same time a handy rubric for differentiating those persons *more like me* from those *less like me*. John Woolman, the American Quaker, issued the invitation to "look upon our treasures, the furniture of our houses, and our garments, and try whether the seeds of war have nourishment in these our possessions."[10] The Dharma goes even further and invites one to look upon one's everyday speech and try whether that, too, has the seeds of dissension within it. And, of course, it does—in just about every last one of its manifestations.

Even the seemingly *right* ones. One may well be ready to grant the vacuity of the neighborhood yenta's idle gossip or the triviality of most social media posts but still make exception for whatever one thinks *must* be weighed in on, those things that seem so important that the word simply *has to* get out. Social activists, moral reformers, and religious zealots of every stripe share at least this much in common: they assume that if people only knew what they knew, then they, too, would be as eager to see it as they do.[11] Therefore, they simply *must* be told about it. Consciousness- or awareness-raising campaigns, political rallies and demonstrations and tent revivals, yard signs, billboards, bumper stickers, coded ribbons, and slogan-emblazoned T-shirts, socks, and hats are all so many attempts to elbow one's message into the public arena and to stand out among the crowd. Success here becomes measured by crowd size, the number of social media followers, the number of posts liked or retweeted, or the amount of coded consumer products sold. And because the field is already oversaturated, the more flashy or provocative the presentation of the message, the better the chances of it being noticed. Rhetoric is ratcheted up to incendiary levels, and graphic displays become ever more

10. Woolman, *Journal*, 241.

11. The frequently seen bumper sticker, "If you're not angry, you're not paying attention," is most assuredly an abridgement of the root sentiment, "If you're not angry *like I am*, you're not paying attention." I affix it to *my* car, not anyone else's, precisely to indicate exactly where I stand on the matter and to differentiate myself from any and all who do not share my feelings on the matter. My position is, to my mind, so incontrovertible, that if you don't agree, there clearly must be some deficiency about you, and my bumper sticker is there to tell you so.

disturbing. Hyperbole sets in. One simply cannot do enough to rally the troops behind the cause, and if people get ticked off, so the thought goes, one must be doing something right. Making people uncomfortable is certainly one sure way to be sure they remember the message.

There is a long tradition in the West that honors the gadfly, the reformer, the social critic, and, more recently, the activist. Introductory philosophy students are often presented with the example of Socrates's defense before the Athenian jury as an exercise of reason over blind adherence to received opinions. Despite questions of historical accuracy, Martin Luther's "Here I stand, I can do no other" before the Diet of Worms is commemorated as a milestone on the long road to the establishment of individual liberties and an affirmation of personal conscience in the face of all comers. The account of the Berrigan brothers and the Catonsville Nine burning draft cards while reciting the Lord's Prayer continues to be retold as a particularly fitting example of religiously motivated direct action. We hear about them, not because they were necessarily correct or particularly effective, but because of the response they provoked in their respective audiences. We remember the proper names well after the points they were trying to make have long since passed into obscurity.

None of this goes so far as to claim that one should only say agreeable things and never disagreeable ones; insisting on rendering speech as milquetoast as possible is just as misguided as the drive to engage in the most impertinent and shocking speech and action. As we saw in conjunction with the discussion of samsaric worlds, there is no basis for any expectation that everyone will agree with me, and there is every expectation, given some of the many samsaric worlds in play, that someone is quite likely to disagree with me. Agreeableness and disagreeableness are insufficient benchmarks for assessing the skillfulness of speech and action. In the *Abhayarājakumāra Sutra*, for instance, we read that the Nigaṇṭha Nātaputta, head of a rival sect, wanted to see whether the Buddha would use speech that is unwelcome and disagreeable to others. Hoping to catch the Buddha in a contradiction, he pressed Prince Abhaya, a son of King Bimbisāra of Magadha, into going to the Buddha to test him on the issue. The Nigaṇṭha Nātaputta told him that he should ask the Buddha, "Venerable sir, would the Tathāgata utter speech that would be unwelcome and disagreeable to others?" If the Buddha said yes, the Nigaṇṭha Nātaputta continued, then he should be asked why he is then at all different from an ordinary person who would do just the same. If the Buddha said no, then he should be asked why he said of Devadatta, one of his disciples, that he was destined for hell where he would remain for an eon, since such speech was clearly unwelcome and disagreeable to him.[12] So off Abhaya goes, puts his question to the Buddha, and the Buddha deftly responds, "There is no one-sided answer to that, prince."[13]

There are, he continued, three kinds of speech along with their opposites: true, beneficial, and agreeable speech, and untrue, unbeneficial, and disagreeable speech. Untrue or incorrect speech the Buddha would not utter, for all the obvious reasons, but even if the speech were true or correct, the Buddha would not utter it if it was at all unbeneficial. As for speech that is true, correct, and beneficial, the Buddha continued, "the Tathāgata knows the time to use such speech,"[14] both in cases where it makes the hearer uncomfortable and in cases where it does not. The paradigmatic case here, of course, is that of the teacher-student relationship, in which the teacher can custom fit the praise or admonition to the situation and the individual student's state of mind. The teacher is free to say yes or no, even though the student may not necessarily be pleased with what he or she hears. A related situation would be that of a more senior member of the assembly toward a more junior one.

Agreeableness or disagreeableness aside, under no circumstances would it be appropriate to trumpet broadsides or endorsements indiscriminately into the public arena, which is exactly what the gadfly, the reformer, the critic, and the activist do. Doing so reinforces the idea that one's view is the only right one, and that it is simply the job of others to receive the message. Those who would characterize their own or others' activity as "speaking truth to power" have already staked out who has the truth and who does not. Far from anything that could be of service to the

12. Devadatta had, on the basis of his limited attainment, thought he, not the Buddha, should lead the Saṅgha. The Buddha, of course, declined Devadatta's offer, but that did not stop the aspiring schismatic. He enlisted the assistance of Prince Ajātasattu, heir to King Bimbisāra, a supporter of the Saṅgha, encouraging the prince to kill his father and send mercenaries to kill the Buddha. When the mercenaries failed, Devadatta tried to kill the Buddha himself. When that plan failed, he fomented schism in the Saṅgha, but that strategy, too, eventually failed. Devadatta became something of a case study for other bhikkhus to reflect on: "Because he was overcome and obsessed by gain . . . by loss . . . by fame . . . by disrepute . . . by honor . . . by lack of honor . . . by evil desires . . . by bad friendship, Devadatta is bound for the plane of misery, bound for hell, and he will remain there for an eon, unredeemable." Bodhi, *Numerical Discourses*, 1118.

13. Ñāṇamoli and Bodhi, *Middle Length Discourses*, 501.

14. Ñāṇamoli and Bodhi, *Middle Length Discourses*, 500.

world, such speech simply further entangles one in the sticky threads of saṃsāra:

> Settling [on his own] as supreme among views,
> whatever a person esteems as best in the world,
> [in comparison] he says all others are "inferior":
> therefore he has not transcended disputes . . .
>
> The skilled speak of that as a knot
> when one is attached and regards others as inferior.
> Therefore a bhikkhu should not be attached to the seen,
> to the heard or sensed, or to good behavior and observances.[15]

One may be speaking the truth all right, but it is hardly liberating—not for oneself, since it further binds one to views, and certainly not for others who now have to deal with the fallout of the speaker's attachments.

The Dharma offers a different model, one that has no room, let alone praise, for the gadfly or the reformer, the critic or the activist:

> Having abandoned what is taken up, not clinging,
> one does not create a dependency even on knowledge.
> Not taking sides among those who are divided,
> one does not fall back on any view at all . . .
>
> How could anyone here in the world categorize him,
> that brahmin who does not cling to any view?[16]

The practitioner of the Dharma who does not engage in social or political commentary is unavailable either as an ally in a partisan fight or as a lobbyist for change, but this is precisely what makes her preeminently positioned to be a fierce friend to all. Because she has no skin in the game one way or the other, she is above categorization as a representative of this or that faction or point of view. Others may well *assume* she is advocating for a particular position (as people often do); she, however, is not trying to *make them* take sides based on what she says and does.

Keeping silent with respect to pointless talk does not at all remove the aspirant from engagement with others, though it might seem to do so to someone for whom the myriad worlds of saṃsāra are the only fields of engagement available. It simply changes the *terms* of that engagement. There are a handful of things to discuss that neither hinder one's own

15. Bodhi, *Suttanipāta*, 295–96.

16. Bodhi, *Suttanipāta*, 296.

development nor create stumbling blocks for some one group as opposed to another—things that are completely in keeping with both the teaching and the practice:

> There are, bhikkhus, these ten topics of discussion. What ten? Talk on fewness of desires, on contentment, on solitude, on not being bound up with others, on arousing energy, on virtuous behavior, on concentration, on wisdom, on liberation, on knowledge and vision of liberation. These are the ten topics of discussion.[17]

These are topics of discussion because they fall in line with the kinds of things the Dharma has only ever been about. They lead to dispassion, detachment, dismantling, fewness of desires, contentment, solitude, the arousing of energy, and being easy to support—precisely those marks one by which one can see "this is the Dhamma; this is the discipline; this is the teaching of the Teacher."[18] They are also not dependent on changing conditions, since they are fitting responses to *any* situation. No matter what comes up or when, the task at hand is to set it to the side. No matter whether the stock market rises or falls, I will develop dispassion towards it. No matter if there is scandal in the halls of government or not, it is up to me to rouse energy and vigor in my practice.

All the same, even these topics of discussion are not matters for general dissemination, either, for even as they may be correct and beneficial, they may not be timely or fitting to the hearer. They are topics that are best addressed in the intimacy of the teacher-student relationship, where a student who is eager and intent on eliminating the defilements and cultivating of the factors of awakening is also ready to learn from one who has gone further along the path and who knows not to burden the student with more than can presently be dealt with. They are topics to be taken up among fellow practitioners as well, but only on the condition that those who weigh in on them are accomplished in the practice and know whereof they speak:

> Here, a bhikkhu is himself of few desires and speaks to the bhikkhus on fewness of desires. This is a ground for praise: "The bhikkhu is himself of few desires and speaks to the bhikkhus on fewness of desires." . . .

17. Bodhi, *Numerical Discourses*, 1424.
18. Bodhi, *Numerical Discourses*, 1193.

> He is himself accomplished in the knowledge and vision of liberation and speaks to the bhikkhus on accomplishment in the knowledge and vision of liberation. This is a ground for praise: "The bhikkhu is himself accomplished in the knowledge and vision of liberation and speaks to the bhikkhus on accomplishment in the knowledge of vision and liberation."[19]

And even though the path of renunciation and solitude is integral to the pursuit of the Dharma, it, too, has to be tempered in accordance with an individual's constitution and frame of mind:

> As *kusa*-grass, wrongly grasped,
> Only cuts one's hand,
> So the ascetic life, wrongly taken up,
> Drags one down to hell.[20]

A teacher or advanced practitioner simply cannot be too reticent and careful, even when it comes to non-pointless, noble speech.

While speaking of the Dharma is contingent upon occasion and hearer and possible benefit, the other half of the Buddha's charge—displaying the holy life fully complete and perfect—is not. The story is told that when the young Siddhārtha went out one night from his comfortable surroundings, he encountered a sick person, an old person, a corpse being carried to the charnel grounds, and a śramaṇa very much at peace. From the first three, so it is said, he caught his first glimpses of dukkha; from the last, his first glimpse of the path to its end. That śramaṇa, forever anonymous, was simply and silently going about his business. He was *just* a renunciant in the same way the sick person was *just* a sick person, the old person *just* an old person, and the corpse *just* a corpse. And no more so than the sick person, the old person, or the corpse could that śramaṇa know that on that evening his mere presence in someone's field of vision would be the spark that would ignite a spiritual quest such as the world had never seen before.

If the Dharma leans in the direction of moral exemplarism more so than toward public moralizing, it is only with the understanding that it is a moral exemplarism that is not at all based on *trying* to be a

19. Bodhi, *Numerical Discourses*, 1425–26.

20. Bodhi, *Connected Discourses*, 143.

moral example. Here we need not rely on the hagiographical account of Siddhārtha's going forth as our only guide. We saw aspects of this already in the discussion of bodhisattvic compassion in chapters 4 and 5, where non-deliberative, non-telic compassion was addressed, and we saw it again in the exercise of patient forbearance in chapters 6 and 7. In the *Sallekha Sutra*, the Buddha was even more direct in addressing the nature of this kind of selfless exemplarism. The sutra opens with the venerable Mahā Cunda asking the Buddha about the matter of relinquishing views concerning self and the world. For the advanced practitioner this comes rather spontaneously with the dawn of awakening, but Cunda is curious about how this works in the case of one who is just at the beginning stages of practice.[21] At the start of one's practice one will still be gripped by views and by the identification of self with one's samsaric worlds. What kind of connection could there be between such a benighted state and the light of awakening?

The Buddha points out that the connection is to be found in the basic disposition to renunciation and abandonment, which is the same for the novice no less than for the adept:

> As to those various views that arise in the world associated either with doctrines of a self or with doctrines about the world: If [the object] in relation to which those views arise, which they underlie, and which they are exercised upon is seen as it actually is with proper wisdom thus: "This is not mine, this I am not, this is not my self," then the abandoning and relinquishing of those views comes about."[22]

One at the early stages of practice will have to make a conscious effort to remember what is known directly and intuitively by the developed practitioner—that none of this, whatever it is, has anything to do with *me*. Each has the same job to do, and so distinctions such as *advanced* and *novice* here ultimately mark out no appreciable difference.

The Buddha then goes through the stages of contemplative development from the attainment of the first jhāna through to the end to demonstrate just how this is the case. (It can be assumed that the preliminary training stages of conforming to the precepts and training rules,

21. Ñāṇamoli and Bodhi, *Middle Length Discourses*, 123. Bhikkhu Bodhi points out Cunda was asking "because some meditators were overestimating their achievement, thinking they had abandoned such views, while they had not really eradicated them." Ñāṇamoli and Bodhi, *Middle Length Discourses*, 1182n103.

22. Ñāṇamoli and Bodhi, *Middle Length Discourses*, 123.

moderation in bodily sustenance, mindfulness, and the rest have already been established.) With the attainment of the first jhāna and its attendant sustained thought, rapture and pleasure born of seclusion, one might think one has achieved effacement, but the Buddha says such states are called "pleasant abidings here and now";[23] they are not yet effacement, as one is still gripped by views about them. The same is true for any of the other samādhi states achieved with the second through the fourth jhānas. As for the states attained with the supramundane awarenesses—the awareness of the infinity of space and the infinity of consciousness, the base of nothingness, and the base of neither-perception-nor-non-perception—the practitioner would also be mistaken in thinking that these somehow reflect effacement. They are not effacement, the Buddha points out, but "peaceful abidings."[24] The point is clear: no matter how far one has progressed in one's meditative practice, one has not yet come to effacement, the definitive extirpation of the conceit of the self. There is yet another step to be taken.

Language concerning the nature of effacement, or nirvāṇa, is relatively scarce in the canon. It is pointed to, but it is not described, and certainly not in terms that might satisfy those looking for an account of some fantastic mystical experience. So here, where the Buddha is called upon to address it, he makes what might well come across as a surprising move. The focus is turned from the supramundane states of mind to a most straightforward and unvarnished presentation of the practice of the holy life, presented in forty-four different examples of effacement, of which only a few can be listed here:

> Now, Cunda, here effacement should be practiced by you:
>
> "Others will be cruel; we shall not be cruel here": effacement should be practiced thus.
>
> "Others will kill living beings; we shall abstain from killing living beings here": effacement should be practiced thus.
>
> "Others will take what is not given; we shall abstain from taking what is not given here": effacement should be practiced thus . . .
>
> "Others will be shameless; we shall be shameful here": effacement should be practiced thus.
>
> "Others will have no fear of wrongdoing; we shall be afraid of wrongdoing here": effacement should be practiced thus . . .

23. Ñāṇamoli and Bodhi, *Middle Length Discourses*, 123.

24. Ñāṇamoli and Bodhi, *Middle Length Discourses*, 124–25.

> "Others will lack wisdom; we shall possess wisdom here": effacement should be practiced thus.
>
> "Others will adhere to their own views, hold on to them tenaciously, and relinquish them with difficulty; we shall not adhere to our own views or hold on to them tenaciously, but shall relinquish them easily": effacement should be practiced thus.[25]

The content is in large measure simply a compendium of the main aspects of practice—the courses of wholesome action, the factors of the eightfold path, the five hindrances, the sixteen imperfections, the factors of enlightenment, and the like. What is instructive for our concerns is the structure of their presentation: others may do what they will; we (each individual in his or her turn) shall do thus and so.

It is one very important aspect of practice not to engage in unwholesome and unskillful actions oneself. The very first steps of the training sequence involved the aspirant submitting to the precepts or the monastic rules, and subsequent steps were aimed at uprooting the attachment and aversion that gives rise to all possible unskillful actions and states of mind. But effacement, the definitive overcoming of all ego conceit, is particularly manifested in an utter lack of preoccupation with whether others engage in such actions and practices or not. I am not others. Their behavior is not me. None of that is my self. Even Cunda's original question about the situation of beginners is implicated here, however subtly, for it reveals a concern about the actions and attainments of others that belies an ongoing attachment to views on which to base the comparison.[26] In fact, at the end of the sutra the Buddha tells Cunda:

> What should be done for his disciples out of compassion by a teacher who seeks their welfare and has compassion for them, that I have done for you, Cunda. There are these roots of trees, these empty huts. Meditate, Cunda, do not delay or else you will regret it later. This is our instruction to you.[27]

"Just live the holy life yourself, Cunda," the Buddha might have said, "and that is enough."

25. Ñāṇamoli and Bodhi, *Middle Length Discourses*, 125–27.

26. According to tradition, Cunda was a brother of Śāriputra, one of the Buddha's foremost disciples. Śāriputra is often portrayed in Mahāyāna texts as having a hard time grasping non-duality, and it would seem here that Cunda shares his brother's difficulty.

27. Ñāṇamoli and Bodhi, *Middle Length Discourses*, 131.

On another occasion the Buddha used concern with the practice of others as a way to distinguish an untrue person (*asappurisadhamma*) from a true person (*sappurisadhamma*). In the *Sappurisa Sutra* he lists all of the various stages in the gradual training from homeleaving to the attainment of the supramundane levels of insight, along with whatever special ascetic practices one might engage in and whatever material gains (renown, food and clothing, and the like) might follow from them. With the attainment of any of them, he points out, the untrue person will entertain the following thought: "I have attained (or received) thus and so, but these other bhikkhus have not." In this way that person praises himself or herself and disparages others.[28]

The true person, however, does not engage in such comparative exercises. The true person knows that, as far as the mundane attainments go, it is simply a matter of "putting the practice of the way first,"[29] and letting things take their course. There is no *status* to be gained by following the precepts and the training rules. Not taking what is not given, for instance, does not turn me into a saint, and developing dispassion and equanimity does not make me a spiritual hero. These are just what happens in conjunction with wholehearted engagement in practice.[30] As far as the meditative states go, such a true person knows that it is a matter of "putting non-identification first," as the Buddha described it, because however one happens to think or feel about these states in terms of attainment and the like, "the fact is ever other than that."[31] In other words, even advanced meditative states are themselves still conditioned dharmas that do not speak to the true nature of things. As long as I am noting and assessing my meditative accomplishments, no matter how lofty or supramundane, there is still a trace of the self—enough of a self to have an arm with which to pat oneself on the back. In the very end, the Buddha continues, the aspirant whose attachments to dharmas have been thoroughly destroyed with insight "does not conceive anything, he does

28. Ñāṇamoli and Bodhi, *Middle Length Discourses*, 909. In the Mahāyāna, not praising oneself and disparaging others is the seventh of the ten Bodhisattva Precepts. Closely related is the sixth, not speaking of the faults of others.

29. Ñāṇamoli and Bodhi, *Middle Length Discourses*, 909.

30. Recall that the Buddha pointed out that anyone who would praise him for being morally upright was only focusing on "inferior matters." Walshe, *Long Discourses*, 68–73.

31. Ñāṇamoli and Bodhi, *Middle Length Discourses*, 911.

not conceive in regard to anything, he does not conceive in any way."[32] No thought of attainment or non-attainment, no conception of better and worse even enters his mind, and certainly no comparison of his own attainment with the attainment or non-attainment of others.

We find all of this handily summarized in yet another exchange, this time between the Buddha and two disciples, Khema and Sumana. Khema spoke first:

> Bhante, when a bhikkhu is an arahant, one whose taints are destroyed, who has lived the spiritual life, done what had to be done, laid down the burden, reached his own goal, utterly destroyed the fetters of existence, one completely liberated through final knowledge, it does not occur to him: "There is someone better than me," or "There is someone equal to me," or "There is someone inferior to me."

The Buddha agreed, and Khema took his leave. Then Sumana approached the Buddha:

> Bhante, when a bhikkhu is an arahant, one whose taints are destroyed, . . . one completely liberated through final knowledge, it does not occur to him: "There is no one better than me," or "There is no one equal to me," or "There is no one inferior to me.

The Buddha agreed with Sumana as well, and after Sumana too had left he said to the other bhikkhus present, "Bhikkhus, it is in such a way that clansmen declare final knowledge. They state the meaning but don't bring themselves into the picture."[33] There is the holy life. There is awakening. There is no need to speak of *who* lives the holy life and *who* does not, nor need one mention *who* has attained its end and *who* has not, whether that *who* be myself or another.

There is simply no quarter here for that subtle (and frequently not-so-subtle) hubris that has a way of sneaking into spiritual practice. Following these examples from the sutras, we can see that it is, indeed, hubris that would lead one to think one has attained something, take cognizance of the fact that others have not, and then use that differentiation as a pretext for drawing attention to their lack of attainment by making quite sure they know about mine. Whether it be in relation to everyday matters or to the finer points of the Dharma, it is enough to know for oneself; one need not be known as "one who knows" on top of it:

32. Ñāṇamoli and Bodhi, *Middle Length Discourses*, 912.

33. Bodhi, *Numerical Discourses*, 921–22.

> When it was said: "This Dhamma is for one with few desires, not for one with strong desires," with reference to what was this said? Here, when a bhikkhu is one with few desires, he does not desire: "Let people know me to be one with few desires." When he is content, he does not desire: "Let people know me to be one who is content." When he resorts to solitude, he does not desire: "Let people know me to be one who resorts to solitude.[34]

We can go much further with this line of thinking. It is enough not to be antisemitic; I do not need to be known as "one who is not antisemitic." It is enough not to be homophobic; I do not need to be known as "one who is not homophobic." I may value the dignity of all and appreciate the countless ways in which that dignity has been denied this group or that over the course of time; I do not need to be known as such a person, either. The same would hold for bodies of people as well. It is enough to be a welcoming community; there is no need for the lawn sign or window placard out front or the statement of principles on the home page of the website to say so.

Even the Buddha himself had no use for this kind of renown, and in the *Nāgita Sutra* we find a rather illustrative account of the Buddha's refusal to be turned into the latest spiritual sensation and to parlay that into an advantage. It seems the Buddha and a retinue of bhikkhus had stopped to stay in the woods near the brahmin village of Icchānaṅgala in the territory of the Kosalans. Having heard reports of his spiritual accomplishments, and eager for a chance to see the Blessed One for themselves, the Icchānaṅgalans gathered up a bunch of fine food and made their way toward to the encampment, where they stirred up quite a ruckus to let the Buddha know of their arrival. The Buddha asked one of the bhikkhus, Nāgita, what all the commotion was about: "Who is making such an uproar and a racket, Nāgita? One would think it was fishermen at a haul of fish." Nāgita explained that it was the villagers come to make their offerings, to which the Buddha replied:

> Let me never come upon fame, Nāgita, and may fame never catch up with me. One who does not gain at will, without trouble or difficulty, this bliss of renunciation, bliss of solitude, bliss of peace, bliss of enlightenment that I gain at will, without trouble or difficulty, might accept that vile pleasure, that slothful pleasure, the pleasure of gain, honor, and praise.[35]

34. Bodhi, *Numerical Discourses*, 1163.

35. Bodhi, *Numerical Discourses*, 652.

Nāgita tried to get the Buddha to consent to their offerings, pointing out that wherever he went he was sure to come upon such admiration and praise on account of his wisdom and virtue, just as surely as water flows down a hillside after the rain. There was no point in trying to stop it.[36] But the Buddha simply repeated what he had just said and went further:

> Nāgita, what is eaten, drunk, consumed, and tasted winds up as feces and urine: this is its outcome. From the change and alteration of things that are dear arise sorrow, lamentation, pain, dejection, and anguish: this is its outcome. For one devoted to practicing meditation on the mark of unattractiveness, revulsion toward the mark of the beautiful becomes established: this is its outcome. For one who dwells contemplating impermanence in the six bases for contact, revulsion toward contact becomes established: this is its outcome. For one who dwells contemplating arising and vanishing in the five aggregates subject to clinging, revulsion toward clinging becomes established: this is its outcome.[37]

Everyday people raise a clamor about whatever they happen to find interesting—that is an outcome of being an everyday person. Renunciant-contemplatives understand the fleeting nature of things, have given up defining themselves by them, and walk away from such situations—that is the outcome of living the holy life.

A religious tactician like Nāgita will see this as a missed opportunity, because he is still caught up in gain and loss and cannot but measure crowd size and territory covered accordingly. It is an opportunity cost the Buddha was willing to pay, wholly in in keeping with his own understanding of the place of the Dharma in the world:

> The Tathāgata has no concern whether the entire world will be emancipated, or half the world, or a third of the world. But he can be sure that all those who have been emancipated, or who are being emancipated, or who will be emancipated from

36. Mengzi relied on precisely this phenomenon to support a theory of benevolent government: "People turn toward benevolence like water flowing downward or animals running into the wilds . . . At the present time, if there were a ruler in the world who was fond of benevolence, then the various lords would all be driven toward him. Even if he did not wish to become King, he would be unable to stop it." Van Norden, *Mengzi*, 94.

37. Bodhi, *Numerical Discourses*, 652–53. Bhikkhu Bodhi notes that the commentaries say that these five are five ways of discussing insight (*vipassanā*). *Numerical Discourses*, 1725n999.

> the world first abandon the five hindrances, corruptions of the mind that weaken wisdom, and then, with their minds well established in the four establishments of mindfulness, develop correctly the seven factors of enlightenment. In this way they have been emancipated or are being emancipated or will be emancipated from the world.[38]

Whether or not the Dharma enjoys broad hearing, it is salvific for those who, having heard it, pursue the holy life without gloss, without guile, and without pretense—no matter what anyone else does or does not do. And that is enough.

The noble practitioner lives alone in a world of wounds not only in bearing with patience the afflictions of the world but also in living a life of *traceless anonymity in the heart of the world*. With no new nest in which to settle, one walks right past the bully pulpit and the social media platform, sets aside all thought of whether or not others do likewise, and devotes oneself wholeheartedly to that unshakable deliverance of mind toward which the path conduces. One becomes just as traceless and anonymous as the śramaṇa Siddhārtha encountered on that fateful evening—fully alive in flesh and blood, not hiding from the streets and the marketplace, but never lingering long enough to shoot the breeze about the affairs of the day or even notice what others might be up to. The meaning of the holy life will be manifest in the world whole and complete, but no self will have been brought into the picture. And that is enough.

38. Bodhi, *Numerical Discourses*, 1471.

Conclusion

Not Quite So Alone

The Dharma is not the exclusive property of something called *Buddhism*, even as the teaching of the Buddha presents it as straightforwardly and as contrivance-free as humanly possible. The Four Noble Truths, far from being a revelatory dispensation come from elsewhere, have always been presented as a concise account of "facts on the ground," so to speak, the fundamental reality we all share, even as it takes a good deal of effort to clear away the obstructive hindrances that keep any one of us from actually seeing it. It is all too easy to get caught up in the technical vocabulary and particular forms of expression that have served as vessels for the transmission of the Dharma from generation to generation and, in the process, lose sight of what they are trying to express—the unshakable deliverance of mind and the path that leads to it. That path, no matter what language or cultural form it is expressed in, is characterized everywhere and always by the same distinguishing signs:

> Those things of which you might know: "These things lead (1) to dispassion, not passion; (2) to detachment, not to bondage; (3) to dismantling, not to building up; (4) to fewness of desires, not to strong desires; (5) to contentment, not to non-contentment; (6) to solitude, not to company; (7) to the arousing of energy, not to laziness; (8) to being easy to support, not to being difficult to support," you should definitely recognize: "This is the Dhamma; this is the discipline; this is the teaching of the Teacher."[1]

1. Bodhi, *Numerical Discourses*, 1193.

Wherever any of these are found, the Dharma can never be far off.

At various points throughout this study I have had occasion to highlight certain aspects of the teaching of the Buddha and Dharma Ancestors against the backdrop of some common religious and spiritual ideas that, I assumed, might be familiar to the reader. These were taken from the Christian tradition, not because I was looking to take issue with Christianity, but precisely because of their widespread familiarity. Moreover, because much of the language of social transformation has been drawn from some distinctively Christian ideas and, however secularized, still retains traces of its origins, it was not unwarranted to take a look at some of those origins themselves to see where they might part ways with a Dharmic response to the ills of sentient beings; as we have seen, some of the drive to create an engaged Buddhism has itself come from trying to imitate certain contemporary forms of Christian practice such as liberation theology. Still, Christianity is no monolith, and the tension between the idea that the gospel commands a reconstruction of the social order and the idea that the gospel bids the surrender of all such aims is every bit as strong among the brothers and sisters of Christ as it is between parallel understandings of the Dharma among the sons and daughters of the Buddha. It should therefore be possible to find in the Christian tradition some examples of the same impetus to the holy life that animates the Dharma—the impetus to a life lived free of attachment, free of pretense, but also very much free of the drive to rely on or influence society or political authority in the service of a spiritual or religious agenda; in other words, a life utterly free of any trace of self. There are, indeed, many. Here I will mention only a few.

Recall that chapter 6 began with the account of the bhikkhu Puṇṇa who lived as a free man, able to enter any country no matter how the locals might treat him. In the *Fioretti di San Francesco*, or the *Little Flowers of St. Francis*, we find a remarkably similar exposition of patient forbearance. It happened that Francis was walking some distance with Brother Leo, and along the way Francis rather offhandedly remarked to Leo that if the ranks of the friars were to grow so much that they spread out across the face of the earth, that would be a fine thing, but it would not be perfect joy. After walking on a bit, Francis said that even if a brother was so accomplished in learning he could understand all the workings of nature and could discourse on them eloquently, such would not be a ground for perfect joy either. Walking on still further, Francis added that if a brother could preach so eloquently that he converted everyone, even sworn infidels, to the Christian faith, even that would not constitute perfect joy. The success of the order, the mastery of all knowledge, and the conversion of every nation to the gospel now all off the table, Brother Leo could contain himself no longer: "Father, I ask you in God's name to tell me where will I find perfect joy!" And Francis answered:

> When we arrive at Saint Mary of the Angels so drenched by the rain and frozen by the cold, spattered with mud and suffering from hunger, and we knock on the door of the place and the porter comes and angrily says: "Who are you?" And we say: "We are two of your brothers"; and he says in return: "You are, in fact, coarse fellows who go about the world stealing alms from the poor," and he will not let us enter but keeps us standing in snow and water, in cold and hunger until it is night, and then if we patiently endure such insults and rebuffs without being disturbed or murmuring, and humbly and charitably feel that even this porter knows us for what we are and that God loosened his tongue against us, O Brother Leo, write that this is perfect joy. And if we persevere in knocking, and the porter, disturbed at our importunity, comes out and attacks us with very hard blows and says: "Leave here, you worthless idlers, and go to an inn! Who do you think you are? You certainly are not going to eat here!" And if we bear these things patiently and with love accept the insults wholeheartedly, O Brother Leo, write that this is perfect joy. And if thoroughly suffering from great hunger and painful cold as night comes on we continue to knock and call out and tearfully cry out for admittance, and the aroused porter says, "These men are very impudent and bold, and I will quiet them!" Then coming out with a knotty club and grabbing us by the capuche, he throws us to the ground in mud and snow, and so beats us with the club that we are filled with wounds on all sides. And if we endure so many evils, so many insults and blows with joy, thinking that we ought to bear and endure most patiently these pains of the blessed Christ, O Brother Leo, among all the gifts of the Holy Spirit which Christ gives to his friends is to conquer oneself and willingly endure abuse for Christ and for the love of God.[2]

Francis, too, lived as a free man. He understood that overcoming one's self was the greatest task and gift one can enjoy. As anyone familiar with the story of Francis knows, the Christ he loved was the Crucified One, who, among Christians, represents the highest exemplar of patient forbearance

2. Armstrong et al., *Prophet*, 449–50.

flowing from the deepest kenosis. As the hagiography recounts, so complete was Francis' identification with the Crucified that he came to bear the wounds of crucifixion, the stigmata, in his very flesh. Whatever there is to say about resurrection and eternal life, Francis knew that the first focus and final joy of the Christian aspirant can be none other than taking up and living out the self-emptying of the cross.

Thomas of Celano, Francis's early biographer, relates that at one time the Holy Roman Emperor Otto IV was traveling through the area where Francis and some of the brothers were living. Even though the road the imperial retinue was taking passed within feet of the friars' hovel, Francis would not even go out to take a look, and he forbade the brothers with him from looking as well. Celano's commentary gives us some indication why:

> The glorious holy one, living within himself and walking in the breadth of his heart, prepared in himself a worthy dwelling place of God. That is why the uproar outside did not seize his ears, nor could any cry intrude, interrupting the great enterprise he had in hand. Apostolic authority resided in him; so he altogether refused to flatter kings and princes.[3]

Otto IV would go on to become embroiled in a power battle with Innocent III, who by some accounts exercised the greatest secular authority of any pope before or since. Even with the political fate of Europe and its peoples in the balance, Francis understood that his only task was to conform to the example of the One who bid him to surrender all (Matt 19:21)—not to weigh in on the developments of the day.

We also had occasion in chapter 6 to look at some of Ryōkan's responses to thieves. Seems living an unassuming, rather solitary life on the outskirts of town almost always leaves one open to being stolen from, and the early Christian anchorites in the Egyptian desert had their share of thieves to deal with, too. Like Ryōkan, some of them also knew how to deal with such folk:

> Once some robbers came to the monastery and said to one of the elders: We have come to take away everything that is in your cell. And he said: My sons, take all you want. So they took everything they could find in the cell and started off. But they left behind a little bag that was hidden in the cell. The elder picked it

3. Celano, "Life of Saint Francis," in Armstrong et al., *Saint*, 221.

> up and followed after them, crying out: My sons, take this, you forgot it in the cell![4]

Even if a monk did not abet the pilferer outright, at least he could shield the perpetrator from others who might not be as inclined to turn a blind eye to the matter: "A brother being burgled said to the robber: Make haste before the brothers come."[5] In both of these cases, the crime was already well underway, but on another occasion it had not quite begun. Rather than taking preemptive measures against the impending deed, the monks were encouraged by one of the elders to maintain their station: "Another priest said to the brothers when evil doers were arriving at the time for the *synaxis*: 'Let them perform their own tasks and let us do ours.'"[6] Monks engage in renunciation and prayer. Evildoers do evil. Neither Ryōkan nor these anonymous monks of the Egyptian desert would have ever suggested that stealing is a virtue, but they also understood that it was not their task to ensure others acted virtuously or even to shield themselves from others and their harmful actions.

Hakuin's equanimity and patient forbearance in the face of being wrongfully accused of fathering a child was offered in chapter 8 as a way of illustrating the skillfulness of patient forbearance over justice-seeking resentment. Pinning untimely pregnancies on unsuspecting monks was not at all a peculiarity of Hakuin's time and place, it seems, and yet another of the Desert Elders, Macarius of Egypt, happened to find himself in just such a situation:

> Blessed Macarius told this story about himself saying: When I was young and lived alone in my cell, they took me against my will and made me a cleric in the village. And since I did not wish to remain there, but fled to another village where a pious layman helped me out by selling my work, it happened that a certain young girl got herself in trouble and became pregnant. And when her parents asked her who was responsible for it, she said: That hermit of yours committed this crime. So out came her parents and seized me and hung pots around my neck and led me about along all the roads beating me and insulting me, saying: This monk has raped our daughter. And when they had just about killed me with their sticks, one of the old men said to them: How long are you going to beat this foreign monk? . . .

4. Merton, *Wisdom of the Desert*, 59.
5. Wortley, *Anonymous Sayings*, 487.
6. Wortley, *Anonymous Sayings*, 487.

> And the parents of the girl asserted: We will on no condition let him go unless the livelihood of the girl is provided for and unless someone will vouch for this man in case he absconds. So when I made a sign to the old man to do this, he offered a guarantee and took me away. So, returning to my cell, I gave him all the baskets I found, to sell and provide food for myself and my wife. And I said: Well, Macarius, now you've got yourself a wife, you will have to work harder in order to be able to feed her. So I worked day and night in order to make her a living.[7]

When the time for the birth arrived, the young woman was afflicted with a difficult labor that lasted several days with little progress. At long last she admitted that it was not Macarius but the young man next door who had gotten her pregnant. Hearing of her confession, Macarius quietly slipped out of the area, lest there be a clamor around him in light of the whole affair. It was enough that the matter was over; he did not need to hear the apologies of the young woman's family and those of the other villagers on top of it, nor was he at all interested in the fuss of their admiration for having so patiently endured the young mother's lie.

One can only assume that had the ruse not been confessed, Macarius would have labored for years to support the woman and her child, much as Hakuin himself had been prepared to do. As it turns out, he would go on to establish a monastic community in Scetis (present-day Wadi El Natrun), which persists to this day. Even this might not have come to pass, however. Under the Arian emperor, Valens, and at the instigation of the Arian patriarch of Alexandria, Lucius, Macarius and another desert monk, Macarius of Alexandria, were sent into exile on an island where no Christians were to be found, only to be allowed to return some time thereafter. One can only imagine that had the emperor not changed his mind, the two would likely have lived and died there instead, continuing even among strangers to engage in their commitment to the holy life without complaint about unfair treatment, just as they would have among their brothers back home.

These examples help underscore the idea that what the Dharma teaches is not something exotic come from the East that somehow needs to be Westernized (whatever that might mean) or even modernized for the twenty-first (or any) century. The relevant distinction is not between East and West, between Buddhist and Christian (or any other religion), or between ancient and modern (wherever that line is set between them).

7. Merton, *Wisdom of the Desert*, 79–80.

The relevant distinction is between setting oneself to living the holy life rather than going on living as an everyday person, and that distinction is as poignant and compelling in our own day and place as in any other. How could it not be, since the stark alternative offered the aspirant by any renunciant-contemplative tradition is always one and the same: cling or abandon clinging, adhere or set aside, surrender the self or defend it at all costs?

A son or daughter of the Dharma may live alone in a world of wounds but he or she is not, for all that, friendless. There are others. They are found wherever the facts of life are squarely faced, the holy life is lived, and the conceit of the self is abandoned. They have little enough dust in their eyes to appreciate and set themselves to realizing what the Buddha knew—that nothing in this world is worth adhering to. They do not get a lot of press, and most of their names are lost to the historians. They don't care about any of that, of course. In fact, most of them, like the Buddha, actually prefer it that way. They bear witness to the truth of the emptiness of themselves and the world in their very lives, however they turn out and whatever anyone around them does in response. There are not many of them, but that is just fine, too. There is nothing here worth adhering to.

Postscript

THE BUDDHA CAUTIONED THOSE who would speak or write about the Dharma to tread carefully: "Bhikkhus, there are these two things that lead to the decline and disappearance of the good Dhamma. What two? Badly set down words and phrases and badly interpreted meaning."[1] I have every reason to believe that, despite my best efforts, both are to be found in these pages. May whatever here has been set down or interpreted well redound to the stillness, ease, and benefit of many, and may whatever here has been set down or interpreted poorly be swiftly forgotten and never heard of again!

1. Bodhi, *Numerical Discourses*, 150.

Bibliography

Aitken, Robert. *The Mind of Clover: Essays in Zen Buddhist Ethics.* San Francisco: North Point, 1997.

Anālayo. *Compassion and Emptiness in Early Buddhist Meditation.* Cambridge, UK: Windhorse, 2015.

Ariyesako, Bhikkhu. *The Bhikkhus' Rules: A Guide for Laypeople. The Theravadin Buddhist Monk's Rules.* Kallista: Sanghāloka Forest Hermitage, 1998.

Armstrong, Regis J., et al. *The Prophet.* Vol. 3 of *Francis of Assisi: Early Documents.* 34 vols. New York: New City, 2001.

———. *The Saint.* Vol. 1 of *Francis of Assisi: Early Documents.* 34 vols. New York: New City, 1999.

Asaṅga. *The Bodhisattva Path to Unsurpassed Enlightenment: A Complete Translation of the Bodhisattvabhūmi.* Translated by Artemus B. Engle. Boulder, CO: Snow Lion, 2016.

———. *The Realm of Awakening: A Translation and Study of the Tenth Chapter of Asaṅga's* Mahāyānasaṅgraha. Translated by Paul J. Griffiths et al. New York: Oxford University Press, 1989.

———. *The Summary of the Great Vehicle.* Translated by John P. Keenan. Berkeley: Numata Center for Buddhist Translation and Research, 2003.

Barnhill, David Landis. "Great Earth *Saṅgha*: Gary Snyder's View of Nature as Community." In *Buddhism and Ecology: The Interconnection of Dharma and Deeds*, edited by Mary Evelyn Tucker and Duncan Ryūken Williams, 187–217. Cambridge: Harvard University Press, 1997.

Bentham, Jeremy. *An Introduction to the Principles of Morals and Legislation.* Edited by J. H. Burns and H. L. A. Hart. New York: Oxford University Press, 1996.

Bluck, Robert. "The Path of the Householder: Buddhist Lay Disciples in the Pāli Canon." *Buddhist Studies Review* 19 (2002) 1–18.

Blumenthal, James. "Toward a Buddhist Theory of Justice." *Journal of Global Buddhism* 10 (2015) 321–27, 328, 339–49.

Bodhi, Bhikkhu, trans. *The Connected Discourses of the Buddha: A Translation of the Saṃyutta Nikāya.* Boston: Wisdom, 2000.

———. *The Noble Eightfold Path: Way to the End of Suffering.* Onalaska: BPS Pariyatti Editions, 2000.

———. *The Numerical Discourses of the Buddha: A Complete Translation of the Aṅguttara Nikāya.* Somerville: Wisdom, 2012.

———. *The Suttanipāta. An Ancient Collection of the Buddha's Discourses Together with Its Commentaries.* Somerville: Wisdom, 2017.

Bommarito, Nicholas. "Bile & Bodhisattvas: Śāntideva on Justified Anger." *Journal of Buddhist Ethics* 18 (2011) 355–81.

Brassard, Francis. *The Concept of Bodhicitta in Śāntideva's Bodhicaryāvatāra.* Albany: State University of New York Press, 2000.

Buddhadāsa Bhikkhu. *Dhammic Socialism.* Translated by Donald K. Swearer. Bangkok: Thai Inter-Religious Commission for Development, 1993.

———. *Heartwood of the Bodhi Tree: The Buddha's Teaching on Voidness.* Translated by Dhammavicayo. Somerville: Wisdom, 2014.

———. *Under the Bodhi Tree: Buddha's Original Vision of Dependent Co-Arising.* Translated, edited, and introduced by Santikaro. Somerville: Wisdom, 2017.

Buddhaghosa. *The Path of Purification: Visuddhimagga.* Translated by Bhikkhu Ñāṇamoli. 5th ed. Kandy: Buddhist Publication Society, 1999.

Buddhist Text Translation Society. *The Śūraṅgama Sutra: A New Translation with Excerpts from the Commentary by the Venerable Master Hsüan Hua.* Ukiah: The Buddhist Text Translation Society, 2017.

Chang, Garma C. C. *The Buddhist Teaching of Totality: The Philosophy of Hwa Yen Buddhism.* University Park: The Pennsylvania State University Press, 1971.

———, ed. *A Treasury of Mahāyāna Sūtras: Selections from the Mahāratnakūta Sūtra.* Translated by The Buddhist Association of the United States. University Park: The Pennsylvania State University Press, 1983.

Conze, Edward, trans. *The Large Sutra of Perfect Wisdom.* Berkeley: University of California Press, 1975.

———. *The Perfection of Wisdom in Eight Thousand Lines and Its Verse Summary.* San Francisco: City Lights, 2006.

Cook, Francis H. *Hua-Yen Buddhism: The Jewel Net of Indra.* University Park: The Pennsylvania State University Press, 1977.

Dayal, Har. *The Bodhisattva Doctrine in Buddhist Sanskrit Literature.* Delhi: Motilal Banarsidass, 1932.

Dhammapāla, Ācariya. *The Commentary on the Verses of the Therīs.* Translated by William Pruitt. Therīgāthā-aṭṭhakathā Paramatthadīpanī 4. Oxford: The Pali Text Society, 1998.

———. *A Treatise on the Pāramīs: From the Commentary to the Cariyāpiṭak.* Translated by Bhikkhu Bodhi. Kandy: Buddhist Publication Society, 1996.

Dōgen. *Moon in a Dewdrop: Writings of Zen Master Dōgen.* Edited by Kazuaki Tanahashi. New York: North Point, 1977.

Eckel, Malcolm David. "Gratitude to an Empty Savior: A Study of the Concept of Gratitude in Mahāyāna Buddhist Philosophy." *History of Religions* 25 (1985) 57–75.

Fischer, Norman. "Acupressure Point of the Heart." In *All the Rage: Buddhist Wisdom on Anger and Acceptance*, edited by Andrea Miller, 68–77. Boston: Shambhala, 2014.

Foucault, Michel. "What Is Enlightenment?" Translated by Catherine Porter. In *The Foucault Reader*, edited by Paul Rabinow, 32–50. New York: Pantheon, 1984.

Frankfurt, Harry G. *On Bullshit.* Princeton: Princeton University Press, 2005.

Fronsdal, Gil, trans. *The Dhammapada: Teachings of the Buddha.* Shambhala Library. Boston: Shambhala, 2008.

Fuller, Paul. *The Notion of* Diṭṭhi *in Theravāda Buddhism: The Point of View*. New York: Routledge, 2005.

Garfield, Jay L. "Nāgārjuna's Theory of Causality: Implications Sacred and Profane." *Philosophy East and West* 51 (2001) 507–24.

———. "What Is It Like To Be a Bodhisattva? Moral Phenomenology in Śāntideva's *Bodhicaryāvatāra*." *Journal of the International Association of Buddhist Studies* 33 (2011) 333–57.

Gethin, R[upert] M. L. *The Buddhist Path to Awakening*. Oxford: One World, 2007.

———. "Cosmology and Meditation: From the Aggañña-Sutta to the Mahāyāna." *History of Religions* 36 (1997) 183–217.

———. *The Foundations of Buddhism*. Oxford: Oxford University Press, 1998.

Giustarini, Giuliano. "Faith and Renunciation in Early Buddhism: Saddhā and Nekkhamma." *Rivisti di Studi Sudasiatici* 1 (2006) 161–79.

Gross, Rita. "Buddhist Theology?" In *Buddhist Theology: Critical Reflections from Contemporary Buddhist Scholars*, edited by Roger R. Jackson and John J. Makransky, 53–61. Surrey, UK: Curzon, 2000.

———. "'I Go for Refuge to the Sangha': A Response to Rosemary Reuther's Paper." *Buddhist-Christian Studies* 11 (1991) 230–39.

Gyatso, Ven. Lobsang. *Bodhicitta: Cultivating the Compassionate Mind of Enlightenment*. Translated by Ven. Sherab Gyatso. Ithaca, NY: Snow Lion, 1997.

Hakuin. "Master Hakuin's Chant in Praise of Zazen (Zazen Wasan)." In *Chants & Recitations*, 34–35. Rochester: Rochester Zen Center, 2005.

Harris, Nigel. "The Revolutionary Role of the Peasants." *Debate* 41 (1970) 18–24.

Ireland, John D., trans. *The Udāna & The Itivuttaka*. Onalaska: BPS Pariyatti Editions, 2018.

John Paul II, Pope. "Apostolic Journey to Poland." http://www.vatican.va/content/john-paul-ii/en/speeches/1979/june/documents/hf_jp-ii_spe_19790602_polonia-varsavia-autorita-civili.html.

Jones, Ken. *The New Social Face of Buddhism: An Alternative Sociopolitical Perspective*. Boston: Wisdom, 2003.

Kant, Immanuel. *Critique of Judgment*. Translated by Werner Pluhar. Indianapolis: Hackett, 1987.

———. *The Metaphysics of Morals*. Edited by Mary Gregor. New York: Cambridge University Press, 2017.

Keenan, John P. "The Prospects for a Mahāyāna Theology of Emptiness: A Continuing Debate." *Buddhist-Christian Studies* 30 (2010) 3–17.

Keown, Damien. *A Dictionary of Buddhism*. New York: Oxford University Press, 2008.

Kornfield, Jack. *Bringing Home the Dharma: Awakening Right Where You Are*. Boston: Shambhala, 2012.

———. *A Path with Heart: A Guide through the Perils and Promises of Spiritual Life*. New York: Bantam, 1993.

Kraft, Kenneth. *The Wheel of Engaged Buddhism: A New Map of the Path*. New York: Weatherhill, 1999.

Lamotte, Étienne, and Sara Boin-Webb, trans. *Śūraṃgamasamādhisūtra: The Concentration of Heroic Progress: An Early Mahāyāna Buddhist Scripture*. Honolulu: University of Hawai'i Press, 2009.

Largen, Kristen Johnston. "Introduction to Liberation Theology and Engaged Buddhism." *Buddhist-Christian Studies* 36 (2016) 51–53.

Leighton, Taigen Daniel. *Bodhisattva Archetypes: Classic Buddhist Guides to Awakening and Their Modern Expression*. New York: Penguin, 1998.

Lele, Amad. "Disengaged Buddhism." *Journal of Buddhist Ethics* 26 (2019) 239–89.

Leopold, Aldo. *Round River: From the Journals of Aldo Leopold*. Edited by Luna B. Leopold. New York: Oxford University Press, 1993.

Lindtner, Christian, trans. *Master of Wisdom: Writings of the Buddhist Master Nāgārjuna*. Berkeley: Dharma Publishing, 1997.

Loori, John Daido. *Invoking Reality: Moral and Ethical Teachings of Zen*. Boston: Shambhala, 1998.

Loy, David. *The Great Awakening: A Buddhist Social Theory*. Boston: Wisdom, 2003.

———. "Why Buddhism and the Modern World Need Each Other: A Buddhist Perspective." *Buddhist-Christian Studies* 34 (2014) 39–50.

Lyotard, Jean-François, and Jean-Loup Thébaud. *Just Gaming*. Translated by Wlad Godzich. Minneapolis: University of Minnesota Press, 1985.

Maitreyanātha/Āryāsaṅga. *The Universal Vehicle Discourse Literature Mahāyānasūtrālaṁkāra together with its* Commentary (Bhāṣya) *by Vasubandhu*. Translated by L. Jamspal et al. New York: American Institute of Buddhist Studies, 2004.

Makransky, John J. *Buddhahood Embodied: Sources of Controversy in India and Tibet*. Albany: State University of New York Press, 1997.

———. "A Buddhist Critique of, and Learning from, Christian Liberation Theology." *Theological Studies* 75 (2014) 635–57.

———. "Confronting the 'Sin' out of Love for the 'Sinner': Fierce Compassion as a Force for Social Change." *Buddhist-Christian Studies* 36 (2016) 87–95.

Marra, Michele. "The Development of *Mappō* Thought in Japan (I)." *Japanese Journal of Religious Studies* 15 (1988) 25–54.

———. "The Development of *Mappō* Thought in Japan (II)." *Japanese Journal of Religious Studies* 15 (1988) 287–305.

Merton, Thomas. *The Wisdom of the Desert: Some Sayings of the Desert Fathers*. New York: New Directions, 1960.

Mill, John Stuart. *Inaugural Address Delivered to the University of St. Andrews Feb 1st 1867*. London: Longmans, Green, Reader, and Dyer, 1867.

———. "Speech on Capital Punishment." In *Utilitarianism*, by John Stuart Mill, edited by George Scher, 65–71. Indianapolis: Hackett, 2001.

———. *Utilitarianism*. Edited by George Scher. Indianapolis: Hackett, 2001.

Mochizuki, Shinjō. "The Compassionate and the Wrathful: Kannon and Fudō in Japanese Sculpture." *Japan Quarterly* 13 (1966) 340–47.

Moretti, Cosantino. "The Thirty-Six Categories of 'Hungry Ghosts' Described in the *Sūtra of the Foundations of Mindfulness of the True Law*." In *Fantômes dans l'Extrême-Orient d'Hier et d'Aujourd'hui*, edited by Marie Laureillard and Vincent Durand-Dastès, 43–72. Paris: Inalco, 2017.

Nāgārjuna. *Nāgārjuna on the Six Perfections: An Ārya Bodhisattva Explains the Heart of the Bodhisattva Path: Exegesis on the Great Perfection of Wisdom Sutra Chapters 17–30*. Translated by Bhikkhu Dharmamitra. Seattle: Kalavinka, 2009.

———. *On Generating the Resolve to Become a Buddha: Three Classic Works Encouraging the Resolve to Pursue the Bodhisattva Path to Buddhahood*. Translated by Bhikshu Dharmamitra. Seattle: Kalavinka, 2009.

Ñāṇamoli, Bhikkhu, and Bhikkhu Bodhi, trans. *The Middle Length Discourses of the Buddha: A New Translation of the Majjhima Nikāya.* Boston: Wisdom, 1995.

Nattier, Jan. *A Few Good Men: The Bodhisattva Path According to the Inquiry of Ugra* (Ugraparipṛcchā). Honolulu: University of Hawai'i Press, 2003.

———. *Once Upon a Future Time: Studies in a Buddhist Prophecy of Decline.* Berkeley: Asian Humanities, 1991.

Nietzsche, Friedrich. *On the Advantage and Disadvantage of History for Life.* Translated by Peter Preuss. Indianapolis: Hackett, 1994.

Nyantiloka. *Buddhist Dictionary: Manual of Buddhist Terms and Doctrines.* Onalaska: BPS Pariyatti Editions, 2018.

O'Malley, Joseph, ed. *Marx: Early Political Writings.* New York: Cambridge University Press, 1994.

Orzech, Charles D. *Politics and Transcendent Wisdom. The* Scripture for Humane Kings *in the Creation of Chinese Buddhism.* University Park: Pennsylvania State University Press, 1998.

Parkes, Graham. "Kūkai and Dōgen as Exemplars of Ecological Engagement." In *Japanese Environmental Philosophy,* edited by J. Baird Callicott and James McRae, 85–110. New York: Oxford University Press, 2017.

Pine, Red, trans. *The Diamond Sutra: Text and Commentaries Translated from Sanskrit and Chinese.* Washington, DC: Counterpoint, 2001.

Rahula, Walpola, and Paul Demiévielle. *What the Buddha Taught.* Rev. ed.. New York: Grove, 1974.

Raud, Rein. "The Existential Moment: Rereading Dōgen's Theory of Time." *Philosophy East and West* 62 (2012) 153–73.

Reps, Paul, and Nyogen Senzaki, eds. *Zen Flesh Zen Bones: A Collection of Zen and Pre-Zen Writings.* North Clarendon, VT: Tuttle, 1998.

Rice, Jeffrey. "Records of Witness of Responses of Guan(g)shiyin in the Three Collections: Image, Icon, and Text." *Sino-Platonic Papers* 182 (2008) 4–24.

Roberts, Peter Alan, and Tulku Yeshi, trans. *Āryakāraṇḍavyūhanāmamahāyānasūtra.* 2021. https://read.84000.co/translation/toh116.html.

Rochester Zen Center, ed. *Chants & Recitations.* Rochester, NY: Rochester Zen Center, 2005.

Ryōkan. *Great Fool: Poems, Letters, and Other Writings.* Translated by Ryūichi Abé and Peter Haskel. Honolulu: University of Hawai'i Press, 1996.

Sahn, Seung. *Only Don't Know: Selected Teaching Letters of Zen Master Seung Sahn.* Providence: Providence Zen Center, 1999.

Śāntideva. *The Bodhicaryāvatāra.* Translated by Kate Crosby and Andrew Skilton. New York: Oxford University Press, 1995.

———. *The Training Anthology of Śāntideva: A Translation of the Śikṣā-Samuccaya.* Translated by Charles Goodman. New York: Oxford University Press, 2016.

Second Vatican Council. *The Documents of Vatican II.* Vatican City: Libreria Editrice Vaticana, 2009.

Sen, Amartya. *The Idea of Justice.* Cambridge: Harvard University Press, 2011.

Senauke, Alan. "Right Anger and the Path to the End of Caste." Buddhist Peace Fellowship, 2014. http://www.buddhistpeacefellowship.org/right-anger-and-the-path-to-the-end-of-caste/.

Sheinfeld, Shayna. "What Is the Righteous Remnant in Romans 9–11? The Concept of Remnant in Early Jewish Literature and Paul's Letter to the Romans." In *Paul the*

Jew: Rereading the Apostle as a Figure of Second Temple Judaism, edited by Gabriele Boccaccini and Carlos A. Segovia, 33–50. Minneapolis: Fortress, 2016.

Shih, Heng-ching, trans. *The Sutra on Upāsaka Precepts*. Berkeley: Numata Center for Buddhist Tradition & Research, 1994.

Sivaraksa, Sulak. *Seeds of Peace: A Buddhist Vision for Renewing Society*. Berkeley: Parallax, 1992.

Snyder, Gary. *Earth House Hold: Technical Notes & Queries to Fellow Dharma Revolutionaries*. New York: New Directions, 1969.

Stevens, John, trans. *One Robe, One Bowl: The Zen Poetry of Ryōkan*. Boston: Shambhala, 2006.

Strain, Charles R. "Is a Buddhist Praxis Possible?" *Journal of Buddhist Ethics* 25 (2018) 71–101.

Sucitto, Ajahn. *Turning the Wheel of Truth: Commentary on the Buddha's First Teaching*. Boston: Shambhala, 2010.

Thurman, Robert A. F., trans. *The Holy Teaching of Vimalakīrti: A Mahāyāna Scripture*. University Park: The Pennsylvania State University Press, 1976.

"Torei Zenji's Bodhisattvas' Vow." https://zensydney.com/Torei-Zenji-s-Bodhisattvas-Vow.

Trungpa, Chögyam. *The Myth of Freedom and the Way of Meditation*. Boston: Shambhala, 1988.

Tsong-kha-pa. *The Great Treatise on the Stages of the Path to Enlightenment*. Translated by the Lamrim Chenmo Translation Committee. Volume 2. Boston: Snow Lion, 2014.

Tucker, Mary Evelyn, and Duncan Ryūken Williams, eds. *Buddhism and Ecology: The Interconnection of Dharma and Deeds*. Cambridge: Harvard University Press, 1997.

Van Norden, Bryan W., trans. *Mengzi: With Selections from Traditional Commentaries*. Indianapolis: Hackett, 2008.

Viévard, Ludovic. *Vacuité (śūnyatā) et compassion (karuṇā) dans le bouddhisme madhyamaka*. Paris: College de France, 2002.

Walshe, Maurice, trans. *The Long Discourses of the Buddha: A Translation of the Dīgha Nikāya*. Boston: Wisdom, 1995.

Walton, Matthew J. "The *Aggañña Sutta* and the Theravāda Buddhist Tradition." In *The Oxford Handbook of Comparative Political Theory*, edited by Leigh K. Jenco et al., 374–93. Oxford Handbooks. New York: Oxford University Press, 2020.

Wangchuk, Dorji. *The Resolve to Become a Buddha: A Study of the Bodhicitta Concept in Indo-Tibetan Buddhism*. Tokyo: International Institute for Buddhist Studies of the International College for Postgraduate Buddhist Studies, 2007.

Watson, Burton, trans. *The Lotus Sutra*. New York: Columbia University Press, 1993.

Willis, Glenn R. "Abandon All Hope of Fruition: Critical Notes on Engaged Buddhism." *Buddhist-Christian Studies* 37 (2017) 247–256.

Woolman, John. *The Journal of John Woolman and A Plea for the Poor*. 1754. Reprint, Eugene: Wipf & Stock, 1998.

Wortley, John. *The Anonymous Sayings of the Desert Fathers. A Select Edition and Complete English Translation*. New York: Cambridge University Press, 2013.

Yü, Chün-fang. *Kuan-Yin: The Chinese Transformation of Avalokiteśvara*. New York: Columbia University Press, 2000.

Subject Index

Abhayarājakumāra Sutra, 237–38, 238n12
Abrahamic religions, 72–75, 90–91
activism
  meaning of, 10
  Western society, 2–5
affective dispositions, 165
Aggañña Sutra, 189–93, 190n16, 191n19, 197
aging, effects of, 166
Aitken, Robert, 4, 148–49
aloneness, 73n1
Ambedkar, B. R., 9n12
Amidism, 176
Anagata-bhayani Sutta, 76
Anālayo Bhikkhu, 101n4
Anamataggasaṃyutta Sutta, 56–57
Ānanda Venerable, 62–63, 78, 82–83, 198–99
anattā (nonself), 12, 153
anger, 149–55, 159, 194–97
anger/aversion (*dosa/dveṣa*), 26
Aṅguttara Nikāya, 110
appamañña (boundless states), 103
apperception (*saṃjñā/sañña*), 24
apratiṣṭhita nirvāṇa (nonabiding nirvāṇa), 118–19
Aquinas, 58
Arab Spring era, 218–19
arhat (*pratyekabuddha*), 117
Asaṅga (Mahāyāna scholar-monk), 47, 158
asappurisadhamma (untrue person), 245
āsavas (taints), 26
asceticism, 28n19
Aśoka (Mauryan emperor), 74n4
Augustine, 193–94n24
Aung San Suu Kyi, 218–19
Avataṃsaka Sutra, 93–94
aversion, 149–50, 195
Avalokiteśvara, 122–23, 131–32, 138
awakening
  circumstances surrounding, 125–27, 126n10
  conduct of the awakening ones, 143–46
  crossing threshold of, 7–9, 8n10
  reality of, 10–11
awareness, unawakened ones and, 30, 129, 151–52

Baudelaire, Charles, 175
begging, 76
benevolent government theory, 248n36
Bentham, Jeremy, 36n40, 186–87
Berrigan, Daniel, 4, 237
Berrigan, Philip, 4, 237
Bhaddekaratta Sutta, 209–10
Bharadvaja, 104
Bhikkhus
  Buddha's exhortation to, 79
  discipline of the mind, 39
  eighteen currents of craving, 25
  five hindrances, 43
  renunciant life, 76–78
  resentment, grounds for, 187–88
  right view, 30–31
  wrong view, 29

Bodhicaryāvatāra, 81, 133
bodhicitta (mind proceeding toward awakening), 8
Bodhisattva
- agenda-free action, 140–41
- on anger, 152–53
- Inexhaustible Intent, 133–34, 134n26
- *Lotus Sutra*, 122–25, 133–35, 134n26
- Perceiver of the World's Sounds, 122–25, 135–38

bodhisattvas
- hurt by others, 153–161
- lay bodhisattva, 7, 9n11, 10
- ordained bodhisattva, 7, 9n11
- types of, 7

body/form (*rūpa*), 24, 54
Bojjhaṅgasaṃyutta Sutra, 110n21
Bommarito, Nicholas, 226
boundless states (*appamañña*), 103
boundlessness, 107
Bourbon, Louis, 207
brahmacariya (holy life), 22
brahmavihāras, the "abodes of Brahmā," 103–10
bright guardians of the world, 44n62
Buddha
- *Dhamma-vinaya*, 22
- dukkha and its end, 19
- as efficacious, 6
- entering ordained life, 75–76
- summary of Dharma, 14
- on teaching of, 19–20
- teachings of, 6–7, 22–32
- therapeutic applications of teaching, 28n18
- view from other shore, 7–8

Buddhadāsa Bhikkhu, 92, 115, 207
Buddhaghosa, 12–13, 112–14, 119
buddhahood attainment, 116–20, 127–28, 177, 224–25
Buddhism
- core precepts, 21
- Dharma, distinguishing between, 8–9, 9nn11–12
- effacement, achieving, 243–44
- Eightfold Path, 23
- exhortation to the bhikkhus, 79
- five hindrances, 26, 42–44, 104–5
- four immeasurables, 105–6
- historical sensibility of, 208–9
- identity-forming structures, 72–75, 73n1, 95
- monastic vs. lay, 9n11
- non-Dharmic comparisons, 99–103
- saṅgha, use of, 75
- scandals within, 77n11
- scholar-theologians, 90–91, 230
- social theory, 7
- *Therīgāthā*, 101
- Three Vedas, 104
- Western introduction to, 4–5

Buddhist Peace Fellowship, 4, 10
Buddhist-Christian "dual belonging," 67n24
bullshit, 233–34
bumper sticker, 236n11

calendars, systems of, 207
Camping, Harold, 219
capital punishment, 200–201
Catholic Worker Movement, 3
Catholic World Report, 229
Catonsville Nine, 237
change, as fact of conditioned existence, 208
Chesterton, G. K., 3
Christians
- Buddhism distinction, 252
- Buddhist-Christian "dual belonging," 67n24
- Catholicism (*See* Roman Catholicism)
- on compassion, 101–2, 101n4
- gospel parallel teaching, 37–38n43, 64n19, 102, 103n7, 128–29n15
- Great Commission, 79n15
- identity-forming structures, 72–75, 95
- as a kerygmatic religion, 229–31
- no salvation outside the church, 79

on righteous anger theory, 193–94n24
salvation history, 208
social environment, 90
social transformation/change, 229–31, 231n4
"Theology of the Body," 166n4
Theresa of Ávila, 167n6
Trinity, 83
civil authority, 192, 196
Civil Rights era, 217–18
Common Era, history of, 207
Commune de Paris (1871), 207
compassion (*karuṇā*)
Christians on, 101–2, 101n4
fierce compassion, 195–96
grief and, 113–14
meaning of, 100–109
near enemies of, 12, 110–15
. *See also* Bodhisattva
compassionate action, 12
conditioned phenomena, 163
Confucian tradition, 123
conscious awareness (*vijñāna/viññāṇa*), 24, 118
contemplative prayer, 21
corporate religious body, 72
cosmos, eternality or non eternality of, 222–23
craving (*tṛṣṇā*), 24–26
Critique of Judgment (Kant), 22
Cūḷa-Assapura Sutra, 109
Cūḷamālunkya Sutta, 222–23
Cunda, Mahā, 242–44, 244n26
"Curious Accounts of the Zen Master Ryōkan" (Yoshinge), 157–58
currents
of craving, 25, 86–87, 107–8
moving against, 143–45

Daoist tradition, 123
"The Declining Age of the Dharma," 175–76
delusion (*moha*), 26
dependent co-arising, 91–93
Devadatta, 237–38, 238n12
Dhammapada (Buddhist scripture), 8–9, 83, 150–51, 153–54
Dhamma-vinaya, 22
Dhammic socialism, 207
Dharma
Buddha's summary of, 14
Buddhism, distinguishing between, 8–9, 9n12
caution to speakers and writers, 259
concept of God and, 91
Dhammapada on, 8–9
external compliance, 32–35
gradual training for, 32–50, 33n29
internal compliance, 36–44
meditation and, 20–22
social activism versus, 5
social theory and, 12
teachings of, 231–33, 240–42, 251–52, 256–57
Dharma Ancestors, 5–6, 103, 228, 252
dharmakāya (reality body), 125
Diamond Sangha, 4
The Diamond Sutra, 120, 131, 220, 221–22
Dionysius Exiguus, 207
divine abodes, 103–10
Dōgen, Eihei, 70, 126n10, 167, 173, 214–17, 228
(*dosa/dveṣa*) anger/aversion, 26
doubt, nīvaraṇa of, 234–35
dukkha (suffering), 6

Eckel, Malcolm David, 128
Edict of Milan (313 CE), 229
Edict of Thessalonica (380 CE), 229
effacement, achieving, 243–44
ego-attachment, 34n34
eight types, saṅgha, 80–81
eight worldly conditions, 170–71
eighteen currents of craving, 25, 86–87, 107–8
Eightfold Path
ascetics, 84
components of, 28–29
on friendships, 82

Eightfold Path (*continued*)
  gradual training and, 23
  to liberation, 42
  as the *Middle Way*, 31–32
embodiment, 39, 54, 118, 164–67
embracing, as antidote to anger, 158
emotional dispositions, 165
emptiness, 62–63, 142–43, 176
Engaged Buddhism, 4–5, 4–5n4, 7–8, 91–93
Enji, Torei, 69–70
enlightenment, 116–21
environmental conditions, 166
equanimity, 202
eternal life, term usage, 27–28

fearlessness, 135–36, 138–39
Fellowship of Reconciliation, 4
Feuerbach, 3
fierce compassion, 195–96
Fioretti di San Francesco, 252
First Things, 229
Fischer, Norman, 211
five aggregates, 24, 26
five hindrances, 26, 42–44, 104–5
Focus on the Family, 10
Foucault, Michel, 174–75
Four Bodhisattvic Vows, 223–24
four immeasurables, 105–6
Four Noble Truths. *See* Noble Truths
four pairs, saṅgha, 80–81
four requisites, 39, 76, 76n8
Francis (Saint), 252–54
Frankfurt, Harry G., 234
French Republican Calendar, 207
friendships, 81–83
Fuller, Paul, 31–32n26

Garfield, Jay, 73, 224–25
Gaudium et spes (Vatican II), 3
gay marriage, 219
gender, 165
Giustarini, Giuliano, 33n31
Glassman, Bernie, 4
global effects of climate change, 2
Golden Rule, 106
Goldilocks way, 168
Gotami, 101–2, 141
gradual training in the Dharma, 32–50
gratitude, 148–49
The Great Treatise on the Stages of the Path to Enlightenment, 153
greed/attachment (*rāga*), 26
grief, term usage, 113–14
Gross, Rita, 73n1, 90–91, 94
Guangshiyin yingyan ji, 123
Guarding the doors of sense faculties, 37, 39, 118n38

Hakuin (Zen master), 204–5, 255
Hekiganroku, 176–77
hindrances (*nīvaraṇas*), 26, 234–36
hiri (moral shame), 35
historical moments, 220–21
Hobbes, Thomas, 74, 191
holy life (*brahmacariya*), 22
Hosts of Māra, 44n62
household life, 32–33, 41, 202
Huayan Buddhism, 93

"I" statements, 12, 86–87
identity, of self, 55–58, 68
Imitation Dharma Age, 175
Innocent III, Pope, 254
interconnectedness, 12, 92
inward non-mental dharmas, 164

Jambudvīpa, term usage, 156n25
jhānas practice of, 44, 105, 243
John Paul II, Pope, 230
Jones, Ken, 10, 94

justice
  anger and, 194–97
  capital punishment and, 200–201
  civil authority, 192, 196
  defense of others, 201–3
  Dharma view on, 183–84, 187–89
  do-nothing response, 203–5
  King, Jr. on, 184
  moral wrongs, consequences of, 197–200

passage of time and, 206–7
resentment and, 187–88
social structures and, 173, 189–93, 193n23
Western society and, 184–85, 194–95

Kakacūpama Sutra, 202
Kant, Immanuel, 22, 200
Kāraṇḍavyūha Sutra, 124
Kassapagotta, Venerable, 88–89, 94, 231
Kauśāmbī monks, 159–160
Khema (disciple), 246
King, Martin Luther, Jr., 4, 184, 208
Kornfield, Jack, 110–12, 114n29
Kropotkin, Peter, 3

Largen, Kristen Johnston, 195
Last Dharma Age, 175, 176
lay bodhisattva
activism and, 10
difficulty of, 7, 9n11
Leighton, Taigen Daniel, 116, 133n23
Leo XIII, Pope, 3
Leopold, Aldo, 1–2, 178
"Letter from Birmingham Jail" (King), 184
liberation, 49–50
Liberation theologians, 3, 90
Little Flowers of St. Francis, 252
livelihood, term usage, 40n49
Locke, John, 74, 191
Loka Sutta, 52
Lotus Sutra
Inexhaustible Intent, 133–35, 134n26
Parable of the Medicinal Herbs, 129
Perceiver of the World's Sounds, 122–25
loving-kindness (*mettā*)
Buddhism and, 109, 156
term usage, 47–48
Tevijja Sutra and, 104–5
Loy, David, 11n14, 76n8, 109m16
Lucius of Alexandria, 256

Luther, Martin, 237
Lyotard, Jean-François, 74

Macarius of Alexandria, 256
Macarius of Egypt, 255
Macy, Joanna, 109m16
Maha Prajnaparamita Shastra, 221
Mahākammavibhanga Sutra, 14, 197
Mahāparinibbāna Sutta, 84
Mahāprajñāpāramitā Upadeśa Sutra, 13, 146
Mahāyāna tradition
Buddhahood, attainment of, 116–20
conduct of the awakening, 144
literature of, 118
scholar-monks, 47–48
six *pāramitātas*, 144
stream-entry path, 81
three poisons, 26
trikāya teaching, 125
upāsaka/upāsikā precepts, 33, 33–34n33, 133–34
Vimalakīrti Sutra, 115–16
Makransky, John, 117, 195
Mañjuśrī/Mujaku interchange, 176–77
mappō theory, 175–76, 218
Māratajjanīya Sutta, 42
Marx, Karl, 2–3, 74–75, 89
mass shootings, 2
meditation, 20–22, 41–44, 41n55, 42n58
Mengzi, 248n36
mental activity (*saṃskāra/saṅkhāra*), 24
Mettā Sutra, 46–47, 160
Middle Way, 31, 168
Mill, John Stuart, 14, 36n40, 185–86, 185nn7–9, 196, 200
mindfulness
practice of, 40–44
training, 28n18
modern exceptionalism, 9–10
modern politics, 74–75
moha (delusion), 26
moral dread (*ottappa*), 35
moral shame (*hiri*), 35

moral wrongs, consequences of, 197–200
Morris, William, 178n23
mortification, 28n19
Mujaku/Mañjuśrī interchange, 176–77
Mumonkan, 225–26

Nāgārjuna
  on anger, 152–53, 155, 202
  on awakening, 144
  breaks the precepts, 49n74
  good I might receive from others, 146–47
  liberation, 117–18
  Mahāprajñāpāramitā Upadeśa Sutra, 13, 146
  on moral purity, 48–49, 49n74
  overview, 13
  unawakened ones, 30, 129, 151–52
Nāgita Sutra, 247–49
Napoléon, 207
Nātaputta, Nigaṇṭha, 237–38
National Catholic Reporter, 229
"Navayāna Buddhism" (Ambedkar), 9n12
near enemies, 12, 110–15
Net of Indra, 91, 93–94
Nietzsche, Friedrich, 81n21
Nikāyas
  on awareness, 41
  Christian gospel parallel, 37–38n43
  core of the Dharma, 15
  on craving, 25
  as the deathless, 27
  directed strategies, 44
  on gradual training, 14, 23
  hiri-ottappa, 35, 38
  on justice, 11
  Middle Way, 31
  three unwholesome roots, 26
nirmāṇakāya (apparition body), 125
nirmāṇas (apparition bodies), 125–27
nirvāṇa, 26–27, 27n16
Nissaraniya Sutra, 184
nīvaraṇas (hindrances), 26, 234–36
Noble Ones, 7
Noble Path, 10
Noble Truths, 6, 23, 31, 33n30, 251
nonabiding nirvāṇa (*apratiṣṭhita nirvāṇa*), 118–19
non-mental dharmas, 164
nonself (*anattā*), 12, 153
non-separation of self, 108–9, 109m16
Nouvelle Action Royaliste, 207

ordained bodhisattva, 7, 9n11
  . *See also* Bhikkhus
Orzech, Charles, 134
ottappa (moral dread), 35
Otto IV, Holy Roman Emperor, 254
outward non-mental dharmas, 164

Pāli Canon, 9n11
pāramitās
  conduct of the awakening ones, 143–46
  patient forbearance, 226
  practicing, 120, 151, 177
  upāsaka/upāsikā precepts, 33, 33–34n33, 133–34
Parker, Theodore, 208
"Pastoral Constitution on the Church and the Modern World," 3
Path of Purification (*Visuddhimagga*), 112–14
patient forbearance (*kṣānti*)
  discarded attraction and repulsion, 171–72
  good I might receive from others, 146–47
  "moving against the current," 143–45
  natural phenomena, 173
  social phenomena, 173
  standing in the midst of rough situations, 159
  toward beings, 163
  toward circumstances, 162–63
  towards those who do me harm, 149–61

perfect joy (Francis), 252–53
The Perfection of Wisdom in Eight Thousand Lines, 120–21
person-like, term usage, 125n9
Phagguna, Moliya, 202
pity, term usage, 111
Pius VII, Pope, 207
Pius XI, Pope, 3
pointless talk, 15, 232–35, 239
practice of others, 245–47
Prague Spring era, 218
pratyekabuddha (private Buddha), 117
"Preferential Option for the Poor" (Vatican II), 3
pretas (hungry ghosts), 233
previous lives, term usage, 174
prophets, 91, 94
protest movements (1960's), 3–4
psychological dispositions, 165–66
Puṇṇa, 142–43, 179, 201, 252

Quadragesimo anno (Pius XI), 3

rāga (greed/attachment), 26
Rahula, Walpola, 184
recluse, 29–30, 34, 109
religions
  identity-forming structures, 72–75, 95
  institutions social transformations, 2–5, 228–29
  theistic systems, 72–75, 90–91
  . *See also* Abrahamic religions; Christians
remnant theology, 90
renunciant life, 75–76
renunciant-contemplative, 4–5
renunciation, 28n19, 38–40, 62
Rerum novarum (Leo XIII), 3
resentment, 14, 187–88
restlessness and remorse (*uddhacca-kukkucca*), 225–26n29
Rice, Jeffrey, 123
right speech, 89
right view, 28–31, 177n21, 188–89
Roman Catholicism
  Catholic Worker Movement, 3
  Catholic World Report, 229
  in Europe, 207
  National Catholic Reporter, 229
  notable Popes, 3, 207, 230, 254
  social transformation/change, 229–31, 231n4
  "Theology of the Body," 166n4
Romero, Oscar, 4
Rousseau, Jean-Jacques, 74
rūpa (body/form), 24
Ryōkan, 157–58, 254–55

Sahampati, Brahmā, 20
Sahn, Seung, 194
Saichō (Japanese Tendai founder), 175
Saḷāyatanavibhanga Sutta, 113
Sallekha Sutra, 242
saṃbhogakāya (bliss body), 125
saṃjñā/saññā (apperception), 24
samma kodha (right anger), 194
saṃsāra
  emptiness, 62–63
  formations, cause of, 61–62
  origin of, 56–60
  as a process, 53–56
  seriously living of, 67–71
  term usage, 53–54
  world, as a whole, 52n2
  world-denying charge, 63–66
saṃskāra/saṅkhāra (mental activity), 24
saṅgha
  noble saṅgha, 80–86
  renunciants, 75–77, 79
  Three Jewels and, 33, 81
  . *See also* Bhikkhus
Sanjūsangen-dō Hall, Kyoto, 131–32
Śāntideva
  on anger, 150, 152
  on awakening, 8n10, 133–34
  on harm, 154, 201
  on hatred, 160
  on patient forbearance, 145
  Three Jewels, 81
Sappurisa Sutra, 245

sappurisadhamma (true person), 245
scholar-theologians, 90–91
Second Vatican Council, 3
self-defense, 186
selfhood, 12
Sen, Amartya, 195
sensations (*vedanā*), 24
sense restraint, 38
Shinran (Jōdo Shinshū founder), 175–76, 218
Siddhārtha, 242, 249
Śikṣā-Samuccaya, 81
Sivaraksa, Sulak, 9n12, 75n7
skandhas (aggregates), 24
Smith, Adam, 170
Snyder, Gary, 4, 4–5n4
social conditions, 169–78
social contract theory, 191, 191n19
social dukkha, 11n14
social environment, 69, 163–64
social revolution, 15–16
social stratification, 190
social structures, 86–95, 88n31, 172–74
social transformation/change, 2–5, 228–31, 237
social transformers, 208, 236
Socrates, 237
Sojourners, 229
sotāpanna (stream entry), 27
Sotāpattisaṃyutta Sutra, 84
speech, types of, 238
stream entry (*sotāpanna*), 27, 80–81
Sucitto, Ajahn, 26–27
Suddhaṭṭaka Sutra, 228
suffering, 6, 23
suicide, 28
Sumana (disciple), 246
Śūraṃgamasamādhisūtra, 127–30
Śūraṅgama Sutra, 124, 136–39
Sutra on the Upāsaka Precepts, 7

taints (*āsavas*), 26
taking refuge, term usage, 33
Tathāgataguhya Sutra, 128
teacher-student relationship, 78–79
teisho of the body (Dōgen), 167
ten topics of discussion, 240–41
Tevijja Sutra, 104–5
theistic systems, 91
"Theology of the Body" (Catholic teaching), 166n4
Theravādin tradition, 15, 27n16, 143–44
Theresa of Ávila, 167n6
Therīgāthā, 101
Thich Nhat Hanh, 4
Thích Quảng Đức, 4
thirst for existence/annihilation, 28n20
Thomas of Celano, 254
Three Jewels, 33, 81
three unwholesome roots/three poisons, 26
Three Vedas, 104
time, passage of
  emptiness of, 221–26
  hope in future, 211
  nurturing delight, 210–11
  overview, 226–27
  perspectives on, 206–9
  present, individual persons, 212–17
  present, social groups, 217–21
timeless simultaneity, 81
Tozan, 136, 139
trikāya (three bodies of Buddha), 125
tṛṣṇā (craving), 24–26
True Dharma Age, 175
true person (*sappurisadhamma*), 245
Tsong-kha-pa, 153
Tutu, Desmond, 4

uddhacca-kukkucca (restlessness and remorse), 225–26n29
Uji (Dōgen), 214–17
untrue person (*asappurisadhamma*), 245
Upāsaka Precepts, Sutra on the, 7
upāsaka/upāsikā precepts, 33, 33–34n33
upāya (skillful means), 133–34
Utilitarianism (Mill), 185

Valens (Arian emperor), 256
Vanasaṃyutta Sutta, 88–89
Vāseṭṭha, 104
Vasubandhu, 118–19, 139
Vatican II Council, 3
vedanā (sensations), 24
vijñāna/viññāṇa (conscious awareness), 24, 118
Vimalakīrti Sutra, 115–16
Visuddhimagga (*Path of Purification*), 112–14

Wadi El Natrun (monastic community), 256
wakefulness, 40
Walton, Matthew J., 191n19
"We" statements, 86–89
"Wheel of Saṃsāra," 56n7
Woolman, John, 236
world, as a whole, 51–53, 52n2
world-denying charge, 63–66
worlds
  diversity of, 67–71
  ending of, 66–67
wrong view, 29, 177n21, 188

Xi Guangshiyin yingyan ji, 123
Xìnxīn Míng, 225
Xu Guangshiyin yingyan ji, 123

Yoshinge, Kera, 157
Yü, Chun Fang, 123

Zen adage, 167
Zen Peacemakers Order, 4
zhiguai genre, 123

www.ingramcontent.com/pod-product-compliance
Lightning Source LLC
Chambersburg PA
CBHW022001220426
43663CB00007B/912
9781666714968